...marvellous stuff ... put ...
shame'   *Observer*

'Di Canio the wordsmith is as free-flowing and entertaining
as Di Canio the ball-playing artist'   *Sunday Times*

'Simply outstanding'

'Has all the ingredien...
absolute elation, and ...
thought-provoking insi...
players'   *...oot*

'A fascinating read from a fascinating person'
                                                Hammers News

'Blitzes the usual bland of rubbish served up by footballers
... an explosive book'   *Manchester Evening News*

'If you read one sports autobiography this year, I urge you
to make it this one'   *Amazon*

'Brilliant, a cracking read'   *Match*

'Like his football, hugely entertaining'   *The Times*

PAOLO DI CANIO

THE AUTOBIOGRAPHY

PAOLO DI CANIO

with GABRIELE MARCOTTI

CollinsWillow

An Imprint of HarperCollinsPublishers

Gabriele Marcotti is the London correspondent for the Italian
daily *Corriere Dello Sport* and knows Paolo Di Canio intimately
through his numerous interviews with the West Ham striker.
A native Italian, he also works for the American magazine
Sports Illustrated, and writes a weekly column on world football for
the CNN/SI website. His work has appeared in publications such
as *The Financial Times*, the *Daily Mail* and *The Sunday Herald*.

First published in hardback 2000 by
CollinsWillow
an imprint of HarperCollins*Publishers*
London

First published in paperback 2001

1 3 5 7 9 8 6 4 2

A CIP catalogue record for this book is
available from the British Library

ISBN 0 00 711598 9

Typeset by Rowland Phototypesetting Ltd, Bury St Edmunds, Suffolk
Printed and bound in Great Britain by Clays Ltd, St Ives plc

The HarperCollins website address is www.fireandwater.com

PHOTOGRAPHIC ACKNOWLEDGEMENTS
All photographs supplied courtesy of Paolo Di Canio with the exception
of the following: **Action Images** 10b, 12t, 12b, 13t, 13b, 15tr, 16t;
Allsport 4b, 6b, 10c, 14, 15b; **Empics** 16bl, 16br; **News Group
Newspapers** 15tl; **Popperfoto/Reuters** 11t, 11b.

I dedicate this book to everyone who has been less fortunate than me, and to those who have made my life what it is: my mother and father, brothers Antonio, Giuliano and Dino, my in-laws Fausto, Franca and Stefania, my wife Betta, and our two daughters Ludovica and Lucrezia. Also, to the memory of Zia Franca, my aunt, to whom I was the son she never had.

CONTENTS

ACKNOWLEDGEMENTS

I would like to thank Phil Spencer, Gabriele Marcotti, Allan Jones, Moreno and Matteo Roggi, and my publishers HarperCollins for all their help on this book.

INTRODUCTION

I fell to my knees, pounding the Upton Park turf.

They had finally broken me.

They had finally made me want to stop playing football, the game I loved, both as a player and as a fan.

My mind flew back to all those who, whether consciously or not, had tried to drag me down, tried to crush me. Faces from long ago chased each other through my brain, a carousel of hatred, stupidity and incompetence. People from my past who said I would never make it, who said I did not deserve to play football, who tried to drive me out . . . it was all coming back to me. I had always believed I could continue, I had always been convinced that the fight, however futile, was nevertheless worth it.

Now, I had lost that conviction. I knew that no matter what I did, no matter what happened, they would not let me win. And I knew that there were others, innocent people whose only crime had been to side with me, to support me, who would suffer as a result.

It was 12 February 2000. The demons had chased me into the new millennium.

I can trace the moment I stopped believing down to the very instant. It was the 12th minute of the second half of West Ham United's home fixture against Bradford City. We were losing 2–4 at Upton Park, in front of our own faithful.

Bradford had taken the lead through Dean Windass on the half hour, we had equalized with Trevor Sinclair and pulled ahead through John Moncur. Peter Beagrie levelled to score on the stroke of half-time thanks to a dubious penalty – or at least a penalty which in Italy would be bread-and-butter but in the Premiership few referees ever grant.

We had been ready to storm back after the break, but a player named Jamie Lawrence, a winger with hair dyed bright red, had scored twice in the first six minutes of the second half to give them a 4–2 lead.

I had been battling furiously, scratching and clawing my way to an opening, willing myself to succeed. For my troubles, I had been kicked and shoved, grabbed and gouged, often just a few feet away from referee Neale Barry. Earlier, I had been felled in the penalty area, right under Barry's watchful gaze.

Nothing.

Not even an acknowledgement that I had hit the ground.

In the 12th minute of the second half, it happened again. This time, there was no question about it, this time, even if the referee had not seen it, he would have felt the force of the blow which caused me to lose my balance and crash to the ground.

Again, there was no call. Again, I had been summarily ignored.

That's when I sunk to my knees. That's when my world caved in.

I had been telling myself over and over again that referees are only human, that they are part of the game, that they make mistakes. But this was beyond anything I had experienced. This was total and utter humiliation.

I felt a rage well up inside me. I felt the anger of a million injustices, a million wrongs that went unpunished, a million vendettas that went unserved.

I waited for the adrenalin to kick in. I waited for that fire to engulf my body, that passion that had carried me through so many setbacks in the past, the spirit that made me pick myself and charge back into battle.

But it wasn't coming.

In its place, wave after wave of frustration was rattling my brain. The realization that the struggle was over, that my enemies had triumphed.

I felt it was time for the warrior to go home and rest.

I rose to one knee and signalled to my manager Harry Redknapp. I motioned to be taken off, to be substituted. Redknapp, perched on the edge of the dugout, looked at me and slowly shook his head. I saw his lips move. Even if the infernal din of Upton Park hadn't drowned out his words, I would not have heard him. But I knew what he was saying.

'Paolo, you're not coming off. Now get back out there and FIGHT!'

Seeing that this man, this middle-aged figure who had faith in me thirteen months earlier when to most Britons I was either a madman or a disease blighting the national sport, still believed in me was the adrenalin injection I craved.

It started slowly and then it all came rushing back.

I was going to be stronger than my enemies. I would continue the struggle, because I was not alone, because I had supporters, teammates, friends who were behind me.

And because there would always be more glory in fighting on and losing than simply walking away.

All this happened in thirty, maybe forty-five seconds. I thundered back up the pitch, screaming at my teammates, calling for the ball, trying to get into space. The noise from the fans made me high with rage, but this time, a healthy rage.

I was possessed, I was in overdrive. I felt my skin close to bursting with the fire inside, I struggled to keep it focused, to keep it channelled on making me run harder, think clearer.

Eight minutes passed and Paul Kitson, who had come on just as I was asking to be substituted, clattered into a Bradford defender and tumbled to the ground. Had I been in Kitson's boots, I can guarantee no English referee would have given the penalty.

In this case, Barry blew his whistle and pointed to the penalty spot.

Penalty to West Ham and a chance to reopen the game.

Frank Lampard strode up confidently, but I ran over and ripped the ball out of his hands. He protested, he asked me what the hell I thought I was doing. I must have said something to him, I don't remember what. At that moment, I was so fired up, so over the top, that I'd be surprised if I could even articulate a sentence.

There was no way I was not going to take that penalty. This wasn't just about revenge. I had missed a penalty a month before against Aston Villa in the Worthington Cup, but I knew this was going to be different. Seventeen years as a footballer had left me with few certainties on the pitch.

That I was going to take and convert this penalty was one of them.

Lampard backed off, somewhere between puzzled and bemused. He was our midfield leader, the assistant manager's son and a future England star. But he knew it was best to take a back seat.

There was venom inside me, built up over many years of suffering, of making the difficult choice and facing the consequences.

It all came out in that one kick.

The goalkeeper was beaten and we rushed back up the pitch for the restart. Barely five minutes passed before the boy wonder, Joe Cole, danced his way past two defenders and rifled the ball home. It was a great goal by one of the greatest pure talents in the game, an exploit worth celebrating, but I hardly raised a fist in the air.

I rushed to the ball and brought it back to the centre circle. The game had to go on, my vengeance had to be completed.

It all happened seven minutes from the end. I led the counterattack, thundering towards the Bradford penalty area. I ran past one defender, avoided another, stepped past a third.

For a second, I thought about cutting into the area and beating yet another defender, but I thought better. I knew I would be hacked down and the referee would look the other way.

Instead, I hit a low cross across the box. Trevor Sinclair faked to the ball and then let it run through his legs. It reached Lampard, steaming in behind Sinclair, and he thundered the ball home.

The final whistle was my personal triumph.

Not the victory itself. As always, it was a team effort. My triumph was the way I once again managed to lift myself and fight on.

Looking back, I have suffered more setbacks in my life than I care to recall. Some were sheer fate, like the time an injury almost cost me my leg or when a mental breakdown drove me to seek psychiatric help. Others were of my own making, like the push on referee Paul Alcock which cost me an eleven-match ban.

But perhaps the majority occurred when I stood up and spoke my mind, when I failed to bow my head in front of the rich and powerful. Gianmarco Calleri, chairman of Lazio, Luciano Moggi, general manager of Juventus, Fergus McCann, chairman of Celtic – men like that, men who are used to having their way, tried to crush me.

I stood up to them and paid the price.

But I never stopped fighting, even in the face of certain defeat.

And while it may not be up to me to determine whether I have won or lost, the mere fact that I am playing in the Premiership, playing the game I love in a country I have come to love, in front of fans and with teammates who I love, makes me think that I haven't done so badly after all.

Games like the victory over Bradford are a microcosm of my life. Struggle after struggle, defeat after defeat, and, always, the fight goes on.

Unlike the Bradford game, the final whistle hasn't sounded yet (and you'll understand if I say that I hope it doesn't for a long, long time).

Am I winning?

Am I losing?

I don't know.

What I do know is that I'm fighting.

CHAPTER ONE

'LOOK AT THIS BEAUTIFUL, TALENTED BOY!'

I was born in 1968. The 9th of July, to be precise.

Looking back, 1968 was a seminal period in Italy and around the world. It must have been an exciting time to be alive.

Students were rioting in universities from Tokyo to Turin. Paris was brought to a standstill by a general workers' strike. In Prague, Alexander Dubcek became the first leader of an Eastern European country with the guts to stand up to the Soviet Union. Across the Atlantic Ocean, Dr Martin Luther King Jr and Robert F Kennedy were assassinated by men afraid of their ideas. The United States government launched its first spy-satellite, while the three Apollo 8 astronauts orbited the moon and caught the very first glimpse of the darkside. Somebody invented windsurfing and somebody else designed the first colour television. A man named Charles Cockerell built the very first hovercraft while a guy named J D Watson thought of the double-helix, the theory on which modern DNA research is based.

They were building one of the modern wonders of the world, the Aswan Dam, in Egypt, and, when they realized that it would threaten the age-old temples at Abu Simbel, on the Upper Nile, they simply moved them, brick for brick, to higher ground.

All this, crammed into the space of twelve months, made you think that anything was possible, that the human mind could achieve anything, that human endeavour could conquer any foe.

Yet, back at the Quarticciolo, where I was born, it all barely registered.

You can live in Rome your entire life and never visit the Quarticciolo, even by accident. It probably won't ever come up in conversation either. That's because, in many ways, it is a parallel dimension, a neighbourhood planned and constructed with one thing in mind: to house people. Nothing else, just a gigantic closet in which to stow humans.

There's nothing there. Just a bunch of public housing estates, tightly packed together on the southern outskirts of Rome. It's a classless society, mainly because there are no rich people, no middle-class people and no homeless people there. Just the working class, neatly tucked away in tiny flats. The buildings all pretty much look the same, perhaps to destroy the notion that the family down the street somehow got lucky and were given a nicer flat. No such luck. In fact, to further reinforce the concept of sameness, somebody had the bright idea of not naming the blocks. Instead, they had numbers. We were in the Settimo Lotto, the Seventh Block, all around us were other numbers, Quinto Lotto, Decimo Lotto and so on. We were defined by numbers.

A few decades before, this was probably somebody's vision of an urban utopia. In the 1950s, Italian cities swelled with people. Many had left the countryside in search for jobs. Others, who had been abroad during the War, had experienced different cultures and varied lifestyles and realized there was more to life than their little villages. Throw in the demographic boom and you suddenly had a severe housing shortage. Which is why the Quarticciolo was built. They needed a place to stuff bodies and it worked well in that capacity.

I know that sociologists have devoted acres and acres of text to the issues and problems in urban estates. They talk about alienation, about crime, about lack of outlets and services. I can only speak of my own experience. It was a tough place to live, it was easy to fall into a bad crowd, to take a wrong turn down a road of drugs, crime and despair.

An outsider may see only working-class families crammed into cubbyhole apartments, men forced to commute for hours to reach their low-paying jobs, kids with nothing to do but stand around on cement courtyards or in dingy videogame arcades.

Yet when I think back, it was a wonderful place in which to grow up. We did not have much, but I never felt like I was missing anything. Most of all, what I cherish is the closeness I developed with my family. It could not have been otherwise; there were six of us living in a one-bedroom apartment. This meant we were pretty much together all the time. I was either out in the courtyard playing football or at home with my family. They were always there and it helped build a closeness, a comfort zone, which I might not have had if I had lived elsewhere.

I was the fourth of four brothers. Looking back, I'm not sure how my mother, Pierina, coped with five male Di Canios running around the house. Inevitably, she was over-matched in all the gender wars. There were five of us and just one of her, but like all intelligent women, she knew how to handle us and get her way. Men would be lost without women like my mother or her four sisters. All five of them lived in the Quarticciolo, a stone's throw from each other. All of them faced the same issues my mother did, and they all overcame them without missing a beat.

Antonio, my oldest brother, was my idol growing up. He was nine years older than me, he always seemed so big and strong, it was like nothing could stop him. For the first five years of my life, he and I shared a sofabed in what was sup-posed to be our living room. One of my earliest memories is waking up in the middle of the night and feeling his body next to mine as he slept. If I was cold, and I often was, I would cuddle up next to him, feeding off the warmth of his body. I knew that I was completely safe there, that it was the happiest, coziest place in the world.

In retrospect, I probably felt too safe. When you're totally comfortable, completely relaxed, you sometimes just let yourself go: in every sense of the word. I felt so content with him that sometimes, when I needed to go to the bathroom, I simply wouldn't. I would just wet my bed right then and there.

I'm sure it was some kind of psychological thing, trig-gered by the cocoon of warmth and safety I enjoyed with

Antonio. You would have to ask Sigmund Freud. When you're in the safest place in the world, you don't want to leave it, especially not to fumble your way through a dark, cold apartment to go to the bathroom.

Bed-wetting is something I had to deal with until I was ten or eleven. But the strange thing is that Antonio never got cross with me. It was as if he understood me, as if he knew why it happened.

It was Antonio who made me want to become a footballer. He was a phenomenal talent, the pride of the Quarticciolo, and had been signed to Lazio's youth teams, just as I would be nine years later. I loved watching him play. He had natural flair, talent, creativity, vision, all the ingredients you need to succeed as a footballer. All but one: he wasn't right in the head. His personality could often be abrasive, both with teammates and coaches. He would speak his mind, always and often with little tact. And when he got angry, he did not train the way he should have. He was considered a loose cannon, a genuine talent cursed by an unpredictable temperament.

Sound familiar? Let's just say I inherited some of Antonio's qualities. But the main difference is that, to me, training and hard work have always been the release valve in the face of adversity. Like Antonio I have never allowed myself to be silenced, I have never been afraid to speak my mind. And I have often paid the price. But when things went wrong, when the going got tough, I simply threw myself into my work with even greater tenacity. It has always been the best outlet for my anger, the ideal channel for my emotions. I think in the long run that is what has enabled me to bounce back time after time. Every setback only made me stronger, because it was followed by hours and hours of hard, intense work.

My other brothers, Dino and Giuliano, are eight and six years older than me respectively. My relationship with them was different. I loved them, of course, but I never idolized them. I viewed them as equals, which naturally led to a number of confrontations. Nothing serious of course, just standard fare among growing boys who literally spent the entire day one on top of the other in a small apartment.

I was the baby of the family, coddled and spoiled by all, especially my mother and Antonio. When I think back to the way things were, I realize I was a little pest, in every sense of the word. I knew from an early age that I could get away with just about anything and I abused my position whenever I could. I loved picking fights with Dino and Giuliano.

I would bother them when they played checkers or when they were watching television, stupid things like that. Nothing major, just minor harassment, like poking them or pulling their hair or disturbing them any way I could. Ideally, I would succeed in setting them against each other and watching them fight. Or, more often than not, they would get angry with me and chase me around the flat. When that happened, I would always run to Antonio, usually crying my eyes out. He would take my side, no matter what. Together, we would hunt down whichever brother was after me and sort him out. Antonio was always older and stronger anyway. I'm not particularly proud of it, but I was just a kid and, to be honest, it was a lot of fun at the time, watching their fury build up and then seeing them skulk away as soon as I called in Antonio.

It's funny how things work out. What makes you a footballer? My four brothers and I all have the same parents, presumably similar genes as well. I am a professional footballer, but Antonio could have been one too, probably even a better one than me. Dino would have liked to become one, but he had about as much skill as a mannequin, while Giuliano never gave a damn about football.

As a boy, football was everything to me. It's nothing new, it's the same with children everywhere, from the favelas of Rio to the housing estates of Belfast. There's something wonderful in watching children chase a ball on a street or on a small patch of cement. It's a scene that repeats itself around the world, but it has an enduring quality to which, I believe, everybody who loves the game can relate.

I would wake up in the morning, and all I wanted to do was go outside and play football. It was the first thing I thought of. During the school year, I'd get back home around 1 pm, eat something quickly and be out there until it got dark. In the summer, it was even more intense. I would spend eight or nine hours outdoors, regardless of the weather.

Whoever built our estate thought it would be a good idea to lay the buildings out around these cement courtyards, maybe fifty feet long and twenty, twenty-five feet wide. It wasn't meant to be an aesthetic element, there was nothing pretty about them. They were purely functional: their main purpose was as a place to hang the washing. They were called 'stenditoi', or 'hanging places'.

There were metal clothesline wires cutting across them horizontally, about five or six feet above the ground. I'm sure it seemed like a bright idea at the time, providing a place where women could hang the washing. Except the architects didn't consider that these patches of concrete would make ideal playing fields for the kids of the Quarticciolo. In effect, we commandeered the stenditoi and turned them into our version of the San Siro or the Olympic Stadium. No sane woman would ever choose to hang her underwear or sheets out there, not with twenty hyperactive children running around.

They weren't ideal pitches of course, and not just because you risked cutting your leg up and bleeding to death each time you fell over. There were all sorts of built-in obstacles: steps, gutters, the odd, scraggly tree trying to wind its way skyward out of the cement. Not to mention the clothesline wires themselves. We were small, so we could comfortably play under them, but occasionally there would be a clothesline which hung low, either because it was twisted out of shape or because some older boys had decided to tear it down. Then it would become the ultimate hazard, a veritable injury threat to spice up our marathon games. I've seen more than one breakaway run halted by a near decapitation in my time and it wasn't a pretty sight.

I developed my skills on those stenditoi, but I also learned the first lessons of life on those cement rectangles. Without them, I would be neither the player nor the person I am today.

From a technical standpoint, I couldn't help but improve my skills. Anybody can trap and control the ball on a picture-perfect billiard table smooth pitch. But where I played, you had to learn how to control the ball no matter what, regardless of whether it bounced off the rubble or skidded along the gutter. I learned how to dribble up steps, how to run non-stop for hours (there was no such thing as 'out-of-bounds') and how to thread my way through tight spaces (we played eleven-a-side on a pitch which would have been tight for a five-a-side). I guess much of my close control and dribbling ability originated on the stenditoi.

Beyond the basic footballing skills however, the days spent in the stenditoi taught me a whole range of values which I might never have otherwise learned. You could argue they were the values of the street, an education based on toughness, on independence, but they were nonetheless crucial to me.

Think about it. To most children, sport is the first time they encounter genuine difficulties and obstacles. Until they start playing sports, they are usually coddled and pampered by their parents and, even if they aren't, they are still enveloped in a family cocoon, surrounded by people who love them unconditionally. It is once they go out into the world, even if it is just playing with other children, that they first realize that not everyone will bend over backwards for them, not everyone has their well-being as their number one priority. School has the same effect in some ways, but it too is different from sport, because there is still adult supervision.

But when you go out in the street or the park and play football with other children for the first time, you are immersed into a world you do not control and of which you are not the centre. There is no safety net. You have to learn how to relate to the other children, you have to learn how to get along, how to resolve disputes, how to get by. In my case, it was only magnified because I lived in a place like the Quarticciolo where you inevitably tended to grow up much quicker anyway.

When I played in the stenditoi, I soon learned that winning was fun and fulfilling. Except I couldn't always win and, when I lost, I'd often come home crying. I came to realize however that if I practiced more than the others and worked harder, it increased my chances of winning. Which is exactly what I did.

It may sound like simplistic pop psychology today and maybe it is. But to me, at the time, it worked. The competitiveness of those games, even at an early age, made me hate losing and the best way to avoid it was to concentrate more intensely, to put in more effort than my opponent. It's a lesson which served me very well and which I have carried with me throughout my life.

I've often wondered if we spent all our time outdoors playing football because there was nothing else to do. Back then my options were simple: sit at home with my mother and stare at the wall or run around with my friends, competing in imaginary World Cups. Naturally, it was no contest.

Today, I'm not so sure. I go back to the Quarticciolo and occasionally I still see the kids out there, but a lot less than before. Children have more options nowadays, there are dozens of television channels, even a working-class family can afford a computer and Internet access. The city of Rome built a public swimming pool in the area, transport links have improved. There are other things to do, maybe better things. I am not one of those nostalgics who begrudges this.

Would I like it if things were exactly as I remember them? Yes, but I also realize that you cannot live in the past. We all have idyllic memories of how things once were, but it's just as important to know and understand that progress and change are what fuel human development, both on a societal level and on a personal level. Sure, something has been lost, perhaps the children of the Quarticciolo aren't learning the same lessons I learned twenty-five years ago. But at the same time, perhaps they are learning other, more important things. Perhaps there are doors being opened for them, doors I did not even realize existed in my day.

As I grow older, I realize more and more that what makes us human is our will to do something. It doesn't matter what it is, as long as it challenges us and pushes us. I love thinking back to the stenditoi, because the experiences I had, the fun and the victories as well as the bloody noses, scraped knees and tears, all helped me develop. They taught me that willpower plus hard work usually equals success. But even when you don't succeed, and I can accept that many times you simply might not have the ability to succeed, the mere striving for success, the effort alone, makes it all worth it.

Growing up, we didn't have much in the way of material possessions. My father, Ignazio, was a builder. When I say builder, I mean a real builder, not just a guy who lays down bricks. To him, construction work was an art, there was a deep, quiet pride involved in everything he did. I look at the things builders are asked to do and I am fascinated. Their work involves careful planning, geometry, dexterity and strength. And yet, builders, like many other manual workers do not seem to get the respect they deserve.

A man in a suit sits behind a desk in an office building, calls people up and sells them financial products and he is seen as respectable. But a builder spends days using his mind, his skills, his tools and his bare hands to construct something tangible, functional and often beautiful and to many he's just a guy in a hard hat who whistles after women.

I've never felt that way. Maybe it's because of the respect I have for my father's work and manual labour in general. After all, being a footballer is manual labour, too. There is this sense that manual labourers don't use their minds. That could not be further from the truth. Whether you are a footaller or a builder, the quality of your work has a direct correlation with your intelligence and work ethic.

Of course, raising four kids on a builder's wages wasn't easy. As I mentioned, our apartment was simple and cramped. You walked in the front door and were immediately confronted by a tiny hallway. To the right was my parents' bedroom, just beyond it, a small kitchen. Straight ahead was our bathroom, which was so small it didn't even have a real door, just a screen which folded up like an accordion when you opened it. The technical term for them is concertina door or bifold door and I suppose at the time it was meant to be some kind of hip innovative design.

And if you made a left coming in the front door you would end up right in what was supposed to be the reception room. In reality, it was where we spent all our time in the flat. It was here that I shared the sofabed with Antonio until I was five, while Giuliano and Dino slept on bunk beds. It was also here that the family ate, watched television and performed virtually all household activities. Did it feel cramped? Not really. Space, especially private space, is a relative concept. To some a room is enough, others aren't even satisfied with a whole house. In my case, I had neither, but it did not matter. Privacy was something in your mind, a place to retreat to mentally more than anything else. If you wanted to shut others out and have a quiet moment, all you had to do was ignore those around you and collect your thoughts.

But that wasn't our way. It was the epitome of communal living, not just as far as my family was concerned. We lived on the first floor of a five-story apartment block. There were two flats on each floor, and one of my mother's sisters lived across the landing from us with her two sons, Ezio and Alvaro. I lived there for seventeen years and I hardly ever recall their front door being closed. It was like an extension of our own apartment. We could walk in and out whenever we wanted, what was theirs was ours and vice versa.

My cousins, Ezio and Alvaro, were like brothers to me. I knew I could wander in at any time and find something to do. They had a record player and we would spend hours listening to old LPs. When we got bored with that, we would just sit around and talk, or go outside, or watch television. It really did not matter, the point was that you were never lonely and you were always at home.

Our housing situation improved a little when I was five. My father figured out that there was an empty space behind the wall in the bedroom. Essentially, it was a windowless rectangle, perhaps ten feet by twelve feet, separating our flat from the one next door. I never understood why it was there. It didn't seem to make sense to construct a building and not use all the available space within the four walls. Perhaps it had something to do with the structural integrity of our apartment block, or perhaps whoever built it simply got lazy and, rather than finishing an extra room, with windows, fittings and the like, simply put up a wall and pretended it wasn't there.

There were six of us crammed into two rooms and the idea that you could knock down a wall and magically add a room to the flat was very appealing. Since my father was a builder anyway, it was something he could do fairly easily and inexpensively. So, working nights and weekends, he began chipping away at that wall and when he finally broke through he found a room which was dusty and dark, but nonetheless represented extra space for the family. He renovated it in his spare time and eventually moved in there with my mother. Dino and Giuliano moved to my parents' old bedroom and Antonio and I remained in the living room.

What he did was certainly illegal (we did it quietly, without telling anyone and, naturally, without getting a single permit), but he didn't think twice about it, especially because he wasn't harming anyone. All that was important was that his four growing sons had enough room to live decently. In those situations, you're not going to get any help from the government, so you might as well help yourself.

When I was very young, they called me Pallocca, a dialect term which you could loosely translate as 'Fatty'. It may surprise you, but as a small boy I had serious weight problems. I was grossly overweight, and I don't mean just baby fat. I wasn't chubby, I was bordering on obesity. It was a medical dysfunction which worried my parents no end. My legs were so fat that when I look back at old photographs I realize I had no knees to speak of. At the same time, the added weight I was carrying put an additional strain on my legs, which were crooked to begin with. I had what they call X-legs, which is the opposite of being bow-legged. I had to wear orthopaedic shoes to straighten them out, but even then doctors were sceptical about whether I would ever walk properly.

They put me on an intense swimming regimen. I would spend hours in the pool, back and forth, back and forth. At first I hated it; remember, I was only six or seven at the time. After a while, I started enjoying it, especially the thrill of pushing myself harder and harder. Maybe that's where I began to learn to like training. I loved the idea of challenging myself, of constantly driving myself forward. I found out at an early age that I am a perfectionist. If I wasn't the best at something I would force myself to go back and do it over and over again until I was the best. Of course, perfection can never be attained, but that's not the point. The thrill, the rush, is in the search for perfection.

Anyway, my time spent in the pool soon started having an effect. In the space of six months, my body tightened, the excess flab disappeared. Soon, the doctors allowed me to remove those horrible orthopaedic shoes. I look at myself now, thin and wiry, all nerves and muscles, and it's hard to believe that I was once a fat little boy.

I was lucky. Nobody ever made fun of me (or if they did, I don't remember it), maybe because by the time I was eight I was no longer fat and kids don't become cruel until they turn ten. Or perhaps it was simply the presence of Antonio which struck fear into potential bullies.

Whatever the case may be, looking back I know that I was very close to spending my entire life as an obese man. Everything would have been different. I would not have become a professional footballer, I would never have met Betta and I probably wouldn't have two beautiful daughters. I look at a lot of overweight children today, kids with problems, both physical and psychological and I wish I could somehow tell them that it doesn't have to be this way. You can bounce back, you can change the way you are. I did it and so can they.

By the time I was nine, I was a happy, smiling boy. So much so that my mother decided to enter me into a talent search. Okay, so maybe it was a typical thing for an Italian mother to do. After all, most Italian mums are honestly convinced that their children are the brightest, most beautiful little creatures in the world.

Remember Zorro, the dashing, masked sword-wielding adventurer who galloped across Mexico, righting wrongs and wooing women? Well, Italian television decided to film a new series of the show, one which focused on his early childhood. They put up billboards all over Rome, inviting boys aged between eight and ten to attend auditions to play the part of Zorro as a little boy. For a while, it was all people talked about. My mother took me down to the television studios. I didn't quite know what to expect, I was just excited to be in a new and different place.

There were around a thousand of us, each one with a number pinned to his shoulder, rather like cattle at a county fair. Some children were visibly nervous, others were crying, still others were as stiff as mannequins, rigidly clamped on to their mother's hands. We had all been cleaned up, given new haircuts and dressed in our Sunday best. I had new clothes, which I didn't really mind. I enjoyed the feel of brand-new shirts and trousers, even back then I liked to dress smart.

But it was nothing compared to the mothers. They were much more nervous than the children and much more dressed up. You would think they were the ones on display. Make-up, floral-patterned skirts, beads; it was the mid-seventies after all. They chattered amongst each other, while jealously keeping an eye on their children, making sure no shoes got scuffed and no shirts got wrinkled.

We did a brief screen test and then went on stage to read for the part. Some kids were scared to death, others just stared back in blank confusion. You could feel the intensity of the mothers' laser-like gaze burning a hole in their little faces. I don't know where everybody came from, but I assume that, like us, they were mostly working-class families. For many this would be their one and only chance to break the cycle of monotony, to actually go and do something different, something glamorous. Throw in the fact that in the end it all boiled down to a cattle market ('M'am, your son is beautiful and talented, but not as beautiful and talented as the next kid') and the pressure was unbearable. You have to understand the mentality of the times and the attitude of the mothers present. Their child was a direct reflection of how well they were doing their job as mothers.

Had they produced a beautiful, beaming boy? Was he articulate and bright? Did he have charisma? To these people, if the boy was less than perfect, it was the mother's fault. They were really the ones on trial here.

For some reason, I was neither scared nor nervous. Even at that age, I figured there was nothing I could do about the way I looked, so I should just concentrate on the way I acted. Since they were looking for Zorro as a little boy, the best thing to do was to act just like Zorro did as a child. But since I had no idea what Zorro was like as a boy, I figured it made sense to pretend that the young Zorro was exactly like me. That way I could just be myself and speak my lines the way Paolo Di Canio would speak them, not Zorro junior.

It worked. The organizers seemed to love me. For my part, I relished being on stage and having all the eyes in the room planted on me. It was almost like the attention gave me confidence. I immediately knew it had gone very well and I could feel the disappointment rising from the other mothers as the judges whispered among themselves. When the results were announced, I had won. Out of two hundred little boys, I was chosen to play Zorro in a national television series. My acting career was about to take off.

Except it didn't. In our excitement, my mother had failed to read the fine print. The talent search I had won merely selected the boy who was most suitable for the part. Final approval rested with the show's producer and director, who weren't actually present at the talent search. Still, the organizers assured us that we would be selected, all we had to do was take a few more photographs and go through a couple more screen tests. They would be happy to arrange them for us, in exchange for the modest and reasonable fee of 50,000 lire, around £30 at the time. The problem was that my mother had already spent money on new clothes and on the entrance fee for the talent search. Forking out a further 50,000 lire was not going to be easy.

'Signora Di Canio!' cooed one of the organizers. 'Look at this beautiful, talented boy! He will be the next Zorro! He has a wonderful future ahead of him! How can you let 50,000 lire stand in the way of a glorious acting career?'

My mother went silent and stared straight ahead. Maybe a part of her felt like she had been duped and that she would be further scammed if she handed over more money. Maybe she simply did not have the heart to go and ask my father for more cash.

'Signora, he is so close to stardom!' The organizers wouldn't let it rest. 'He will be working with professionals, it is imperative that he have a professional screen test and photos done. It will only take an afternoon of your time, no more. Think of it: an afternoon in exchange for a career on the television!'

We walked out in silence. My mother held my hand as she shuffled towards the bus stop. I looked at her quietly, the number I had been assigned still pinned to my chest. We did not talk about it again, but I think I learned a lesson even then at that young age.

Bringing me to that Zorro audition was really the only

time my mother projected her dreams on me. It was the one time I saw stars in her eyes, the one time I felt like she was steering me towards something she wanted me to do. It was her brush with glamour, her glimpse into a world that was different and far away. Of course, years later I would become a professional footballer and would experience fame and glory, but that was a different sphere. She could not relate to it in the same way. Even though she was always very happy for me and shared in my success, it was not the same.

To think that her dreams were shattered by 50,000 lire, by money alone and not that much money at that, is heart-breaking. I think the worst part was that 50,000 lire was an in-between sum, which made it all the more painful. Had we been rich, or even middle class, we would not have thought twice about it. Had we been dirt poor, we would not have worried about it either, because it simply would not have been an option. But 50,000 lire was a sum large enough to seriously affect the running of the household and at the same time small enough that we could have afforded it, if we really, really needed to. That was the difficult part: the dilemma, the realization that to aid her dream and to help me, Paolo, she would have had to take something away from the rest of the family.

I wonder sometimes how things might have worked out if I had become an actor. To me, there is something wonderful about being on stage or in front of a camera. Life, in its purest form, is about experiencing emotions. Think about it. Everything you do generates some kind of feeling, whether it be happiness, contentment, relief, anger, whatever. In our free time, we actively seek out emotions. We might go for a nice meal or read a book or take a shower or make love to our wives and girlfriends. Each of these activities stimulates us, it generates an emotional response which may be more or less pleasant, more or less intense. Actors, and by extension films or plays, bring out emotions within us. We may feel sorrow, passion, anger, humour, pleasure, all because an actor is performing for us. It's a beautiful thing, the relationship between an actor and an audience.

The parallels between that and being a footballer are obvious. When I play football, I generate emotions, both inside myself, but, just as importantly, among the spectators. That's why some people compare a game of football to an opera: it grabs you, you feel a part of it, you become one with the action, rising and falling in synchrony with the events on the pitch. It is the ultimate communal emotional experience.

When I am on the pitch, I am on stage. This does not mean I am there only to entertain. There may be an aesthetic quality to a dribble, or a trap or a shot or a tackle and that will generate one kind of emotion. But I am also there to win, by any means necessary. And that, the sheer relief of victory, is a totally different emotion. That is why football is like an unscripted opera. There is a flow of raw emotion between the performers and the audience.

Like actors, footballers operate on a combination of natural ability and constant practice. There certainly are innate qualities, a basic foundation of talent which is necessary. If you are not expressive, if you are unable to transform yourself into another character and project it to the audience, you cannot be a succesful actor, just as if you cannot control the ball, you cannot be a successful footballer. Having said that however, without the hard work, without the hours of daily training, you will not get far in either field. I have seen hundreds of talented footballers, people who, in terms of strength and ability, were far superior to many Premiership or Serie A players, fail to make the grade because they were unwilling or unable to put in the effort. It is the same with acting.

I suppose that is why I am drawn to it. A number of athletes have become actors. Some have merely played themselves on the screen, but the really good ones have put in the work and gone to the next level. Look at Vinnie Jones and what he has achieved. Okay, some might say that his goon character in *Lock, Stock and Two Smoking Barrels* wasn't a big departure for him. But if you watch the film closely as I have, you will see that there is a sophistication in his performance that you only really see with professional actors. That's why he's received offers to work on a number of other projects and is considered a real actor. Contrast that with Eric Cantona. He may have a strong presence and a very familiar face, but have you ever seen his movies? He's wooden, he generates no emotion whatsoever. I don't know if he's not cut out to be an actor or if he has not had the chance to study acting properly. Either way, I hope I did not look like that when I was on screen.

In the summer of 1998, some twenty-one years after the Zorro audition, I finally got my chance in front of the camera. A guy named Luca Borri, a young director trying to make a name for himself, asked me if I'd be interested in starring in his short film.

Luca had studied under Carlo Rambaldi, the Italian special-effects guru who created ET, the Extraterrestrial, and who worked on the film *Dune*. I think he approached me with some trepidation; the film would take two weeks to shoot, which meant I'd spend my entire time in Terni on the set. It was quite a big commitment for me, but the idea was intriguing. Maybe, deep down, I had never given up on the idea of acting.

The film was called 'Strade Parallele', or *Parallel Roads*. It's the story of two friends who live life as a perpetual competition. They are close, but they are also constantly challenging each other, one way or another. To them, nothing is straightforward. Every day is a new opportunity to compete, to fight, to win. Everything becomes a battle. Their rivalry knows no bounds.

It all reaches a peak when they compete for the love of the same woman. They decide that settling things requires the ultimate winner-take-all competition: a pistol duel. It is the only way to stop the competition which has spiralled out of control. Needless to say, the final gunfight costs them both their lives. They kill each other in the name of competition.

Luca picked me to play one of the two rivals. While I obviously had no acting experience, I prepared as best I could and I think I was particularly suited to the role. In many ways I too lived life as a constant challenge, always on edge, always looking for an opening. It couldn't have been otherwise, growing up on the streets of the Quarticciolo. If you don't quickly learn how to hold your own, if you don't relish and thrive on the pressure of competition, you don't get very far.

You develop a victim's mentality, and that can lead to only one thing: becoming a victim. Somebody once said that on the street there are only two kinds of people: victims and victimizers. I don't know if it's true, I don't want to think of myself as a victimizer, but I know for a fact that I am not a victim.

We shot every single day, for fifteen days straight. Some days it was only three or four hours, others it could be as many as seven. All this to produce a film that was all of twelve minutes long.

The thing which struck me most about acting is the constant repetition. You do a take over and over again until it's perfect. In football you obviously repeat the same action endlessly as well, that's what practice is all about. The key difference however is that, in football, you can rehearse it as often as you like, but you only get one chance to get it right on the pitch. Actors on the other hand can rehearse it as many times as necessary, which can be just as gruelling. Except they are faced with a different kind of doubt. At some point, they have to say, 'Enough! That's as good as it's going to get.' If you're a perfectionist by nature, as I am, it's a difficult concept to swallow, because my natural instinct would be to continue re-shooting the take forever.

I wasn't fazed by the idea of being in front of the camera. What I found interesting was the process by which I had to search inside myself for the emotion to portray on film. As I said, growing up on the street, I could relate to what my character was feeling, which is why I think the role came naturally to me. I was acting, yes, but what I was really doing was releasing some of the anger, some of the passions, which had developed inside me from the time I was a small boy.

Perhaps the strangest part of the experience came at the end of the film, when my character and his rival kill each other in the pistol duel. Pretending to die on-screen was weird, unsettling in some ways. After all, most of acting consists of going into character and repeating actions which you perform in your daily life, except you're repeating them in a different context and through the eyes of another person. But dying, obviously, is not something you do every day. In fact, it's something no actor has ever experienced. The best you can do is imitate, which is what I did. I thought back to other films I had seen, plays, instances where I had witnessed extreme pain or desperation or just the realization that something you care deeply about is about to end.

I know it wasn't a big-budget Hollywood feature, I know I'm not a real actor. But the experience taught me a lot and I genuinely enjoyed it. It's too early to say if I might be cut out for that kind of career. Still, it's something which will remain in the back of my mind.

CHAPTER TWO

KING OF THE QUARTICCIOLO

To most Italian children, the happiest time of the year is summer. No school, empty streets, hours and hours of sunshine in which you could do anything from chasing a football to lying on the grass (or in my case, the asphalt). Italian cities seem to shut down in the summer, particularly in August. Businesses close, people go on holiday, everything moves at a slower pace.

Of course, Rome gets overrun by tourists as well, but they never came to my neighbourhood. No, the Quarticciolo was the exclusive domain of its inhabitants and in July and August, it felt as if the kids had taken over. The parents still had to go to work, but with no school shackling us to a daily routine, we could do whatever we wanted.

I would wake up late, around eleven, and wander down to the corner shop or, as we called it, 'il fornaio'. It was all so reassuring. The shopkeeper, Edoardo, would make me a mozzarella sandwich and pour me an extra-large cola drink. He would then put it on our tab. It seemed that every family had a 'credit book', usually a notebook like the ones we had in school, where Edoardo would keep track of which kids spent what and then charge it to the parents at the end of the month. I don't know if that's still done today, these days it feels like you can't trust anybody and no one is willing to trust you. But back then it was easier, simpler. I can still see Edoardo carefully writing up my breakfast in that big black notebook, his gnarled fingers gingerly gripping the ballpoint pen.

Sandwich and coke in hand, I would sit on the front doorstep of his shop reading *Corriere Dello Sport*, Rome's sports daily. Every day, it brought us 30 broadsheet pages, brimming with news on Roma and Lazio. It was our bible. Many foreigners are perhaps more familiar with *Gazzetta Dello Sport*, the pink newspaper you can find at many newsagents in London and throughout Britain. *Gazzetta* is based in Milan and is better known worldwide but there was something wonderful and irreverent about *Corriere*. It was our newspaper, focusing on our clubs, Roma and Lazio and, to a lesser degree, Napoli. It did not matter that at the time, Lazio were stuck in Serie B, that Napoli always seemed threatened by relegation or that Roma was forever the bridesmaid, as northern clubs like AC Milan, Inter and Juventus dominated Italian football.

Corriere was Rome's paper and it gave us what we wanted: pages and pages (usually four to six every day) offering every detail, even the most mundane, on Lazio and Roma. Later, when I experienced this blanket coverage as a player, it could sometimes get a little overwhelming. I wondered if people really needed to know which players missed penalties in training or how many wind sprints we did the day before or even that so-and-so arrived at the training ground wearing a yellow-checked shirt. But to a boy of twelve who was in love with Lazio, this kind of detail was fantastic and I gleefully soaked up every inch of information.

After reading the paper, I would meet my friends at the video-game arcade. Those were still the early days of video games, we're talking Pac Man, Space Invaders, Asteroids, that sort of thing. Compared to today's games, it was pretty dire stuff, but at the time it seemed wonderful. And then there were the pinball machines, each with its own theme, each with its own array of sounds. Most of the time was spent chatting or watching others play, none of us ever seemed to have much money (and, unlike Edoardo's shop, we couldn't really put video games on the family tab). Still, it was a place to meet, a haven from the midday sun.

A couple of hours later, we'd be out on the 'stenditoi' and our afternoon of football would begin. Those were marathon games, lasting well into the evening, when our mothers would emerge from the apartment blocks and call us back in. Around 8 pm, Rome's twilight would reverberate to the sounds of boys' names.

'Paolo!'

'Ezio!'

'Stefano!'

More often than not it would end with an irate mother chasing her son up and down the cement stenditoi after the boy had ignored the umpteenth call to supper in order to finish off his own personal Quarticciolo World Cup Final.

When I was twelve I had my most serious run-in with my brother, Giuliano. As I said, I love my brothers, but I have to admit I was a serious pest. Money had been tight for several weeks and my mates and I spent more than one afternoon in the games arcade, watching wistfully as other kids fed the pinball and video-game machines. Something clicked in my brain. I wanted to do something special for my mates, give them a day of fun, a day where we could live large with video games, ice cream and sandwiches. It was no big deal, it's not like I was asking for the moon. I just wanted a fun day out.

But of course, I had no money. So I got to thinking: how does a twelve-year-old kid in the Quarticciolo raise a fair amount of cash in a hurry?

I kept asking my brother, Giuliano, who was eighteen at the time, for money. He had done some odd jobs and was earning a little, so it seemed only logical that he should share it with me. Except Giuliano, probably remembering all the times I put him through hell, refused to budge, especially since he knew I would just blow it all in the video arcade.

Naturally, this displeased me no end. I had to get him back. He had one of those old bicycles, the kind where you would brake by pedalling backwards. It wasn't much of a bike, but at least it worked and it was all he had.

One day, I took his bike and rode it down to a used bike shop, a few blocks from where we lived. The owner, Peppino, bought, sold and repaired bikes and scooters. He looked at me in a strange way when I offered to sell him the bike.

'Pallocca, why are you selling this bicycle?'

'Because I don't like it,' I replied. 'I'm going to get a new one. Now, do you want it or not? How much will you give me for it?'

He looked at the bike closely.

'Whose bike is this?'

'It's mine!' I replied, indignant. 'Whose bike would it be? Of course, it's mine, otherwise I wouldn't be selling it, would I?'

'It looks familiar, it's just that I've never seen you riding it . . .'

'I told you, I don't like it!' I snapped. 'Now, how much can I get for it?'

Peppino shrugged and scratched his chin. The fact that a twelve-year-old boy was selling him a bicycle may have seemed suspicious, but then, it wasn't his problem, was it?

'I'll give you 10,000 lire for it,' he said.

At the time, that was around £6. Probably not a fair price for a used bicycle, but to me, it seemed like a fortune. Remember, this was some twenty years ago. The things I could do with 10,000 lire! I didn't think twice about it and took the cash.

For the next thirty-six hours I was the King of the Quarticciolo. Friends came out of the woodwork, everybody wanted to be around me. We hadn't seen that much money in a long, long time.

I was like the guy who wins millions in the lottery and buys drinks for everybody in the pub. We blew the cash quickly and efficiently. First, we played every game in the video arcade. Then, I treated everybody to lunch, deep-filled sandwiches with big bottles of coke, followed by ice cream.

It has always been my nature to share. I don't even think about it. It's an old saying, 'giving is better than receiving', but it's true. In fact, at the very heart of it, if you think about it, the sentiment behind giving is almost a selfish one. You feel good about yourself because you are making somebody else happy. You do it because it makes you feel better about yourself. Maybe it's not a conscious thought process, but giving is as much something you do for yourself as something you do for others.

Anyway, the money dried up quickly, very quickly. I was left with a great memory of a wonderful day out and that is what mattered to me. Little did I know that I would soon have to face the consequences of stealing my brother's bike.

That night, Giuliano was a nervous wreck.

'Where's my bike? Who took my bike? Did you see my bike?'

He was like a broken record, but it was understandable. That bicycle, however old and rusty it may have been, was more than just his prized possession. It was his means of transportation, it was his way of getting out of the Quarticciolo, at least temporarily, and it opened up the rest of Rome to him. Without it, he was stuck here, just like the rest of us.

'I can't believe it!' Giuliano was desperate. I genuinely felt bad for him. 'Somebody stole my bike! Pallocca, tell me, you must have seen something . . .'

'Sorry, Giuliano,' I replied, playing dumb. 'I have no clue. It could have been anybody, probably someone from another neighbourhood. Maybe the gypsies took it.'

Giuliano was shattered, but I held my nerve. I thought I had got away with it, but in retrospect, I was foolish. The Quarticciolo simply wasn't that big, sooner or later Giuliano would get wind of something.

Which is exactly what happened. A few days later he walked past Peppino's shop and saw the bike outside, with a 20,000 lire price tag on it.

'What the f**k is going on!' he roared at Peppino. 'That's my bicycle! You're selling stolen goods! I'm calling the police, you're going to jail!'

Giuliano doesn't quite have the same temper as I have, but when he gets angry, there's no stopping him. And I guess I would have blown my top as well in that situation.

'Cool it, son,' Peppino told him. 'I don't know what you're talking about. Pallocca came in and sold me this bicycle. He told me it was his and I had no reason to doubt him.'

'It's my bike! He had no right to sell it! Give it back!'

'Sorry, Giuliano. I paid him good money for it. If you want it back, you'll have to buy it back. You'd better go and sort it out with him . . .'

That's when Giuliano came looking for me. I have never seen him so angry. I saw him in the distance and I'll never forget the look on his face. Rage doesn't quite describe it. He looked almost like a cartoon character, I could just about see the smoke coming out of his ears.

I didn't give him time to get any closer. I bolted. I just ran and ran, with Giuliano in close pursuit.

I was very fast even then, but there is no way a twelve-year-old can outrun an eighteen-year-old. My legs were just shorter than his. I was running for my life, he was fuelled by sheer fury. I ran into the house, thinking that maybe my mother or Antonio or Dino or anybody would be around. I stormed up the stairs, frantically hoping to find a family member.

There was nobody there. What's worse, there was no way out. I was cornered in my living room.

The punishment began, almost without saying a word. He didn't need to. We both knew what I had done. He beat me black and blue with an assortment of slaps, kicks and punches. I fought back, but there was nothing I could do. I had been asking for it. He started banging my head against the table, once, twice, three times. I was screaming at the top of my lungs.

Just then the door burst open and my Aunt Franca stormed in. There is nobody in the world I would have rather seen at that moment. Aunt Franca adored me. She was a big, tough, no-nonsense woman. A hardcore Lazio fan, she never had any kids, and I became like a son to her. She didn't take any nonsense and I can understand why she was always pushing my Uncle Alvaro around. Come to think of it, in many ways, she was like a man herself.

'What the f**k do you think you're doing?' she bellowed at Giuliano. She grabbed his arm and yanked him away.

Giuliano was a big, strong guy, but Aunt Franca could take him. Easily.

'Leave Paolo alone!' she roared. 'Touch my nephew again and I'll kill you! How dare you!'

Giuliano was stunned, he didn't know what to say. Naturally, I sensed the opportunity and exploited the situation to the best of my ability. I did what I always did in these instances. I started crying.

'Aunt Franca, he beat me up!' I sobbed. 'Giuliano attacked me for no reason and beat me up. He's mean, he's vicious! And he did it for no reason, no reason at all!'

My brother protested his innocence and tried to explain his side of the story, but Aunt Franca was having none of it. She shoved him out of the room, closed the door and tended to me. I was in a pretty bad state, I had bruises and a few cuts, though nothing life-threatening.

Most of all, though, I hurt inside. I hated the fact that somebody could come and physically overpower me. Quietly, I began plotting my revenge, though I still had to face my parents.

Aunt Franca was great. She totally took my side, even after hearing from Giuliano what I had done. And she intervened with my parents, begging them to go easy on me.

Giuliano and I were still at each other's throats. My father ended up sorting things out. He went to the bike shop and bought the bike back for ·20,000 lire, which meant that Peppino made a nice little profit on it. He scolded me, but without being too hard. I think he was shocked by Giuliano's violent reaction and figured I had suffered enough. Either that or Aunt Franca bullied him into going easy on me.

I think Giuliano realized he went way over the top in beating me up. From his point of view, he had got his bike back, he had his chance to beat the hell out of me, and now he was satisfied. He let things slide.

As for me, I was still boiling inside. I had to get even. And I did. About a week later, we got into another fight. This time, it wasn't serious, at least not to him. He was just pushing me around, taking advantage of the fact that he was bigger and stronger. He knew there wasn't much I could do to him.

Or so he thought.

After slapping me around a little, he turned his back to me, laughing. I ran into the kitchen and grabbed the biggest fork I could find. I held it in both hands, sneaked up behind him and rammed it into his back, just beneath the shoulder blades.

He let out a blood-curdling scream. His eyes opened so wide, I thought his eyeballs were going to roll out of their sockets. He stumbled around, frantically trying to reach back and pull out the fork. He was blinded with rage, he looked like Polyphemus the Cyclops after Ulysses burned out his one eye. I was laughing, partly because he looked so ridiculous, crashing around the flat with this big fork stuck in his back.

This time, I was clever about it. I exacted my revenge when the rest of my family was around, knowing they would protect me from Giuliano's rage. Antonio extracted the fork. I got yelled at a lot, but didn't really get into serious trouble. I don't remember exactly how I was punished, but whatever I got, it was worth it. As for Giuliano, he was more stunned than angry. I don't think he could ever have expected anything like that.

In the meantime, I had started turning out for a local boys' team, Pro Tevere Roma. It was after-school stuff, nothing too serious, but even at that age most of us really believed we could one day make it as professional footballers. I suppose everybody who loves the game goes through the stage where he thinks, or maybe just dreams, that he will make it.

From the very beginning, I loved training. I took it very

seriously. Don't get me wrong, I was still a colossal pest, an unrepentant pain-in-the-backside to the coaches, playing pranks and joking around with the other kids. But when it came time to run, I always had to finish first and when shooting practice came around, I had to be more accurate or powerful than all the others. I wouldn't stop until I was the best. Once the idea is ingrained in your head that you can improve by training, your natural instinct is to work harder. At least, that was the case with me.

My budding career was put on hold at age twelve, for the most bizarre of reasons. Remember how I said I loved cola drinks? Well, that's an understatement. I was obsessed with it, that fizzy sweetness hitting my throat was like a drug. I would drink two or three litre-bottles a day, furiously guzzling it down whenever I could get my hands on it.

It may seem strange to hear that fizzy drinks can do that to you. I'm not saying they are bad or dangerous products, but if taken in ridiculously large quantities (as I did), they can be very harmful. They contain chemicals which have an acidic effect. Try putting a coin in a glass of cola overnight and see what happens. Now imagine what it does inside your stomach.

As a result, my liver began swelling and the doctors were genuinely worried. They told my parents that if I continued, I could suffer permanent damage. My liver had deteriorated to the point where the rest of my body had to work twice as hard just to keep it functioning. This caused my bones to weaken. Not only did I have to give up cola drinks, I also had to stop playing football. The pounding I took on the pitch was extremely dangerous, as it placed even more stress on my already weakened body.

They ordered me to swim instead, as it was a non-impact form of exercise. And they told my mother in no uncertain terms: 'No more cola, signora. Otherwise, we cannot be held responsible.'

At first my mother banned it entirely from the house. What seemed like a good idea at first, turned into a nightmare. Without cola I became even edgier and nervous than I already was. Every moment outside the flat was spent trying to procure more cola drinks. Edoardo, following my mother's orders, cut me off. I would beg friends to buy me some, or I would scrounge together enough money any which way I could to get my fix. I found places around the flat where I could stash it, hoping to God all the time that my parents or brothers wouldn't find my illicit storage.

It was sheer hell. I was like an addict, and I was only twelve. My mother was understanding. She would water it down and ration it out, no more than half a glass with meals. It was difficult, I had to accept that I had a problem and I had to will myself to overcome it. The swimming helped. The hours spent in the pool at least offered a respite from my cravings. Again, my instinct for training kicked in. I wanted to stay fit so that when I began playing football again I would be ready and since swimming was the only thing I was allowed to do, I threw myself into it. The smell of chlorine followed me everywhere. Perhaps in some ways, the chlorine high, not the chemical itself as much as what was associated with it, the physical exertion of training, the endless laps of the pool which left me exhausted but stronger, replaced the cola kick.

Six months later, I got the all-clear to return to football. The swelling in my liver had gone back down. The doctors told me to steer clear of cola drinks whenever I could. By then I had learned to think of it as a treat, something to have occasionally, perhaps three or four times a week, rather than three or four times before lunch. I continued drinking cola until Christmas Day 1998. On that day, I vowed to give it up altogether and I've been clean ever since. It may not seem like a big deal, but it was a very difficult thing for me to do and I am very proud of it.

When I turned thirteen, I had a trial with Lazio. Pro Tevere was one of their satellite clubs and every year they would select the most promising thirteen-year-olds to join their youth system. A man named Volfango Patarca picked me out immediately. I was the first name on his list, after only a few minutes.

Joining Lazio meant a long, long commute every single day. After school, I would take a tram and two different buses to get from the Quarticciolo to the training ground at San Basilio. It took me anywhere from an hour and a half to an hour and forty-five minutes each way. If you add up all the hours, I probably spent a year of my life on Rome's public transportation system. But at that age, you really don't mind. The mere thought of Lazio's sky-blue colours was enough to make every bus journey seem like a chauffeur-driven stretch-limo ride.

Volfango would become my mentor. I always had a love for training and work, but it was he who took it to the next

47

level, teaching me that how you train is just as important as how much you train. He was also the one who encouraged me to follow my footballing instincts.

'Go ahead, take on the extra man, you never know what's going to happen,' he would say. 'Don't be afraid to dribble. If you see the goal, and it feels right, have a crack.'

I think I was very lucky to work with somebody like that. Most other coaches were preoccupied with winning, tactics and team cohesion, even at that age. They would expect their players to hold their positions, to play it safe, to above all keep possession. In short, even at that age, thirteen or fourteen, they were instructed to play just like adults. And in Italy, playing like an adult means putting tactics above creativity, results above skill.

Ever wonder why Italian teams are so polished technically and tactically but often so unimaginative? It's because they have certain ideas drilled in their head from a very early age. Players turn into robots, losing individuality. That's fine if you're a professional and your manager has to blend eleven players into a cohesive unit. But when you're just a kid, you should be free to develop your personality as a footballer. You should be assertive, creative, allowed to learn from your mistakes. I had all that with Volfango, but to be honest, if I'd had another coach, I'm not sure how it would have turned out.

Even at youth-team level, Italian coaches feel the pressure to win. They'll go 1–0 up and pack the defence, just like the adults do. Playing like that you'll get a string of victories and you'll produce competent defenders, but it will do little to develop your players, especially the midfielders and forwards. The other thing they will do is teach players that winning comes above all else. Often, this can mean being cynical. Nobody ever told me to take a dive (though I wouldn't be surprised if it happened elsewhere), but some of my coaches (though never Volfango) did tell me to go down if I felt contact and thought I could win a penalty or free kick. In fact, many times they would get angry if you were fouled and stayed on your feet, rather than tumbling to the ground.

It's unpleasant to discuss these things, but all I can say is that I was fortunate to have had Volfango as my first coach. He never stifled my creativity or tried to control my instincts. I think he understood right away that I was a talented player and that I should develop my talents rather than transform them into something that could fit into a team framework. There would be plenty of time for that later on; at age thirteen you should only worry about learning the game. Tactics and formations ought to come later, much later.

At Lazio, I began to learn some important lessons. First, even at that age, who you are and where you come from often matters as much as what you do. Lazio had two youth-team academies, San Basilio and Monte Mario. I was at San Basilio, which catered mostly to kids from working-class neighbourhoods, whereas Monte Mario included some of the posher areas of the city. Strangely enough, the boys at Monte Mario had better facilities.

It was also the boys from Monte Mario who regularly got picked to be ball-boys at the Stadio Olimpico when Lazio's first-team played at home. We would all go down there on a

Sunday; between San Basilio and Monte Mario there were maybe thirty-five boys, all competing for the twenty ball-boy slots. The job of choosing the ball-boys belonged to a coach from Monte Mario, a guy we knew only as 'Topolino', or 'Mickey Mouse', because he was short and had huge ears.

I can still hear Topolino's voice now, telling us: 'Alright lads, it's real simple. If Lazio are ahead, take your time getting the ball back into play. Walk, don't run, drop it a few times, just make sure it takes as long as possible. And if Lazio are behind, I want to see you all bust your tail-ends. The ball needs to get back in play as quickly as possible. I'll be watching, so don't screw-up!'

Even back then we were being taught all the little tricks of the trade. See what Italians are like? We'll do anything to get an edge. I didn't like Topolino because he would always pick his own kids from Monte Mario to be ball-boys, which meant the rest of us had to fight it out for the remaining two or three spots.

This struck me as a grave, grave injustice. We were Lazio boys just as much as they were, why should they get all the privileges? One day, I stood up to him in front of all the kids and some parents too.

'Enough of this crap!' I said. 'We are from San Basilio and we are not second-class! I am not taking this!'

With that, I stormed out, even though that day I was one of the lucky ones who was picked to be ball-boy. Topolino got really angry and chased me out. The commotion attracted the attention of other officials who all inquired as to what was going on. They took Topolino aside and spoke to him. I don't know what they said, but from that day on the ball-boy slots were evenly split between San Basilio and Monte Mario.

Even at San Basilio there were some kids who enjoyed a level of favouritism, either because their parents were professionals who knew people within the Lazio organization or because they were relatives of players or officials. Those kids always seemed to get picked in games, year after year they were never the ones who were dropped or asked to leave, no matter how good they were or how much they worked. I was just a runt from the Quarticciolo. I had nobody backing me up. In Italy, we have an expression for this, 'Santi in Paradiso', which means 'Saints in Heaven', powerful people further up the food chain who look out for you and push you along. I had no 'Saints in Heaven', where I came from; if anything, I was more likely to have 'Devils in Hell'.

Still, I had Volfango. In the larger scheme of things, he didn't have much influence, but he always looked out for me. He too was from the Quarticciolo, so he knew what I was dealing with, what kind of a world I returned to every night after training. Often, he would get angry, very angry, but I could always tell it was the kind of anger which is borne out of love.

I'll never forget the night Italy won the World Cup in 1982, beating West Germany in the Final, 3–1. I had just turned fourteen and had got caught up in the excitement of the tournament. My cousin Alvaro and I had bought some green, white and red fabric and sewn together a huge Italian flag. We had spent a lot of money to get the material, we didn't want it to look cheap or corny, and at the final whistle we went nuts.

The plan was to cruise around Rome in a FIAT Cinquecento belonging to Alvaro's mate, while proudly flying the flag out the window. Unfortunately, after a few hundred yards, our flag got caught between the wheel and the axle and was torn to shreds (the fact that we were driving much, much faster than we should have did not help). We were disappointed for the flag, but it didn't dampen our enthusiasm. Italy had become world champions after forty-four years of waiting and we sure as hell weren't going to let a torn flag ruin our celebration.

If we couldn't fly the flag out the window we would do the next best thing. We would roll the windows down and Alvaro and I would sit on the roof, reaching inside the car for something to hold on to. But if you've ever been in a Cinquecento, you'll know that it's a very small car and having two people on the roof is rather awkward. So I got creative. I stood on the hood, balanced myself carefully and rode along there. It was loads of fun, rather like surfing, Quarticciolo-style, even when Alvaro's mate got carried away and the speedometer crept past thirty kilometres an hour. I didn't care. By now the streets were teeming with fans, blowing horns, waving flags and singing at the top of their lungs. I was loving life. Imagine Leonardo di Caprio in that scene from *Titanic*, the one where he shouts 'I'm the king of the woooorld!!!' That's pretty much where I was.

You can imagine then that the last person I wanted to see was an irate Volfango. I spied his face in the crowd while cruising through the Quarticciolo. His was the only one not smiling. We turned the corner, I glanced back and I could see he was trying to fight his way through the crowd. He did not look pleased.

He finally caught up with the car a few more yards up the street. He grabbed my arm and yanked me off the car. He shoved me to the pavement and glowered down at me.

'What the hell are you doing?!!' he yelled. 'Are you trying to kill yourself?'

At that moment, I think he was the only grumpy Italian on Earth. I looked at him in disbelief. I knew he was angry because what I had done was pretty stupid. Dancing on the hood of a moving Cinquecento is foolish at the best of times. It's downright retarded when you're an aspiring foot-baller and one fractured tibia can kill your career before it even begins. I decided playing dumb was the best strategy.

'Volfango, we won the World Cup!' I shouted, trying to pick myself up off the floor. 'It's time to party!'

He shoved me back down.

'You, you're crazy!' he yelled. 'You have a future! You have a gift, you have something special which nobody else here has! You can make it! And yet, you are willing to jeopardize it by being a moron!'

He was more than angry. I could see pain in his eyes. Pain at the thought that a guy like me could waste his talent, ruin his career.

'Why? Why are you like this?' he said, almost pleadingly.

I got up slowly and apologized. He seemed to calm down, he seemed to understand that I was genuinely sorry.

Looking back, I know that riding on the hood of that Cinquecento was one of the dumber things I have ever done. It could have been over before it ever began. And I think I understand exactly why Volfango was so upset. Not only did he know how much I loved football, he knew that I had the tools to succeed. Not just the physical tools (my brother Antonio had those as well) but the attitude, the drive, the toughness to emerge. So many kids dream of becoming professionals. I was one who could have done it, who had everything to succeed. And I risked throwing it all away. And for what? A stupid, teenage thrill. Nothing more.

I'll never know if Volfango saved my career by making me get off that Cinquecento. But I do know that if it hadn't been for him, I might have given up on football altogether. I was fifteen years old. By this point I had moved from Lazio's San Basilio academy to the main youth academy. I had a new set of coaches, but was having a frustrating time. Everybody told me I was one of the most promising kids on Lazio's books, but when it came time to read out the team sheet, I was often on the bench. Or worse, I'd start and get substituted. With Volfango, I could make my own decisions, here I was stuck in a rigid tactical system; if I ran five yards forward, the coach would have a fit and threaten to take me off. It was hell.

One day in training I decided I had had enough. We had just lost 3–1 and I had been kept on the bench. Nobody ever told me why, I don't think there was a logic to it. The coaches had promised me over and over again that they would bring me on, but I just sat there the whole time. It was like they were mocking me, telling me my time would come, and then letting me rot on the bench.

On the tram ride home, I brooded the entire time. I was fighting back tears. I had just got off at the tram stop, when a car pulled over in front of me. It was Volfango, holding his six-month-old son. By sheer coincidence he had been driving by at the exact same time. He could tell I was upset.

'Pallocca, what's going on?' he asked me.

I didn't answer. I just stared down at the ground.

'What's wrong?' he repeated. 'Are you angry? What is it, tell me.'

I couldn't control myself. I just exploded.

'They won't let me play!' I sobbed. 'They don't give a shit about me, they just care about their favourites! We lost 3–1 today, I could have made the difference, but they didn't want me on the pitch!'

He put his hand on my shoulder.

'Pallocca, Pallocca,' he said, trying to be reassuring. 'I know it's upsetting, but you have to be patient. Your time will come. Just remember, hard work and patience are . . .'

'No!!!!'

I screamed. I lost it completely. I took my official Lazio team kit bag and flung it into the middle of the Via Palmiro Togliatti, the main thoroughfare in the Quarticciolo. Because it was open, everything flew out: my boots, shin-pads, shirt, shorts, towel . . . everything ended up either all over the road or on the cars, both parked and moving.

'I've had it! They can all F**K OFF!!!!' I ran away in desperation.

Unbeknown to me, Volfango coolly stepped out into the traffic and collected all my gear, gingerly avoiding the speed-ing cars. He then got into his own car and drove to my house.

When I got home, I found my kit bag on the dining room

table. Volfango, who had come by car, had arrived there before me. I looked up and there he was, next to Antonio. His eyes were bright red and it felt like they were burning holes in my head. He tore into me right away.

'How dare you?' he roared. 'How dare you throw your kit bag like that? How dare you turn your back on the greatest talent you have?'

He stormed forward to get me, with Antonio struggling to restrain him.

'You are a nobody! Understand? A nobody! You can't act this way, you don't deserve the talent you have!'

He broke free from Antonio's grasp and lunged at me. I was terrified. I had never seen him like this. I dived under the table. He would have got on his hands and knees to drag me out if Antonio hadn't been in his way. Since he couldn't grab me, he began kicking me.

'You can't do this! You can't spit on your God-given talent!'

I was crying again, this time out of genuine fear.

'No, boss, no!' I sobbed. 'Please, stop, please! I'll come back, I'll do whatever you say, I'm sorry! I'm sorry!'

Only when he was fully convinced that I was being honest did he calm down. As far as I was concerned, I had changed my mind about giving up football the moment I saw his glare when I walked in the door. The fact that this man would pick up my soiled shirt and muddy boots off a Rome street, bring them back to my house and then threaten to kill me just because he cared enough about me to force me back into football, was more than enough for me to change my mind.

Of course, unbeknown to me, it was all a set-up. After I stormed off, Volfango had sped to my house and told Antonio what had happened. He handed his baby to my mother and agreed with Antonio that I needed to be scared out of my wits. That's why he read me the riot act, while Antonio pretended to restrain him. It had to be believable and it was.

By this time I was also in my second year of secondary school, thanks to Lazio. If it had been up to me, I would have only concentrated on football (at the time, in Italy, you could leave school at fourteen). I attended a trade school for electromechanics called Duca D'Aosta. At first, I liked the idea of having lots of books and studying something electronic. Pretty soon, though, I saw that it was boring and pointless, not to mention inconvenient, as it made my commute to training even longer.

I started hanging out with some of the sixth-formers. I've pretty much always had older friends. Being older, 18 or 19, they cared even less about school than I did and would often take the day off, skipping class to hang out at the bar playing pool or reading the paper. I started joining them on a regular basis, which won me no favours with the teachers. One day they called my parents and told them I hadn't been going to class. They suspended me for a week.

I was blissfully ignorant of all this when I came home from training one evening around 8 pm. I bounced into the flat, happy as pie, smiled widely and greeted my dad: 'Hey Dad, how was your day?'

He replied by smacking me right in the mouth. I realized right away that the lie was up. I had been completely exposed, I had been found out and there was nowhere to hide. Or was there? Gamely, I did what I always did as a kid. I cried and started making things up. Remember the guy who said 'The bigger the lie, the more likely it is that somebody will believe it'? Well, that's the strategy I took.

'Dad, I'm sorry!' I sobbed. 'But, you've got to understand, I can explain! There's unrest at school, there was a big fight between left-wing and right-wing students, there were terrorists, they brought guns and . . . and when the shooting started . . . I, I got scared, Dad . . . I had to get away, the guns, the bullets and . . .'

Big mistake.

'Enough of this bullshit!' my father roared. 'Enough of these stupid, stupid lies! School is something you have to go to!'

I was frozen with fear.

'You made me spend 150,000 lire on books, 150,000 lire for your stupid electromechanical manuals! Do you realize how much money that is?'

More than anything, that's what drove the point home. The money. I imagine that many would frown at that. Many would simply turn up their noses and say 'Education is important for education's sake. It's rather ignorant to suggest that Paolo should have gone to school simply because his father had bought him books.'

Well, everybody is entitled to their opinion. But what those people wouldn't understand is just how important that money was to us. When you grow up where I did, you don't live on academic ideals and intellectual platitudes. You live on food and to get food you need money. I knew what 150,000 lire, around £80 at the time, meant to us. I felt terrible.

'But you know what, if you don't want to go,' he added, softening his tone, 'you don't have to.'

I looked up, surprised.

'I don't?'

'No, you don't. You'll come to work with me.'

At that point, I figured it was best to cut my losses. Anything seemed better than going to school, especially if it got me out of being punished. I told him I would do anything, I'd be happy to work.

The next day my father woke me up at 5 am.

'Paolo, get up!' he said cheerfully. 'Time to go to work.'

I was half-asleep and my bed felt like the warmest, safest place in the world. Getting up was the last thing I wanted to do.

'No, please,' I half-cried, half-pleaded. 'Don't . . .'

After what happened the day before, there was no way he was going to let me sleep. I dragged myself out of bed and got dressed. It was raining, it was cold. That morning, Rome, the most beautiful city in the world, looked and felt like the last place on Earth you would want to be. I was so cold, so miserable, I wore my pyjamas under my jeans and sweater. At least I would have the illusion of still being in bed.

It was still dark. We took a tram, then a bus, then another bus. It took over an hour to get to the construction site. My father was silent. We met the rest of the crew, they didn't say much. They just told me to carry sacks of cement from one area of the site to another. I struggled to even lift them, much less carry them. By mid-morning it felt as if my arms were going to fall off. There was an angry pile of raw, twitching flesh where my back had been. And my legs were heavier than the cement I had been carrying, and about as limber. All I could think was: 'I'm fifteen years old, all I want to do is play football and instead I'm lugging sacks of cement around a construction site.'

Two weeks with my father gave me a glimpse of a different reality. Hanging out on street corners in the Quarticciolo was one thing. That had been my reality until then and it was something I could probably do for another five, ten years. At some point however, if I wanted to have a life, a normal life with a wife and a family, I would have to get a job. And unless I made it as a professional footballer, my reality would be a lot like my father's. Getting up at the crack of dawn, busting my butt for the next fifty years, then ten years of retirement, probably replete with arthritis and backaches, and then death. I didn't have to take that road. I had a gift. I could make it as a professional footballer, playing the game I loved.

If I understood this, it is because of my father. When I think of what he did for me, the sacrifices he made, I shudder and feel like crying. Fragments of memories float into my head, snapshots frozen in time. And I cry, because many times I did not understand what he was doing and would get annoyed.

When I was on loan at Ternana, I made very little money. Every two weeks, Dad would take the train down from Rome, an hour-and-a-half journey each way. I would meet him on the platform at the station. He would get off the train, hug me for a few seconds and hand me an envelope containing 100,000 lire, around £45. All this, in total silence. He would then run off to another platform and hop on to a train in the opposite direction, heading back to Rome.

Again, I get goosebumps when I think about what he did. He would take three hours out of his one day off just to bring me a little bit of extra cash, money he had earned by waking up at 5 am to go to work. He had problems to worry about, four children to raise, he worked six days a week and yet he did that for me. It is unbelievable what a parent will do for his child.

If I succeeded, if I am here now, it is because of him, of what he taught me. It wasn't ever anything he said to me, he taught by example; they were lessons I learned, perhaps unconsciously. He never told me, he showed me.

To me, that is the ultimate skill as a father. That is what it's all about. Passing on your set of values to your child, preparing him or her for the real world. An outsider, viewing my life in a fly-on-the-wall documentary, would conclude that he was a distant father, because we didn't spend hours together doing the things that normal fathers do with their sons.

He too was a Lazio fan, but we never talked football, nor went to games together. He never came to watch me play, he never stood on the sidelines cheering me on like so many of my teammates' fathers when I was at the youth academy.

He never asked me 'So, son, tell me how your day was. What did you learn in school today?' He never told me not to eat sweets or to do my homework or all the other things parents in films do.

He simply set an example for us to follow. We didn't need him to be around all the time, we didn't need him to cuddle us. We knew he wasn't around because he was working. We knew that when he got home and didn't feel like talking to us or doing things with us, it was because he was tired or stressed or both.

I have tried to do for my children Ludovica and Lucrezia what my father did for me. Of course, I can't use the exact same blueprint. Our lives are radically different. Compared to him, I have an easy life, as does my family.

Teaching the value of hard work becomes more complex. I work hard to earn the money I make and I am very well rewarded for what I do. But it's also very true that I was lucky to have been born with certain talents. Without the work I put in and the sacrifices I made, I wouldn't be where I am today, but that is not readily apparent.

In some ways, if you have money, you have to work harder to teach certain values to your kids. You cannot simply set an example, because their lives will most likely evolve differently than yours did. I look at Ludovica. Even at eight years old, she knows she is different from other little girls. She knows not everybody has all the toys she has and that not everybody has a swimming pool in their house. But I don't think she feels different. And I think she knows that the material possessions we have are neither a birthright nor something which simply fell out of the sky. They are the result of hard work, my work and Betta's work, because without my wife, we would not have got this far.

I've tried to teach her the value and importance of the opportunities she has. She has travelled the world, she has learned another language, she has two parents who would do anything for her.

I remember when she was little, she would grab a toy and say: 'Mine!'

I would immediately take it away from her and tell her: 'No, this is everybody's. When you're playing, you're sharing. This belongs to everyone.'

I see the results of this every day. Ludovica is one of the most generous, giving people I know. At times, she goes over the top. She's constantly giving away her toys to her friends. She'll have her friends over and say: 'Mum, Kelly really likes this doll, can I lend it to her?'

A few days later, the doll will be gone and she'll announce: 'Kelly liked the doll so much, I gave it to her as a present! Mum, you should have seen how happy it made her!'

It's heart-warming really, though there are times when I have to rein her in, because otherwise I feel like I'll be buying toys for half the little girls in Britain. Still, I am so glad that she has learned the importance of giving.

It's just as important to me, however, to teach my daughters that things don't come easily. Lucrezia is only two years old, but Ludovica already leads a fairly active life for an eight-year-old. From September to May she attends an English school, but at the same time she is enrolled in school in Terni. Each day, her teacher in Italy sends her homework which she does and faxes back to Terni. Then, at the end of May, after the season is over, she does the same in reverse. She attends school in Terni and has her homework and lessons sent down from London. Basically, she does twice the schoolwork of a normal child.

It's tough, it's demanding, God knows I don't think I could have done it. But it will give her a huge head start in life, she'll be totally comfortable in two different educational systems. And I like the fact that it's difficult, that it's a struggle. I like the fact that she has to fight to do well in both systems.

I fear that kids who grow up with too many material possessions risk losing that edge, that drive to succeed. Maybe they don't have that toughness which you learn where I grew up. Too many rich kids reckon that because they have everything, they don't need to do anything.

I can give her a base, I can give her the tools to succeed in life. I can't give her the hunger, the will to make something of herself. All I can do is challenge her and hope that she responds by developing that drive to succeed.

I have seen her grow up, it seems like only yesterday she was in the hands of her godparents, Ennio and Leda Binocci, at her christening. That day was one of the happiest in my life. I wanted to be with her forever. But I know that one day she will be on her own. And it is up to me to give her the tools to survive in the world.

CHAPTER THREE

LAZIO AND THE IRRIDUCIBILI

While all this was happening, my childhood crush for Lazio had developed into a full-blown love affair. I first became aware of the club when I was six years old. They had just won their first (and, up until 1999–2000, only) scudetto and the echoes of that triumph reached my world in the Quarticciolo. I knew a local team had won and I understood it was a big deal, since just two seasons earlier Lazio were stuck in Serie B. Yet it seemed almost like something which upset many in the neighbourhood.

That's because I grew up in Roma country. The Quarticciolo was solidly yellow and red, Lazio fans stuck out like flies in buttermilk. Apart from my cousin Alvaro and my Aunt Franca, there were few Lazio fans where I lived. Supporting them was a way of being different, of cutting against the grain. Not to mention the fact that I loved their symbol, the Lazio Eagle.

Beyond that, I think I have always felt a special affinity towards the weak, the disadvantaged, the unloved. And, to be fair, after the 1973–74 title, Lazio encountered some pretty meagre times. During the 1979–80 season, some of their players and officials were involved in a match-fixing scandal, as a result of which the Italian Football Association came down hard on them and they were automatically relegated to Serie B.

It was around that time that I began going to the Stadio Olimpico to see them play. I would go with a teammate from Pro Tevere, Paolo Scotti and his father. Paolo was one of the lucky ones – he also made it as a professional and last I heard he was at Triestina, in Serie C. Signor Scotti would always make sure we got to the ground several hours before the game. The anticipation, the long wait for kickoff, was something to savour.

There are many ways to love football. Of course, I love to play, it is something I have done since as far back as I can remember and, while it is my job, it is also one of the single greatest sources of joy and satisfaction I know. At the same time however, there is another way to not just love football, but to live football. And that is as a fan.

There is a bond that links supporters everywhere, that unites those who make sacrifices, who spend money and rearrange their lives to watch their team. It also unites those who suffer, because the suffering of a supporter is very real and, in some ways, tragic. You care desperately about something you really have no control over. And your suffering is borne out of love, intense and unconditional love.

Perhaps that's why, in my mind, the supporters of the teams I have played for have always been special. I know what they go through, I know what they experience because I too went through it with Lazio. I don't think there are many footballers who were also fans when growing up, at least not the kind of fan I was. Maybe supporters can sense that when they see me play, and perhaps that's why I think they appreciate me in a special way.

To a twelve-year-old kid, the Stadio Olimpico was an exciting, magical place. I would get high on the atmosphere inside. Even today, twenty years later, I can taste what it was like: the sounds and the smells, the buzz and the burning, the idle chitchat and the impassioned discussions.

By the time we got to our seats in the Curva Nord (the North Stand), the stadium would be perhaps one-quarter full. We were off to the side of the Curva Nord, the middle was the domain of Lazio's Ultras, the hardcore fans. They would be busy setting up banners, flags and drums for the match. They all had their scarves, they would be laughing and joking, preparing their smoke bombs and flares. They looked strong and united, warriors ready to fight for the Lazio cause.

They were true fans, because they were fans who had suffered. Their beloved Lazio was now in Serie B, broken and humiliated after winning the title, but they were still there, always at Lazio's side. I dreamt that one day I could be in their midst, firing a flare, banging a drum or simply just holding up a scarf and singing my lungs out for Lazio. It was something I wanted almost as much as becoming a professional footballer. And, sure enough, a few years later, both wishes were granted.

Lazio were hurting back then. Our two best players, Lionello Manfredonia and Bruno Giordano, had received long bans for match-fixing. Before the ban, both had been capped for Italy, and it looked like they were heading for long and successful careers.

We all felt like they had been punished more than they deserved. Paolo Rossi was also involved in the scandal, but his ban was reduced in time for him to play in the 1982 World Cup where he was top scorer and became a national hero. Giordano and Manfredonia, on the other hand, were pilloried. Their careers were nearly ended by the scandal, even though they were just youngsters at the time.

To me, they were heroes. I close my eyes and I can see Giordano cutting into the penalty area, slamming a blistering shot past the goalkeeper and watching the black nets (at the time Lazio's goalnets were black for some reason) billow up in the air. Or I can feel the strength and personality of Manfredonia, marshalling the defence or winning a 50-50 ball.

They were a very real inspiration, but what made them all the more special is that they didn't just revel in being Lazio legends. They might have thrown in the towel after their bans. They might have simply accepted their lot as a big fish in a small pond, or at least a losing pond. Instead, they battled on and enjoyed incredible success elsewhere.

Manfredonia later went to Juventus, where he won a scudetto and the World Club Championship. As for Giordano, he had the greatest honour of all. He played for Napoli with Antonio Careca and Diego Maradona in one of the greatest frontlines ever. Their three-pronged attack was known as Ma-Gi-Ca, (Maradona-Giordano-Careca) and they broke the northern clubs' hegemony on the scudetto by leading the Naples club to two titles in the late 1980s.

My other hero at the time was the Dane, Michael Laudrup. He was considered the greatest prospect in world football. Juventus had bought him so that he could eventually replace the legendary Michel Platini, and, as a short-term measure, had loaned him out to Lazio. Watching him play was a real treat. Later in his career, he changed, he became a central midfielder and a playmaker; but at the time he was a forward, all flair and creativity, just like me. I would watch him dribble past opponents on a Sunday and then spend the next week imitating his moves in training.

By the time I turned 14, I was going to games with my cousin, Alvaro, who lived across the hall from me at the Quarticciolo. When I was younger, I was always cruising around with him and his brother Ezio. The two of them have taken distinctly different paths in life. Ezio became a priest, while Alvaro dropped out of school at age 13. Not surprisingly, it was Alvaro who joined me on the roof of the Cinquecento after Italy won the 1982 World Cup. Alvaro was one of my role models. He was older, tougher, he had a motorbike, he had done his military service in the Brigata Folgore. 'La Folgore', as it was known, is Italy's elite paratrooper unit. I know people make jokes about the Italian armed forces, but the Brigata Folgore regularly wins awards at NATO training exercises. It's like the SAS, only better. And it's one of the top forces in the world, it really is.

Alvaro wasn't just tough, he was cool, he dressed well, albeit in typical Roman fashion. He had a camouflage jacket, which was all the rage at the time, hair back, sunglasses, motorcycle boots, and was a hit with women. Alongside Alvaro, I always felt safe, which is why we started following Lazio away from home.

To this day, I've experienced few things which can compare to the buzz and excitement of an away trip with the Lazio Ultras. Traditionally, Lazio had two main groups of Ultras, the Eagles and the Vikings. As the Viking group grew older, it began to disband, and the Eagles gained supremacy. We were part of the Eagles, but after about a year a splinter group was born: the 'Irriducibili'. 'Irriducibili' means unyielding. Think of that old chant: '*We shall not, we shall not be moved! We shall not, we shall not be moved!*' That was the basic philosophy.

The Eagles had become so big, it was difficult for them to have a defined identity. Their leaders were older, they had reached their mid-thirties, some were in their forties. They had done a lot for Lazio, but their priorities had changed. They had families, responsibilities. They still followed Lazio everywhere, but they lacked that edge which the Irriducibili had.

Naturally, I had to keep the club in the dark about my travels. If they had known that I spent my Sundays with the Irriducibili, visiting far-flung corners of Italy, they would probably have kicked me out of the youth academy. They knew how dangerous it could be. I was only found out once, but got away with it. A Lazio player had got injured near the away stand. The team physio, an old guy named Doriano, came to tend to him on the sidelines. As he was jogging back to the bench, our eyes met in the crowd. I immediately hid my face, hoping he wouldn't recognize me. But it was too late. The next day, at training, he grabbed me and shoved me against the wall.

'You are a moron, Paolo!' he said. 'I saw you with the Irriducibili in Bergamo. Don't let me ever catch you again! Do you know what the club will do to you if they find out? You'll be toast. You'll be out of here in a split second!'

Indeed, it would have been very bad PR for the club if it emerged that one of their star youth players was also a member in good standing of the Irriducibili. I knew it was risky, but I couldn't give it up. The thrill was too much.

Alvaro and I were among the first to join the Irriducibili, just after they were created. In fact, we knew many of the founders. Several things set the Irriducibili apart from the Eagles and indeed from most Italian Ultras at the time. The Eagles, like most Italian 'tifosi' adopted a Latin or South American style of support. If you're familiar with the 'torcida' in Brazil or Argentina, you'll know what I'm talking about. It was very colourful, with flags, banners and flares. For big matches, like the Rome derby, they would construct huge cardboard floats recreating slogans or caricatures of the players. The Irriducibili, on the other hand, were partly inspired by English fans. They would sing and clap in unison throughout the game, their songs were longer and more elaborate. They had a certain look about them, they were the younger, wilder, hardcore. They were also among the first to produce their own scarves and banners bearing the Irridicubili logo.

But most of all, what I loved about the Irriducibili was that they only ever travelled at night. Normal supporters might get up early on match-days, sometimes at the crack of dawn, to make kickoff in a faraway city. But the Irriducibili always left at the same time, just after 11:15 pm, on Saturday night. This meant that if we were travelling to the extreme parts of Italy, say Puglia or Sicily in the South or Udine or Trieste in the North, we might arrive at 11 am or noon, a few hours before kickoff. But if we were going to places like Perugia or Florence, we would arrive in the middle of the night, say 3 or 4 am, which left us plenty of time to roam the streets and wake the local population.

The trips were often more memorable than the matches themselves. Alvaro and I would leave the house around 10 pm on Saturday night, giving us plenty of time to get to Termini, Rome's main railroad station, by 11 pm. Lazio's youth teams played on Saturdays, so I would have had a few hours to rest after my match. As we neared Termini, the excitement would rise. You could see cars parked haphazardly, on sidewalks, in driveways, all over the place. The next day was Sunday, which meant nobody would be getting a parking ticket.

Several hundred yards away from Termini, you would see the first small groups of fans arriving. Somebody would begin to sing: 'Dove stanno i Laziali?' ('Where are the Lazio fans?')

Any group of fans within earshot would then reply: 'Siamo qui, siamo qui!' ('We are here, we are here!')

You could hear voices rising out of the darkness, echoing from alleyways, booming down the underpass. Once in the station, we would buy beer, drinks and sandwiches and stake out our spot on the train. We were on special trains, organized exclusively for fans. The police set them up for us because otherwise we would simply ride on the normal trains and would become more difficult to monitor. This way, we were all in one place and were considered easier to control.

Not that they controlled us in any way. We pretty much did whatever we wanted on those trains, it was a constant party. Dancing, singing, loud music, there were no limits. Those were *our* trains, we were LAZIO and were going off to battle. It was the best feeling in the world.

I'm not naive, I'm not going to pretend that there wasn't some bad with the good. The Ultras have a bad reputation, some of it justified. There were people who were armed with knives and chains, arguments could break out. Others did drugs, mostly marijuana, but sometimes harder stuff. It could be ugly and dangerous and ideally most 14-year-old kids shouldn't be exposed to those types of things.

Having said that, it did not affect me. I grew up in the Quarticciolo, a place which could often be a jungle. You couldn't avoid drugs, you couldn't stick your head in the sand and pretend they did not exist. Everybody who lives in the Quarticciolo personally knows either a drug addict or a drug dealer. Everybody. And when I say drug addict, I mean drug addict. I don't mean a guy who smokes a joint once a week.

If you're in that kind of environment, you can hold out for awhile but eventually you either give in or risk becoming an outcast. If you refuse to do drugs, in the long run, you can feel like a moron. Sure, you'll go out with your mates, you'll have a good time and at some point they'll all get stoned or start popping pills. Then what do you do? You're stone cold sober and they're all in another world. You just can't relate. After this happens once, twice, three times, you just stop going out with them. And you lose your friends.

That's the problem with those 'Just Say No' campaigns. They don't seem to understand that they're asking kids to not only say 'No' to drugs, they're asking them to say 'No' to their friends. And that is a very, very difficult thing to do.

When I think back, I'm almost surprised that I didn't get into drugs in a big way. I think there are two reasons for it, one simple and mundane, the other more complex.

The first reason is that I simply don't like smoke. When I first tried marijuana, it didn't do anything for me, but that's normal, I don't think anybody gets high and loves it the very first time. But what really stayed with me from that experience was the disgust I felt at having smoke in my mouth. The taste of smoke inside me made me feel sick; that's why I've never smoked cigarettes either. I simply couldn't bring myself to smoke, which pretty much ruled out joints for me. It helped that I was stubborn. No matter how many times I was offered drugs after that, I would always say 'no', not because I wasn't tempted, but because that revolting taste of smoke was fresh in my mind.

The other reason it was easier for me to stay away from drugs has to do with the fact that I always had very good role-models in my parents, of course, but also my brothers. I never saw them do drugs or even be around drugs in any way. It was like a different dimension and the fact that I always knew that when I returned home I was entering a drug-free zone made it that much easier for me.

Drugs were never a big part of the away trip for me, but

they were to some Irriducibili. There was always police with us on the trains, but they left us alone. It was the same cops every time, they got to know us and they looked the other way, provided we didn't get too out of control.

Once we arrived at the opposition's city, we began to make our presence known. Usually the police followed us everywhere we went, so it wasn't as if you could really do much. But the sheer thrill of marching through enemy territory as part of a group, singing your songs, waving your flags, feeling you've taken the city and made it your own, is difficult to describe to people who haven't had similar experiences.

When you're in a group, a mob, you feel invincible. Any type of fear or apprehension you may have had dissolves as you feel the power of the mob flowing through you. It didn't matter, we were never scared, no matter how dangerous things became. I've had rocks and bricks hurled at me by rival fans, I've been teargassed and clubbed by the police, I've seen things I wish I hadn't. I have lived the life of the travelling Ultra and, all told, I'm glad I did.

I remember our train arriving in Bergamo and stopping a few hundred yards before reaching the main train station. We were playing Atalanta and we knew their fans were among the most violent and rowdy in Italy, so we were on our guard. But we had no clue why the train had stopped.

We soon realized. We heard loud thuds on the roof of our carriage, then the sound of glass shattering. The Atalanta fans had ambushed us! They had blocked the train tracks and were showering our carriages with bricks, rocks, cinder blocks, anything they could get their hands on. Glass was everywhere.

Later, our boys got their revenge outside the ground. Running battles were being fought everywhere. I was maybe five yards away when the Bergamo Chief of Police was knifed. I can still see him screaming in pain, holding a bloody hand above his head while running through the crowd.

The following year, they took no chances with us. Our train had a police escort all the way in. We arrived at 10 am and were marched directly to the ground under police guard. There must have been two cops for every supporter. We got to the stadium at around 10:30 am and stayed there, in the pounding sun, for five hours. We couldn't leave, we couldn't do anything. We couldn't even get something to drink, because the vendors were scared of approaching us. The funny thing is that we didn't mind. It was miserable but, because we were all together, because we were the Irriducibili, it was still fun.

Today there is a lot of talk of fan violence, much of it from people who have never travelled with their club, who have no idea what they're talking about. Sure, a minority are utter psychopaths, people who are only there to dish out violence, but most are simply passionate fans who get carried away.

The thing to remember is that when you're in a mob, everything changes. All of a sudden, there is a mental transformation, you are no longer the same person. I've seen the calmest, most mild-mannered guys turn into absolute thugs. There's always a flashpoint, a moment when the strength and power of the mob overcomes you and you lose your sense of right and wrong. Or rather, you develop a different sense of right and wrong.

It's not something I really enjoy talking about. After all, I'm 32 years old, I am a father with two daughters, I should be an example to them. But I cannot turn my back on my youth, because that has contributed to making me what I am today. I do not live with regret, I accept my past. I have walked with the Ultras and I have stepped over the line, more than once.

I remember one time in Padova when it happened. We had lost 2–0 and were making our way out of the ground. When you go to an away ground to support your team, there are two things that will make you happy: one, obviously, is winning, the other is grabbing some sort of trophy, a souvenir from the opposing fans. Since we had obviously missed out on our first goal, we concentrated on the second.

There were three of us and we were all buzzing at the thought of grabbing a Padova flag or scarf and making it our own. We scoured the stadium forecourt for the right people to jump. All of a sudden, my mates steamed in to a group of five Padova fans. I'm not sure why they picked them, they were a little older than we were and we were outnumbered, five to three. But we did have the element of surprise and besides, the Irriducibili were never afraid, even when the numbers weren't in their favour.

We thought it would be over quickly: a few shoves, grab the scarf and then run off to safety. Instead, they fought back bitterly, they wouldn't let go of the scarf. It all blew up, I had to help my friends, fists were flying. I knocked the guy with the scarf to the ground, my friend was still pulling on the other end. Even lying there, he would not let go of his scarf, of his colours, in a way, of his team. That's the spirit of the Ultra.

I knew right away my mate wasn't going to let go of the guy's scarf, either. That too is the spirit of the Ultra. So I kicked the Padova fan while he was lying on the ground. Two or three times, I don't remember how many. He cried out in pain and rolled over on his stomach, letting go of the scarf. We had what we wanted, so we dropped everything and sprinted off, laughing all the way until we were reunited with the rest of the Irriducibili. I don't think my mate let go of that scarf for the entire train-ride home.

I was high from the adrenalin rush. I had no regrets whatsoever about what I had done. Yes, I had hurt another man, humiliated him, kicked him while he was lying on the ground. But I rationalized it. I told myself that I had done it to defend my mate, a fellow Irriducibili member. I told myself that we were badly outnumbered, that I had no choice but to get involved. Most of all, I told myself that I was part of a group and it was my duty to back up my mates.

I tell this story not because I am proud of what I did. Violence is wrong in principle, especially violence over a football match. I should never have done what I did. But I'm talking about this now because I want people to know that I understand a thing or two about fan violence. Not because I have a doctorate in sociology, but because I lived it. I was there, on the front line.

There is so much talk these days of hooliganism, of fans getting stabbed, like the two Leeds supporters who were tragically killed in Turkey during the UEFA Cup tie against Galatasaray. That is another matter. Punch-ups and fist-fights have been a part of football support for a long time. My father used to tell me stories of Rome derbies which ended in fisticuffs among fans. There is such a thing as a healthy punch-up. It's when it grows out of control, when it starts involving fifty, sixty people running at each other with knives or bottles, injuring innocent bystanders, that's when it becomes a problem.

That's the difficult part; there's a fine line and in some areas, it's pretty much invisible. But while violence is wrong in principle, physical confrontation can be beneficial. Or rather, if it does happen, it's not a tragedy.

Punch-ups are a fact of life. I'm not urging people to beat each other up, I am just saying that they happen and they can actually teach you a thing or two. Again, perhaps it's a function of where I grew up, but I got my ass kicked many times by people who were bigger, stronger or just meaner than I was. It's about having an edge, it's about having that toughness. In the Quarticciolo we have a saying: 'Chi mena primo mena due volte.' Which means: 'He who hits first, hits twice.' Essentially, the point is that if you hit the other guy first, you will succeed next time as well.

That's what it was like in the Quarticciolo. You had to hit the other guy before he hit you. It was about surviving and it's a philosophy that I have taken with me on the pitch. Football doesn't have to be a battle, but if you treat it as one and you're a warrior you will come out on top. On the pitch, you need that edge, that hunger which allows you to get to the ball first. You have to anticipate, you have to be first and be hard, whether you are chasing the ball or going into a tackle. It's a state of mind.

To me, that's what the British bulldog spirit is all about. Being first, being tough, never giving up. I don't want to evoke the usual stereotypical images of Winston Churchill and all that, but I have a deep and genuine admiration for the British spirit and the British people. It's probably because I, too, growing up in the Quarticciolo, learned similar values.

It's a mentality which is reflected in British footballers as well. Britain values the strong, the tough, the hard workers over the talented. I cannot tell you the number of times people have come up to me and said: 'Paolo, you're the greatest! I can't believe you never played for Italy! I mean, you and Gazza are the most talented players I've ever seen!'

It's very flattering, but I think it also speaks volumes about British football. Over the past forty years, how many genuine world-class talents has British football produced? I don't mean world-class players: from Bobby Moore to Bobby Charlton, from Gary Lineker to Bryan Robson, there have been plenty of those. I mean genuine world-class talents, people with top-notch technique and vision, flair and creativity.

I can think of two: Kevin Keegan and George Best. Maybe Gascoigne, if he hadn't had his problems. Beyond that, Britain hasn't produced too many artists, guys with genuine skill. That's why the Keegans and Bests remain untouchable even today.

But when I think of Italy, a guy like Bruno Conti, who played in three World Cups and without whom we would have never won the title in Spain, is virtually forgotten. And, with all due respect, Conti was worth three Keegans.

Players who are too skilful are almost viewed with suspicion in Britain. Think of Glenn Hoddle or, to a lesser degree, Steve McManaman or David Beckham. Instead, the British value fighters, people with spirit and commitment. Billy Bremner is a God in Leeds. Today, British heroes include guys like Dennis Wise, David Batty, Paul Ince and Roy Keane. Kids worship them.

In Italy, it's the reverse. I don't think too many Italian kids idolize Demetrio Albertini or Gigi Di Biagio. And I'm not so sure it's a good thing. They are quality footballers, they are strong and hard-working, but you cannot compare their toughness, their hunger with that of British players.

That's why there are so few Italian players who are genuinely tough and committed. Two come to my mind right away, and in both cases, there is a good reason for it. Ciro Ferrara is like me, he grew up on the street, except in his case it was Naples, not Rome. And Paolo Maldini, well he's just an exception. In his case I think he became incredibly driven because as a young player coming through the ranks at AC Milan he was constantly being compared to his father. As a result, he became obsessed with winning and his succeed-at-all-costs mentality isn't too different from that of say, Roy Keane.

But those are the exceptions. And notice, they are both defenders. In other positions, there is little toughness to speak of. Look at a guy like Christian Vieri. He is bigger and stronger than most defenders, he should have the same viciousness, the same hunger, after all, few can match him, both physically and technically. Yet, compared to say, Alan Shearer, he seems fragile, unwilling to mix it.

I think the British understand that if you give everything you have, if you fight to the end, you will be recognized, even if you lack the skill or the strength to succeed. Not all British heroes may have been winners, but they were all fighters, people who had the tenacity to never give up. I feel a special kinship towards that, every day I feel myself absorbing more and more of that bulldog spirit. I have a long way to go before I become like, say, Julian Dicks, a true gladiator and a genuine inspiration, but I'm getting there.

This need to dominate, to fight, to never give up, is what allowed Britain to build an empire. They didn't have the greatest generals or scientists or statesmen, they simply refused to give in. This goes hand in hand with a certain arrogance, because you will only put your life on the line if deep down you believe that you can succeed, that you are the best. It's that feeling that says: 'I am better than you are. Now, I will show you.' It is what allowed them to colonize the entire world, just about. It doesn't even really matter if you are the best or not. What matters is that, after you get your ass kicked, you pick yourself up and dive right back in.

Contrast that with Italy. We had the greatest empire the world has ever seen, the Roman Empire. We gave the world art, culture, laws, everything. And then we threw it all away. Why? Because we didn't have the spirit the British have.

In Italy, as long as we have our pizza, our Coke, our women, we're happy. That's all we need. I was one of the exceptions, because I was a fighter. Ask anybody in Italy, I always gave my all on the pitch. Even when I didn't play every week, even when I was relegated to the bench, the fans always loved me.

That's why the English Premiership is the best place in the world for me. I am in a country that appreciates a fighter, that loves commitment and spirit. And that's why there are times when I don't want to ever return to Italy.

CHAPTER FOUR

PAINKILLERS, PSYCHIATRISTS AND FAITH HEALERS

By this time I had moved through the youth ranks at Lazio and basically progressed as far as I could. In 1985–86 I was part of the Lazio team that won the Italian youth title by beating Cesena at the Stadio Olimpico. At the time, the first team was struggling in the lower reaches of Serie B, but our youth system was producing some talented players. I played alongside guys like Antonio Rizzolo, a striker who became an Under-21 international, and Gigi Di Biagio, who is now at Inter Milan. It's ironic, Di Biagio never quite made it at Lazio, he bounced around the lower divisions and eventually ended up, of all places, at Roma. It was there that he really made a name for himself and became an Italian international (you may remember him for missing the decisive penalty against France at the 1998 World Cup, but that's another story).

Anyway, Lazio finished twelfth that year, just four places clear of relegation to Serie C1. The chairman was making promises, talking about injecting new funds in the club and restoring us to our rightful place in Serie A. I desperately wanted to be a part of Lazio's re-birth. The previous summer however, another match-fixing scandal rocked Italian football to its foundations. Once again, Lazio were in the thick of it. A few weeks after the 1985–86 season had ended, the Italian Football Association issued its sentences. Lazio were to be docked nine points in the 1986–87 season.

This meant the club would start the new season with minus nine points. It was a huge deficit to make up; remember, at the time, it was still just two points for a win. The club had promised us youngsters that we would get a chance to shine that season, but that was before the nine-point penalty. As things stood, there would be no room for experiments, no room for the kids. The team needed solid veterans, players who could do battle in the trenches of Serie B and save the club from the unthinkable, relegation to the third division. We youngsters were sent out on loan. I was to sign my first-ever professional contract with Ternana, in Serie C2, the fourth division.

My father and I were called into Lazio's headquarters. Since Dad didn't have a driving licence, Lazio sent a car to pick us up. When we walked into the office of the general manager, Felice Pulici, a shifty-looking man in a dark suit was sitting next to him. Pulici introduced him as Domenico Migliucci, chairman of Ternana.

'Paolo, the time has come for you to gain some experience,' Pulici told me. 'There is no room for you in the first-team this coming season. But Ternana is a good place to further your education as a footballer. Do well and you'll be back with us.'

I knew that was why I was there and I had accepted the fact that I would have to leave Rome. What I did not expect

Far left: Here I am at age five with my parents. Notice how my legs were so fat that you can barely see my knees!

Left: Mum and I at the audition to play the young Zorro for an Italian television programme. I won, but we were ripped off…

Right: At my flat in the Quarticciolo with my brothers Dino (left) and Giuliano (right). Wasn't I adorable?

Below: One of my early teams, Rinascita '79. I'm standing next to the skipper, looking away.

Right: Receiving an award at a youth tournament in Rome. I seem much happier than the other lad!

Below: Nothing quite like doing wheelies in front of your house on a friend's scooter. Incidentally, the graffiti in the background ('Roma is shit and the Curva Sud stinks') is my handiwork. Originally it was an anti-Lazio message, but, with the help of some spray paint, I put everything right.

Right: On the road with the Lazio Ultras. This is before I joined the *Irriducibili* when I was still with the Eagles.

Below: The Lazio side that won the Italian Youth title in 1986. You might recognize Inter star and Italian international Gigi Di Biagio (front row, second from left).

Right: Moments after scoring the only goal in the Rome derby, I had the temerity to celebrate right under the Roma fans' noses. It won me a place in Lazio history.

Left: Celebrating Napoli's qualification for the UEFA Cup in 1993/94 with Marcello Lippi, one of the finest managers around, and teammate Sergio Buso.

Below: The goal of the season against AC Milan when I was at Napoli in 1993/94. Stefano Eranio and Christian Panucci are totally befuddled by my trickery.

Left: Celebrating with Roberto Baggio at Juventus.

Below: Yes, that's me after Gianluca Vialli shaved my head. Don't I look ridiculous

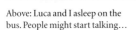

Above: Luca and I asleep on the bus. People might start talking…

Right: Managerial legend Giovanni Trapattoni. We had our times, mostly bad, but he remains one of the all-time greats, and now, of course, Italian coach.

Celebrating Milan's victory over Arsenal in the 1995 European Super Cup.

Another team, another hairstyle, though I'm not sure the mohawk suits me…

Below: AC Milan's Christmas card. We're all there, looking suitably stiff and spontaneous.

Above: After winning the scudetto with Milan in 1996. I'm top left, with (*clockwise*) Christian Panucci, Roberto Baggio, Franco Baresi, Marcel Desailly, Milan chairman (and former Italian Prime Minister) Silvio Berlusconi, Demetrio Albertini, Stefano Eranio and Paolo Maldini.

Above: Baresi and I flexing by the pool during our pre-season trip to China. Everybody thought Franco was dour and humourless, but I brought out the kid in him.

Left: Fabio Capello. The expression says it all. It's very hard to be a good manager and a good friend at the same time.

Left: Ludovica and I. She and her sister Lucrezia are everything to me.

Right: My mother-in law Franca with Lucrezia and Ludovica.

Left: Celebrating with my wife Betta. Without her, things would have turned out much differently.

Right: A West Ham convert – Ludovica wearing Daddy's No 10 shirt. She insisted I buy it for her and always wears it at the beach.

Left: On holiday at the seaside with Ludovica and Lucrezia.

Below: My shop in Terni, Il Conte. Clothes have always been a passion of mine.

Below: In Egypt with two mates (no, I'm not the one sitting down with the huge gut). Notice how black I get with a tan. I might get mistaken for Marcel Desailly!

Right: With Betta's father, Fausto, at Juventus' Villar Perosa training camp in 1992.

was Migliucci's offer: he was going to pay me 350,000 lire a month in salary. That's per month, not per week. 350,000 lire was the equivalent of £150 at the time. Granted, the club would provide meals and lodging, but £150 wasn't going to get me very far.

My father stepped in.

'I am not an agent, I don't know much about football,' he said firmly. 'But I do know something about the value of money. And, believe me, my son cannot survive on 350,000 lire a month.'

Migliucci was a little taken aback. He thought my father was just an ignorant labourer, instead he found a man who would not let himself be pushed around. He agreed to pay me 750,000 lire a month, which at least was something approaching a fair wage. As it turned out, it was all a moot point, because Migliucci ran into massive financial difficulties, which left the club on the verge of bankruptcy. I would go seven months without drawing a salary at Ternana, which made my father's visits twice a month absolutely essential.

Ternana may have been in Serie C2, but it was still the big-time. I had achieved the first part of my dream of becoming a professional footballer. Now it would be up to me to go further. I had to use this as a stepping stone to greater things.

I settled into Terni quite well. The team wasn't very good, so I was given a chance early on and won a starting place in the lineup. I was happy and hopeful, the only things I really missed were my family and travelling to see Lazio with the Irriducibili.

I had been there for a few months when my life changed

forever. I met Betta. Ternana's digs were in San Gelmini, some five miles outside the city. They had put me up in a local hotel, the Hotel Duomo. After training, I would while away the afternoons sitting in the hotel manager's office, watching television.

I was at my usual post in the hotel manager's office, feet propped up on the desk (I had befriended him immediately, he didn't care), when I spied a familiar face in the lobby. It was my teammate Romualdo and he was with a girl. Not just any girl, but the kind of girl who makes everybody stop and take notice when she walks into a room.

Romualdo was from Terni and he was still enrolled in school. It just so happened that on that day, by sheer coincidence, their school had taken them on a class outing to San Gelmini. Romualdo and the girl had slipped away from their class and he had taken her to the Hotel Duomo, to show her where the players stayed.

I knew right away that there was something about this girl that was worth investigating. I walked into the lobby as nonchalantly as I could and said hello. Romualdo introduced her as Betta. When she first smiled at me, I was smitten. I had to make an impression.

'Guys, let's not hang out at the hotel, this is boring!' I said. 'Let's all go and get an ice cream. I know just the place.'

Romualdo was keen, but Betta said: 'Are you sure? Maybe we should get back, they might be looking for us. We don't want to get into trouble with the teachers, now do we?'

Even then, Betta was the responsible one. But I was in too deep. I couldn't just let her walk away. So I insisted and she agreed. If she hadn't, I might not be where I am today.

The three of us went for an ice cream. I was like a child the night before Christmas. I had never been nervous around women, but with Betta it was different. I was desperate for her to like me, I guess I was all hyperactive.

The next day I began harassing Romualdo for her number. He tried to act dumb, coming up with a whole series of excuses: he either didn't have it or he'd lost it or she didn't have a phone or whatever.

Much later I would find out that he had called her a few days later and said: 'Hey, remember that friend of mine, that Roman kid from the other day? Guess what, he wanted your number! Don't worry, I didn't give it to him. You don't need a guy like that bothering you . . .'

'What? Are you crazy?' Betta replied. I guess I had made an impression on her as well. 'You should have given it to him right away!'

I suppose Romualdo was a little jealous, he probably liked Betta too. As it happened, I didn't get her number for another week. He gave it to me on our way to an away game at Galatina, a town in the extreme heel of Italy's boot. I couldn't wait for the bus to stop so I could call her. I just had to hear her voice again.

When we got to the team hotel, I was the first one off the bus. I ran up the stairs to my room and burst in, looking for the phone.

There was no phone. Out of all the damn hotels in all of Italy, we had to end up in one with no telephones.

Clutching her phone number, I turned right around and ran back to the lobby. My teammates were looking at me like I was insane.

'Where's the phone?' I screamed at the receptionist. 'I need a phone!'

He looked back at me with contempt, like he might look at a dung fly.

'I have a phone right here,' he said. 'But it's not for customer use.'

Cursing, I ran out on the street. There were no public telephones anywhere. I ran into one restaurant, then a bar, then another restaurant. Nothing. They either didn't have payphones, or they were out of order, or they wouldn't let me use them.

I was frantic. I thought my head was going to explode. I ran through the streets of Galatina thinking: 'What kind of a God-forsaken place is this? They don't have a single telephone!'

I was ready to break into the team bus, hotwire the engine and drive to civilization when I finally found a phone box. I don't know how long I had been running around for, but it seemed forever and I found that I was completely out of breath.

Hands shaking, I dialled her number. She was home. And she was happy to hear from me! I must have poured twenty coins into that phone. We talked for hours, we talked about everything. I had fallen in love.

We didn't get together until New Year's Eve. A few days later, I made my parents come down from Rome so they could meet her parents. To some, that may have seemed premature. We had known each other for a few months, we had been together for a few days. But in my mind, heart and soul, I knew that Betta was the one.

Fourteen years later, we're still together. And every day I discover something new about her. Or, I should say, about us, because it's hard to think of myself separately from her. When we met, we were still kids, we grew up together, in every sense of the word. She has shared all of my experiences and I have shared all of hers.

In many ways, we complement each other perfectly. I am not the most laid-back, easy-going, relaxed kind of guy (surprise, surprise). Betta, on the other hand, is always calm, she always puts things in perspective. She knows how to handle me, she knows how to calm me down, how to smooth my rougher edges.

I think we are a very traditional couple. I play the man, she plays the woman. Which means she knows how to steer me, how to guide me. She doesn't need to stand up and yell back at me. I may scream and shout, but she is the strong one in the relationship. She can communicate more with one look, one gesture, than I can in two hours of shouting. Her silence is her strength; I don't think there is anybody in the world who can relate to me the way she does.

I knew right away that it was going to be like this. I can't explain why, but I knew it was going to work between us. I was a nobody, then. I had no money, no success, just a lot of dreams, like thousands of other aspiring professionals. Betta didn't care. She loved me completely and, just as importantly, she was willing to grow with me, to develop with me. When you make a commitment to somebody, you give up something of yourself. In exchange, you build something new with the other person. From day one, I knew she would be my partner. And we haven't stopped growing together since.

I cannot imagine what my life would have been without her. I don't know if I could have made it through my injury or the long ban at Sheffield Wednesday. She balanced me out, she helped keep me 'calm'. Again, I say 'calm' in quotation marks because I know I'm not exactly a model of tranquility. But believe me, without Betta I would be much, much worse. I wouldn't have the mental lucidity I have now, I wouldn't have had the will to fight back after every setback.

Nowadays, I spend a lot of time thinking about love and what it means. Maybe I see life through rose-tinted glasses, but I firmly believe man's natural instinct is to love. Of course, there are varying degrees of intensity, there are highs and lows, there are different ways it manifests itself, but there is love inside all of us.

I think the strongest love you can have is for your children. With them, it's constant, unconditional love. That's only logical. Your children are your flesh and blood, they are an extension of you. I swear to God, I feel Lucrezia and Ludovica are a part of me. How can there possibly be anything less than total love between us? I would die for them. I am totally convinced of this. Perhaps I'm not saying anything new, perhaps any father would put his own life ahead of his children's, but when I think about them, the intensity of emotion is just so strong, it is natural for me to say such a thing.

The feelings I get when I touch them, when they hug me, when I look at them or even when I picture their faces in my mind is unlike any other emotion I have experienced. I am not a person who lives with remorse, but the greatest regret I have in life is not spending more time with Ludovica when she was born. I was 24, I was having a difficult spell at Juventus, I was edgy and nervous, and I had many worries on my mind. I was still a kid and maybe I didn't fully appreciate the love I could get and receive from my baby daughter. There are times, even today, when I blame myself for what happened. That's probably the reason why I shower her and Lucrezia with affection. I try to share as much as possible with them, whether it's doing homework with Ludovica or playing with stuffed animals with Lucrezia. Every moment is a gift to be treasured.

Given that the love of parents for children is so strong, it's unusual that it doesn't work both ways. Of course, you love your parents, but it's different, you don't display it the same way. As you grow up, you don't appreciate what they do for you and sometimes their love for you isn't readily apparent. You clash, it's inevitable; if you ever want to become an independent, free-thinking person, you almost need to clash with your parents at some point. There are times, growing up, when your parents become the enemy, somebody to fight with, authority figures to question, to tear down. And yes, sometimes you hate them, at least temporarily. You still love them, but you begin to see certain things about them, you begin to understand that they are not infallible. Perhaps that's why you hate them, because there was a time when every little boy thought his father was the strongest, smartest man in the world and his mother the most beautiful, most loving woman in the world. At some point you realize it's not true. At some point, you realize they are just two human beings, nothing more, and perhaps subconsciously you feel let down. Maybe that's when you hate them.

But when you grow older, you grow past that. That's when you begin to understand what they have done for you. There are so many times when I think back to my relationship with my parents and think: 'Why did I behave that way? Why did I treat them that way? Why couldn't I have been more loving?' And when that happens, I truly hate myself.

My love for Betta is another thing altogether. The love for your life partner is the love for the person you are sharing your existence with, the person you make love to, the person to whom you consciously give the very essence of your being. Over time, in some ways, the two of you become one and the same. You have selected this person and there is no turning back. You cannot erase the bond, even if you leave each other, even if you go elsewhere; you cannot escape the fact that this person knows you better than anyone else in the universe.

At the heart of it, however, is the fact that your life partner is somebody who chose to love you. With your parents or your children, it's not really up to you. The love flows naturally. But when you meet your soul mate, you are choosing to commit. Yes, there are natural feelings for that person, but you are electing to pursue them. In a sense, it's a blend of rationality and raw emotion and that is, I think, what makes it special.

Even then, making a commitment is not easy. In my case, things were complicated by the fact that after Terni I moved to Rome and then Turin, while Betta stayed behind. Long-distance relationships are very difficult. We started dating in January 1987, but after that summer I returned to Lazio and, except for the time I was injured, we only saw each other on weekends. It was a tremendous strain and it only got worse after I joined Juventus in the summer of 1990.

We were fighting a lot and I think we both understood that we had to make a decision. Either we tied the knot or we went our separate ways. It was a difficult choice because, after all, I was still just 23. I had not had any other serious relationships, I was very much a kid.

Yes, I knew I loved her, but lifelong commitment is something altogether different.

After our umpteenth fight I rang her back and said: 'We're getting married.'

I knew I wasn't being romantic, but I also knew I risked losing the woman I loved. She did not take me seriously.

'Paolo, no, you don't mean it, it's the same old thing. Just words.'

I was determined and, the next time I saw her, a few weeks later I made it clear I was all too serious.

'Well?' I said.

'Well what?' she replied.

'I'm totally serious,' I insisted. 'We're getting married.'

Her expression changed.

'You're just talking . . .' she said, weakly. Her voice trembled. 'You're not serious? Are you sure?'

I simply nodded. At that moment we both knew. We told her parents and were married the following July.

There was a period when I asked myself many times if I was ready. But then, how do you ever know if you're ready?

What does being ready mean? Some people say that if you're ready, you just know. There is no logic behind it. I'm not so sure. Like everything else, you're taking a chance, trusting your life to someone else. It's not just about love, it's about trust.

Her parents, Fausto and Franca, were delighted. By this point, they had become like another father and mother to me. That year at Terni, they treated me as if I was their son. Around February, I caught a bad fever and Franca insisted I spend the night so she could take care of me.

I would share a bedroom with Stefania, Betta's older sister, and immediately felt part of the family. I owe Betta's parents a tremendous debt, because I was nothing then, just a scrawny teenager with footballing dreams who had just begun dating their daughter.

Having said that, taking care of others has always been their way. Fausto is the kind of guy who shows up for dinner with four homeless people he met on the street. He'd simply find these guys, take him to his house and tell Franca: 'They're hungry and we can give them a warm meal. It's not a problem is it?'

And, to Franca, it never is, because she knows her husband is like that. Fausto has always been that way. He virtually adopted a boy named Vitale, an orphan from the Virgin Islands and raised him as if he was his own son. He shared a room with Betta for fifteen years and, when he left home, Fausto bought him a car. Fausto even paid for Vitale's brother's wedding.

That's the kind of people Betta's parents are. When you are a giver in life, you cannot stop giving.

Around the time I met Betta, I injured my tendon. The doctors whom I saw at that time told me not to worry. They said there were ways of treating it, that I should leave it up to them. Their solution was to shoot me up with painkillers. It was a decision that could have cost me not just my career, but my leg.

For you see, they didn't just give me injections to play in games. They gave me painkillers to train, almost every day, and that is an entirely different proposition. For five months, they would stick a needle in my tendon and pump me full of painkillers.

I didn't know any better. All I knew was that without the painkillers I couldn't run. If I couldn't run, I couldn't train, which meant I couldn't play on the Sunday. Little did I know that nothing, short of lopping my leg off with a chainsaw, could have been more damaging.

Painkillers treat the symptoms, not the problem. The gash in my tendon was still there and it went wholly un-treated. All the injections did was take the pain away. Over time, the injury got infected and the infection spread through the muscle until it attacked the first layers of the bone. I was totally oblivious to all this, because thanks to the painkillers, I couldn't feel anything.

The injury just never healed. I basically had a hole in my leg. If you shone a light down it, you could see the bone. Foolishly however, I had trusted my doctors blindly.

I found out how serious the situation was at the end of the season, when I had my medical for the Italian military service (all healthy Italian males are required to do a year's military duty). The doctor looked at my leg and told me I would probably be excused. At first I didn't realize how serious the situation was. I knew I carried an injury, but if it got me out of military service, that was fine. I knew Lazio's doctors would deal with it. While there are special provisions for athletes, military service is a serious inconvenience to footballers, because you spend your time shuttling between the barracks and training. Lazio had managed to avoid the drop to Serie C1, in spite of the nine-point penalty and the chairman was once again promising that next season, we'd be aiming for Serie A. With a year at Ternana under my belt, I was going to be a part of it.

I ran into Volfango and broke what I thought was the good news.

'Guess what? I might not have to do military service!'

'What?' he replied. 'Why? How are you going to get out of it?'

'Remember the problem with my leg?' I said. 'The one they fixed with the injections? Well, the guy from the army said it makes me unfit for military service!'

Volfango immediately saw how serious the situation was. He came over right away and took me to see Professor Carfagni, the Lazio team doctor. I told him about the cortisone injections. As he was examining the leg, I could see his expression darken. By the time he was finished, he looked like he was at a funeral.

My mother and Volfango came into his office and he broke the news to us.

'Signora, I'm going to be straight,' he said. 'First off, your son needs to forget about playing football ever again. The best we can do is to avoid having to amputate. It will not be easy and you must be prepared for that. You must understand, he may never be able to walk again.'

My mother was crying.

'Doctor, I don't care about football,' she sobbed. 'If I knew this was going to happen, I wouldn't have wanted him to ever kick a ball. All I want is for him to walk like a normal boy.'

Just like that, it was all over.

In forty-eight hours I went from being a carefree, rising young star, one with legitimate aspirations who had just received the good news that he wouldn't have to spend a year in the army, to being a 19-year-old shell of a kid who risked never walking again.

I was in a state of shock. My life had collapsed.

Looking back, I know my doctors were to blame. They didn't care about me, they just shot me up with painkillers to try and solve the problem.

I think the doctors who did this to me were more stupid than evil. I hope for their sake it was just a case of ignorance. Lord knows, I was ignorant at the time. All I understood was that with these injections the pain would go away and I could play. I had no clue that it was the most dangerous thing they could have done.

At that age, you blindly accept what you're told, you're just happy to be playing football. If a manager or doctor tells you to take these pills or those shots, you're going to do it. I just wonder how many careers have been snuffed out by incompetent or negligent doctors over the years. It's a problem few people talk about, but it deserves more attention.

Today, I won't let any doctor near me unless I trust him completely. I'd rather play through the pain than take cortisone shots. I remember at Sheffield Wednesday they tried to give me painkillers and I just refused. I fell for it as a boy, I was not going to be fooled again.

Of course, if there's a crucial match coming up and the team needs me, I'll do it, I'll take the injections. But it must never become a matter of routine. And you never, ever take painkillers to train. Ever.

The next few months were some of the worst in my life. I was prescribed a large dose of antibiotics, which was supposed to attack the infection. They had to be injected directly into the tendon, using a three-and-a-half inch needle. It was painful and it was scary, but over time I got used to it. Every few weeks I would go and see Professor Carfagni and his two assistants Agostine Tucciarone and Andrea Billi. He would examine the hole in my leg. The skin would grow back, giving the impression that perhaps the wound had closed up. But he would poke through the skin and see that there was still a gaping gash in the flesh, right down to the bone. The infection was still there and it was slowly eating away at me.

It was a nightmare and, as often happens in these situations, I coped with it by taking things out on others. I was nervous and irritable, I would snap at everybody. It took the slightest thing to set me off. The worst part was the frustration, the feeling of total powerlessness. My family was close, Betta was close, but it made no difference. I felt totally alone, completely worn out, broken down.

Lazio sent me to see several specialists, but the story was

always the same. The antibiotics had attacked the bacteria that caused the infection, but the bacteria were multiplying faster than they could be killed. Months passed.

One day, Professor Carfagni called me in and said: 'Paolo, I've booked you an appointment with this Belgian specialist. His techniques are very cutting-edge and some-what controversial. He's a pioneer in his field and the things he does are rather unusual. But frankly Paolo, I don't see any other alternative. This could be your last chance. The infection is spreading. Soon we may not have any choice.'

I agreed right away. Faced with this type of situation, some people become zombies, wallowing in their misery. I became a bundle of nerves, a vicious wreck of a person, but also one who jumped at every chance, no matter how slight.

Tucciarone and I had to travel to Cortina d'Ampezzo, a ski resort in the north of Italy, to see the specialist. He didn't say much, he seemed like every other doctor I had ever seen. That was until he pulled out this gigantic needle which resembled a screwdriver. It was scary.

'My God, this guy's a witch doctor!' I cursed to myself. 'Either that, or a butcher.'

He stuck the needle in my leg, explaining that it would extract the bacteria. It took a few minutes, and when it was done, he gave me a vaccine. He said it would help prevent some of the bacteria from growing back, but I still needed to have my leg drained of fluids when I returned to Rome.

Draining my leg took about a month and it was perhaps the worst part of my experience. I was flat on my back for days and days. There was absolutely nothing I could do, save mistreat the people around me. Which I did with passion and brutality.

Throughout my ordeal, Betta would take the train to Rome to see me every single day. She would finish work and take the train, an hour-and-a-half each way, just to be by my side.

How did I repay her? By yelling at her, by ignoring her, by humiliating her. I was so irritable, the slightest thing would set me off. Because she was always there, she was the easiest target. She would start crying and I would tell her to go back to Terni. Again, it's difficult for me to talk about this. When I think back to those times, I hate myself for treating her that way. I would torture her and she would still love me. That is how I began to learn what true love was.

She was always there and it took me a long, long time to fully appreciate what she did for me then and still does today. Until I was in my mid-twenties, I thought I was the centre of the universe. I thought my worries, my concerns were bigger and more serious than everybody else's. I was the breadwinner, so I needed and deserved all the attention.

Even when Betta was pregnant with Ludovica, I did not understand what she was going through. She might complain, or feel tense or simply not be all smiles and I would snap at her, take it out on her. My problems were always bigger than hers. When I think back, it's ridiculous. The fact that I had been left on the bench in some football match became more important than the fact that she was about to give birth to another human being, our daughter, the fruit of our love. It's painful to admit that I treated her that way. If any good did come of it, it's the fact that I value and appreciate her that much more today. She is the beat of my heart and I adore her every day of my life.

Three months after seeing the Belgian specialist I was due back to meet Professor Carfagni. After my leg had been drained, I spent the first few days peering down intently at the wound, looking for some sign that it had healed. The skin began growing back, covering up the hole, but I figured it meant little. Just as before, it was just skin. Poke through it and the gash would still be there, all the way down to the bone.

Perhaps that's why my mind wandered as I lay on Professor Carfagni's table and he fiddled with my leg. I was sure nothing had changed, so I tried not to think about it. He poked around for a few minutes, then he slapped me on the back.

'Son, get dressed,' he said. 'The hole is gone. You start rehabilitation on Tuesday and you had better be ready.'

My jaw dropped, like in those old Warner Brothers cartoons. If it hadn't been attached to my head, it would have landed with a thud. I began shaking. I tried to speak, but I couldn't.

I was going to get another chance at football, another opportunity at life. I started crying, slowly at first, dry heaves from my chest, my hands clutching air. I grabbed Professor Carfagni and broke down. The feelings of relief, of hope, made it one of the greatest and most emotional moments of my life.

I have to thank Lazio for sticking by me throughout my injury. They could have just as easily dropped me altogether. After all, I was just a kid whose career was in jeopardy. From a business standpoint, considering that there was maybe a two per cent chance I'd ever play again, it didn't really make sense to spend all this money on my treatment and rehabilitation. Yes, I was under contract, but that has never stopped big clubs from doing what they want, especially when it comes to 19-year-old kids.

Instead, they believed in me. Maybe they did it out of loyalty, or maybe they did it because they thought I was too good a prospect to assign to the scrapheap. And perhaps they would not have done it for a less-touted youngster. Whatever the case may be, without Lazio's support, odds are I wouldn't be able to walk unassisted today.

By the time I finished the rehabilitation work on my knee, the 1987–88 season was almost over and Lazio were on the verge of gaining promotion to Serie A. I even had the chance to meet up with my old buddies from the Irriducibili and go see a few games on the road, though this time I tried to avoid trouble.

The manager, Eugenio Fascetti, called me into his office before the crucial promotion-decider against Taranto. A win would clinch Serie A status the next season, a loss or draw and our future would depend on results in other games.

'Son, I just want you to know that regardless of what happens on Sunday against Taranto, regardless of whether we are promoted or not, you're going to spend the pre-season with the first-team next year,' he told me. 'I know you've been through hell, just make sure you're ready.'

I was drunk with happiness. My big chance was just around the corner. That Sunday, we beat Taranto 3–1. Betta and I were invited into the director's box, watching the game with the players' wives and those who weren't in the squad that day. I was going nuts: Lazio, my Lazio, were back in Serie A. And I was going to be a part of it.

After the season ended, Fascetti and his players biked to a monastery at Terminillo, a few hours outside Rome. It was a tradition, a way of giving thanks and celebrating promotion. That day, Fascetti wrote a name on a piece of paper and placed it in an envelope.

He said: 'The name in this envelope is the name of the player who will be the young player of the season in Serie A next year.'

A year later I would find out that the name in the envelope was 'PAOLO DI CANIO'.

I couldn't wait to work with Fascetti when, just two days after the trip to Terminillo, I received word that he had been sacked. In a sudden and controversial move, the chairman, Gianmarco Calleri, had axed the popular Fascetti and replaced him with Giuseppe Materazzi, a disciplinarian who had helped Pisa avoid relegation to Serie B the previous season.

The shock move caused widespread riots outside Lazio's headquarters. I was confused, I didn't know what to think. Materazzi was a man of few words, but he tried to reassure me: 'You'll still do the pre-season training with us. Then, in September, we'll probably loan you out. Don't worry, your chance will come, one day.'

Materazzi was true to his word. I busted my butt in pre-season training and I think one or two people took notice. That summer, Lazio played a string of friendlies at the

Flaminio, the older, smaller stadium in Rome, where the Italian rugby team played in the Six Nations.

As often happens in summer friendlies, there were tons of substitutions late in the games and, to me, it was a chance to show what I could do in a Lazio shirt. In England, nobody seems to care about the summer warm-ups, but in Italy, and in Rome especially, they receive wall-to-wall coverage. It's the first opportunity to get a glimpse of next season's team.

Lazio wouldn't even bother listing my name as a sub on the team sheet for those games. They simply wrote the letter 'X'. But then, I didn't even have a proper jersey, my shirt didn't even have a number on the back. The first time I came on, some twenty minutes from the end, the stadium's PA introduced me as 'Mister X' and the fans had a bit of a laugh. Two minutes later, after I had dribbled past three defenders and hit the crossbar, they were no longer laughing, they were on their feet, applauding my every move.

I knew those types of games were just exhibitions, a chance to show what I could do, so I played with reckless abandon – there were dribbles, backheels, flicks, the lot. I wanted people to see my entire range of skills. And I wanted them to know that I was the kind of guy who spilled his guts on the pitch.

The fans loved it and each time would start chanting: '*Mister X! Mister X!*'

Most had no idea who I was, but it didn't matter. I was Mister X and I was entertaining them. We played three friendlies at the Flaminio that summer. Each time, I came on halfway through the second half. Each time, the stadium's PA introduced me as 'Mister X' and the crowd went nuts.

A few weeks later, before an Italian Cup game against Campobasso, Materazzi called me over and said: 'Just so you know, you're coming on in the second half.'

His words took a while to register, but when they did I was out of my skin. I was getting my chance, in a real game. The Coppa Italia begins before Serie A, many teams don't take it seriously until the later stages, but it's still an official competition. I was about to make my debut.

Sure enough, I was on the pitch for the start of the second half. Materazzi had faith in me, I repaid him with an extra-ordinary goal. I received the ball on the right, cut inside, beat one defender, beat another defender, slipped past the third and chipped the goalkeeper. It was my first-ever official match for Lazio and I had scored a goal. And not just any goal, but one which earned me a standing ovation.

It still hadn't really sunk in. A week later, we were in Cesena, preparing for the season opener. I was hoping just to be on the bench. My buddy, Antonio Rizzolo, my old team-mate from the Lazio youth team, was sitting next to me while Materazzi was giving his pre-game speech. Rizzolo and I had become inseparable, we were chatting away quietly, not really paying attention as Materazzi stood at the front of the room, drawing our formation on the blackboard and explaining what to look out for.

All of a sudden, just as I was talking Rizzolo's ear off, he smacked my arm and said: 'Shut up, man! You're playing tomorrow.'

'What the hell are you saying? Don't mess me about.'

'No, he just said that Mister X was going to play. Now shut the hell up. We should be listening to him anyway.'

Indeed, Materazzi had a tendency to drone on and as a hyperactive 19-year-old, attention spans aren't your greatest assets. But then he started running through the team, 'Number one, so-and-so, watch out for high balls, number two, so-and-so, look out for the winger cutting inside,' and on he went until he got to number nine.

'Number nine, Paolo, you're right of midfield . . . take it easy, Mister X, don't get caught out . . .'

I froze. I mean, I became a statue. I could no longer hear his voice, I was just watching his lips move, not hearing a word he was saying. The moment we were finished, I ran out and called Betta to break the news. I was so happy, I could not contain myself.

That day, as I took my place on the pitch, I took a long, hard look at my teammates. There was Oliviero 'Gus' Garlini, the top scorer from Serie B. There was Giuliano Fiorini, the elegant midfielder. There was Mimmo Caso, the wily veteran. Then I looked up at the visiting end, where I could clearly see my mates from the Irriducibili. Four months before, I was standing next to them. Four months before, my teammates were my idols; I would scream myself hoarse, chanting their names. Now, we were on equal footing.

Not only was I playing alongside my heroes, I was playing with overseas stars as well. I saw the two Uruguayans, Ruben Sosa and Jose Gutierrez, who had played in the World Cup. And I was there, with them. On the same pitch, wearing the same shirt. It was incredible.

I was playing well, I had slotted right into the side, even the Under-21 manager had been to see me. But two months in, week nine of the Serie A season, came the biggest test of all: the Rome derby.

I have had the opportunity to play in five derbies. The Juventus-Torino rivalry has deep historical roots, while the Milan derby, Inter Milan versus AC Milan, is probably the best in the world in terms of evenly-matched sides and sheer quality on the pitch. At West Ham, we play four or five local derbies a year, so perhaps it's less of an event, but you know that when we play Arsenal, Chelsea or Spurs, we're totally fired up.

Yet, apart from the Old Firm, which is far and away the biggest rivalry in all of sport, nothing else compares to the Rome derby, or the 'Derby del Cupolone', the 'Derby of the Big Dome' (St Peter's). People begin talking about it six weeks in advance, the preparations begin with weeks to spare. The build-up is huge, nothing else matters. And yes, it's true that for a long time Roma and Lazio fans cared more about winning the derby than where they finished in the league.

Much of it, of course, had to do with the fact that northern clubs have traditionally dominated the Italian game; Roma and Lazio have won only four titles combined. Since you weren't going to win the scudetto anyway, it really didn't matter if you finished fifth or tenth in the league table, as long as you won local bragging rights by beating the other Roman team.

Even today, when both clubs have legitimate title ambitions (Lazio are the defending champions) that attitude perseveres. And in my opinion it's actually damaging. I remember three years ago Lazio and Juventus were neck-and-neck for the title. Juventus were away to Roma, you would have thought that the 'laziali', at least for a day, might support their cross-town rivals. Instead, when Juventus scored, many Lazio fans cheered. Why? Because Roma were losing. Seeing Roma beaten was more important to them than Lazio's title chances.

I had tried to steer clear of the build-up, but it was impossible. My heart was pounding as I walked on to the pitch. It was so loud, I could feel the weight of the noise bearing down on my shoulders. My teammate Ruben Sosa was a few yards away, I could see his lips move but I could not hear anything. Obviously, I had been to many derbies, but this was my first as a player. I knew from being an Ultra how loud, how passionate the fans could be, but I had no idea that it would have this effect on the players.

The Lazio fans had covered the entire Curva Nord with a gigantic flag. It was a white heart, on a sky-blue background. Lazio colours, all the way. It mirrored what was inside my chest. I just kept staring at the fans, even during the coin toss. Somehow I felt like my place was up there, with the Irriducibili. At that moment, I was a fan on the pitch. I was living the greatest dream any football fan can live.

And it was about to get better.

Twenty-five minutes had passed when our playmaker, Antonio Elia Acerbis, received the ball from the full-back, Paolo Beruatto, inside the Roma half. Acerbis cut towards the middle, from right to left and hit a diagonal ball to Ruben Sosa, who was standing just outside the box, to the left of the goal. Ruben Sosa's back was to the goal, it looked like he was going to control it, instead he first-timed a square ball across the penalty area. I began running as soon as he released it. As I stormed in from the right wing, I watched the ball skid along the ground, in between the goalkeeper, Franco Tancredi and the defender, Sebastiano Nela. By the time I got there, it had crossed the entire face of the goal. I smacked it hard, one touch, I was trying to hurt the ball. It exploded off my foot. Tancredi got both hands to it, but the sheer power, the raw violence of my shot was too much for him to stop. I watched for a second as it hit the back of the net and then I took off.

I just ran and ran, straight toward the Curva Sud, where the Roma fans were sitting. The roar at my back, from Lazio's Curva Nord, was spurring me on. I ran right under the fans, finger raised, face contorted in a mixture of ecstasy, relief and fury.

It wasn't planned, it was just a spontaneous eruption. When you score a goal like that, in a situation that means so much to you, you don't think, everything happens naturally. When you're a passionate, emotional person like I am, the moment only gets magnified and multiplied. I'm just glad I never did a similar thing at Ibrox, when I was playing for Celtic. If I had, I would probably be dead now.

Only one player in history had ever run up to the Roma end and given their fans a one-fingered salute. It had happened years earlier when centre-forward Giorgio Chinaglia had made a similar gesture to the Roma faithful, causing a national scandal. The difference was that at the time Chinaglia was a veteran Italian international, whereas I was a twenty-year-old, playing in his ninth-ever game for Lazio.

Chinaglia would go on to join the New York Cosmos of

the North American Soccer League and play alongside Pele and Franz Beckenbauer. Later, he even became Lazio chairman. He is a living legend, a man who will forever be in the hearts of Lazio fans. With that goal, I knew immediately that I too would forever remain in their hearts.

Even now, I get shivers down my spine when I think about it. Scoring the winning goal in the Rome derby was simply beyond words, especially for me, a kid who had spent his childhood travelling the country to support the club.

I am being brutally honest when I say that if I had quit football right then and there, I would have done so a happy man. The joy was so great, I didn't care if I never touched a football again in my life.

After our 1–0 victory, things were different. For many months, I had to be careful every time I left the house. As long as I remained in the Quarticciolo, I was all right. It was teeming with Roma fans, even some hardcore Ultras, but I was on my home turf. Odds are, they were friends of mine, and, even if they weren't, I knew help would always be close at hand.

It was a different story in other parts of Rome and it would be that way for a long time. I was spat at and insulted several times, nobody forgot my goal and most of all, my goal celebration.

It was the only goal I scored that first season, but the press were raving about me and, more importantly, so were the fans. I had an instant rapport with them, which was logical, since just a short while ago I was one of them. I was the hometown hero, the local boy who had worked his way up, who loved Lazio and its colours as much as they did.

We finished tenth that year, not bad for a newly promoted club. The 1989–90 season started well, I scored a few
goals, but by January, things were starting to turn sour off
the pitch. I began to realize that the chairman, Calleri, for all
his talk of rebuilding Lazio and restoring us to our old glory,
had no intention of spending serious money. In fact, not
only was he not going to strengthen the squad, he was going
to sell off the best players.

I was angry enough at that, but what put me over the
edge, what made me feel like somebody had reached into
my chest and pulled out my heart, was the fact that I found
out I was one of the players up for sale. I had waited a lifetime to play for Lazio, to fight for the Lazio eagle and now,
after just two years, I would have to leave.

My agent, Moreno Roggi, told me that several clubs had
made inquiries, but Calleri had already reached a deal with
Juventus. The official price was £3 million, but I now know
for a fact the real figure was closer to £5 million. That was a
hell of a lot of money at the time. To put things in perspective, the British transfer record back then was £2.3 million
for Gary Pallister.

Still, I wanted to stay at Lazio. I asked Moreno what
could be done.

'Paolo, you've got to understand that you are now a professional footballer,' he said. 'Being loyal to your club is a
wonderful thing, but you can't be a fan and a professional at
the same time. You have chosen to be a footballer and that
means you have to accept that you can be bought and sold,
just like that.'

I wasn't convinced. I didn't want to leave my club. But it

was clear that Calleri wanted to sell me. He needed the cash. What he did next was utterly reprehensible.

Calleri knew that sooner or later he would get his way. But he also knew that the fans would never forgive him if he sold me against my will. He knew that if I came out and told the Lazio faithful that Calleri was selling me but that I had no intention of going, things could get really ugly for him. Especially since he was well aware of my relationship with the fans and that many leaders of the Irriducibili and Eagles were my friends.

So he chose to pre-empt all that. Remember the old Quarticciolo mantra, 'Strike first, strike hard'? Well, that's exactly what Calleri did. He tipped off his friends in the press that I had made outrageous contract demands.

The reality was very different. My first contract with Lazio was going to run out after the following season. I was on slightly more than the basic wage for young players; this was to be my first proper deal. We went in to talk to Calleri and it became immediately clear he had no intention of giving me a new contract. He had already decided he was going to sell me, now all he had to do was make it impossible for me to stay.

He tried to do this by saying I had to take a pay cut. His offer wasn't a real offer, it was an insult, it was worse than an insult. I was already making very little money, and he wanted to cut it even further. Even then, saying no, tore me up inside. The fan inside me was ready to play for Lazio for free, hell, even to pay for the right to wear the shirt. But as a human being, I was humiliated. He even had the nerve to tell me that I wasn't playing well, that the club wasn't happy with my performance. This, after a season in which I had won my first Under-21 caps and was the hero of the Curva Nord.

I refused to sign. I wasn't going to be taken for a fool. I felt that, given a little time, the fans would rally around me and Calleri would be forced to keep me. It was a mistake believing I could do that. He had struck a deal with Juventus and Juventus always get their way. Not to mention the fact that players rarely, if ever, win player versus club battles. It's a fact: players come and go and clubs remain.

To avoid embarrassment, Calleri turned up the pressure. He managed to convince the fans that I had asked him for a transfer, that I was trying to force him to sell me. I fought back. Many of the fans were on my side, they knew I would never willingly turn my back on Lazio, and many of them remembered me from my Irriducibili days.

But it's much easier to control public opinion if you're the chairman of a big club than if you're just a 21-year-old footballer. The pressure mounted, I started hearing the first insults from a minority of the fans. Most were still squarely on my side, they refused to believe what was being said about me, but it started becoming very difficult.

The media didn't help. The pressure, especially in Rome, can be enormous. I laugh when I hear certain footballers, particularly foreigners, complain about the pressure of playing in the Premiership. Inevitably, it's people who never played in Italy. Compared to Serie A, the Premiership is a holiday. The English media can be jingoistic, xenophobic and aggressive, but in terms of coverage, they are years behind Italy. In Rome, there are dozens of television and radio stations that provide blanket coverage of Roma and

Lazio. Pick up *Corriere Dello Sport*, the Roman edition, and you'll find pages and pages of stories, every single day.

Naturally, my contract situation was the big story. Everybody wanted to know what was happening. It got ridiculous, but then, that's the norm when it comes to the Roman press. Already, there were stations who would provide live commentary of our training session.

It was stuff like: 'It's 10:33 am and Paolo Di Canio has just parked his car in the players' lot. He's wearing brown slacks and a black shirt. He's heading for the dressing room now . . .'

With people like that, you couldn't escape the controversy. Just imagine something like that happening in England. It's another world.

Every day became more stressful, more of an ordeal. Once again, I was getting nervous, paranoid. It seemed as if everywhere I went there were whispers, rumours, poisons. It made no sense to me. All I wanted to do was play for Lazio and now, because of rich and powerful men and their backroom deals, my dream was being taken from me.

My head would start spinning, there were times when I felt nauseous, times when I thought the world was about to crush me. The Lazio fans were being torn apart by my situation, and I was responsible for this split at the heart of the club. I knew it wasn't my fault, but I was still the catalyst and it killed me inside.

I began to suffer fainting spells, panic attacks. I was terrified, I had no idea what was happening. One morning, I woke up and simply could not get out of bed. I just could not move. I was petrified with fear.

My mother was worried sick.

'Paolo!' she would implore. 'Please! Get up, get out of bed. Tell me, tell me what's wrong, what is it?'

My lips would move but nothing would come out. I just couldn't do anything. The poor woman, it had been less than two years since the injury that almost cost me my leg. And now this. She was seeing her child suffer and she knew she was powerless to stop it.

As for me, I thought I was going to die. I really did. I never knew when the panic attacks would come. When they did, my head would spin, I felt the air being sucked out of my lungs, my eyes would fade to black. I had broken down completely.

Lazio were concerned as well. I was a nervous wreck, I was totally unpredictable, I could collapse at any moment and I had lost a lot of weight. I had always been thin, but now I looked gaunt and sickly, like I had been in a concentration camp for the past six years.

The club sent me to a psychologist, but it didn't help. Next, they tried another guy, a specialist in nervous breakdowns. His office was in Trastevere, just across the Tiber River. I remember going with my brothers, Antonio and Giuliano. The drive over was a nightmare, I became claustrophobic in the car, I wanted to scream, I couldn't breathe. As soon as they parked, I jumped out and ran off, sprinting as hard as I could through the streets of Trastevere. I'm not sure why I reacted that way, I just knew that when I was running, when my body was under stress, sometimes my head would begin to clear. I ran and ran, trying to get away from the poisons and demons in my head, from the rumours and backstabbing which were poisoning Rome, my city, and most of all, Lazio, my club.

I don't even know where I went, I just know that it took my brothers almost an hour to find me. We got to the specialist's office late, but it didn't matter. He still saw me and it was still an utter waste of time. He said I was in the throes of a deep depression, which was obvious to anybody. He prescribed more pills, but they didn't do anything. Nothing could get through to me.

What saved me was Fausto, Betta's father. He took me to see a faith healer. This is something of which I have never spoken before. I didn't believe in faith healing at the time and, I don't think I believe in it now. To me, spells, witches, psychics, it's all junk.

I don't really want to publicize this woman, this faith healer, because I'm not sure how it really worked or whether it would work for others. I just know that the woman whom Fausto took me to see, cured me of my problems and maybe saved my career.

Her name was Luciana and she lived in a rambling house in the countryside, a few miles from Terni. She was in her early fifties, with three teenage kids. When I went to see her, she took me to a room in the back of the house and made me lie down.

Right away she said: 'Paolo, I don't think there's anything wrong with you. You're just filled with negative energy.'

Without touching me she placed her hand, palm flat, facing inward, some ten centimetres from my right arm. Immediately, I felt the entire right side of my body collapse. It was like a house of cards, when you remove the bottom card, or a bathtub, when you remove the plug. It just fell apart, like it wasn't even there. I almost fell over, I had to steady myself. I threw myself on a bed.

She began touching my forehead, my chest, different parts of my body. I could tell that something was happening. I hate saying that she was draining the negative energy from my body, because it sounds so New Age, so ridiculous. Rationally, I don't believe any of that stuff.

All I know is that somehow it worked. A month of popping pills and seeing psychologist and psychiatrists had done nothing for me. Now, after one sitting with this woman, I was already feeling better.

I went back to see her four or five times. Each session was the same and would last a half hour. After the final session she told me I was cured, but there was one more important step I needed to take.

'Paolo, you need to picture your room back in Rome,' she said. 'You have something made of wool with a checker design, you have another object with the picture of a car on it and you have some kind of spherical metal object.'

I pictured my flat in Rome. My mind wandered around my bedroom. The blood froze in my veins. I did indeed own a wool hat with a red and black checked design that I had bought in Verona a few years earlier. My blanket had a racing car on it. And I had a trophy that I had won as a boy, which was shaped like a football.

How could this woman possibly know this? She had never been to my house, I only ever saw her in her home. Neither had either of Betta's parents, they couldn't have told her what was in my room in Rome. Betta had never even met her. How could she possibly have known?

It makes me uncomfortable to think about this, because as I said, I don't believe in magic and mysticism. But not only did she heal me, she knew things about me nobody else did. It was spooky.

'Paolo, you need to burn the hat and the blanket,' she told me. 'As for the trophy, bring it to me and I will take care of it.'

I did as I was told. She never asked for a single lira in payment. She did all this for free, she said she had a gift and she wanted to share it. If anything, that is the only thing which makes me believe in her. That, and the fact that after seeing her I felt much, much better.

Even though my depression was gone, things in Rome were no better, in fact, they were getting very ugly. My breakdown had caused me to miss three matches but when I got back into the squad, Calleri's stance hadn't changed. He told me it was all done, I was being sold to Juventus and I had no choice in the matter. I could either accept the reality now or accept it later. The outcome was going to be the same.

I was gutted but I had no choice. He was playing hardball with me, he had turned some of the fans against me, I wasn't wanted. Deep down, I also knew that you couldn't take on management and hope to win, especially not in a situation where you wanted to stay. There are ways to demand a transfer, but getting a club to keep you when they don't want you is virtually impossible. Grudgingly, I accepted my fate.

One night a short while later, I was out by the Piazza di Spagna, the Spanish Steps, with two friends of mine, Bruno and Antonello who, ironically, were both Roma fans. It was around midnight, we were in Bruno's car, trying to make our way through the narrow alleys around the piazza, when the people in the car in front of us recognized me. They slowed their car to a walking pace and took turns leaning out the windows to insult me.

'You bastard!' they yelled. 'You f**king laziale! Why don't you get out of the car and we'll teach you a lesson!'

It went on like this for a few minutes, we couldn't go anywhere, there were no turns off our street and it was way too narrow to pass them. By now, all of them except the driver were leaning out of the windows, making obscene gestures and threatening us.

It was getting ugly. I knew that if they got carried away, if they jumped out of their car and attacked us, the last place we wanted to be was stuck in Bruno's car. It was best to do something, right away. I remembered the lesson I learned as a kid in the Quarticciolo: 'Strike first. Strike hard.'

So we did. Bruno slammed on the brakes, we jumped out and rushed the car in front of us. We dragged the guys from the car and it all went off. There were four of them, but they weren't expecting us to react so decisively. Fists flew and I was in the thick of it.

We were beating the living daylights out of each other when, all of a sudden, we heard police sirens going off.

'Get the f**k out of here, Paolo!' Bruno yelled.

I hesitated. I didn't want to leave my mates in the middle of a fight.

'I said get out!' Bruno screamed again. 'GET THE F**K OUT!!!'

I turned and ran. Bruno was right. I had already signed for Juventus. If an incident like this hit the papers, I was done for. Juventus were very tough that way, they didn't want any controversy surrounding their players. If word got out that Paolo Di Canio had been arrested for assaulting someone in the centre of Rome, I was finished.

I hid in a restaurant around the corner and waited for news. The cops arrested Bruno, Antonello and the other guys and took them down to the police station. Bruno and Antonello were ready to take all the blame on my behalf. As it happened, they didn't need to.

When they were first taken away, the other guys were yelling: 'Paolo Di Canio the footballer was with them! He attacked us, but he got away! You have to find him!'

They were hysterical, and the cops looked at them like they were crazy.

'I don't see Paolo Di Canio anywhere, so I'm not going to arrest him,' one cop said. 'But if you have something to say, feel free to tell us at the police station when we do the paperwork. For the time being, SHUT THE F**K UP!!!'

Bruno and Antonello were put in the same holding cell as the guys we had been fighting with and they went straight to work on them. My mates didn't mess around, they were not the type of people with whom you really wanted to get involved.

They grabbed one of the guys and shoved him against the wall of the cell.

'I am assuming you want to get out of here alive, so I'm

telling you that you'd better forget all about Paolo Di Canio,' Bruno threatened. 'You did not see him. He wasn't there. In fact, you'd better forget all about pressing charges or even reporting this incident tonight. Do as you're told and we can all go home and forget about this. Press charges, mention Paolo Di Canio again, and you'll be getting out of here in a body bag.'

As I said, Bruno and Antonello were the type of people who looked like they could back up their threats. No charges were pressed, they said it was just a misunderstanding, a bit of argy-bargy, no more. After a few hours they were released and came by the restaurant to pick me up. I had been sitting there, a nervous wreck all that time.

Given this incident and the climate at Lazio, I came to accept that maybe moving on was not such a bad thing. After all, Juventus were the biggest club in Italy, maybe in Europe. I would be getting more money, it was a bigger stage. Who knows, maybe I could come back to Lazio one day. I wasn't thrilled, but I was ready.

CHAPTER FIVE

'YOU'RE FINISHED, DI CANIO!'

Sometimes even dynasties fall apart and need to be rebuilt. The Juventus team I joined in the summer of 1990 was just such a club.

Juventus are the closest thing Italian football has to royalty. Known as the 'Vecchia Signora', or 'Old Lady', it has collected more titles than any other club. In the 1980s, it won four scudetti, a Coppa Italia, a Cup Winners' Cup, a UEFA Cup and a World Club Championship. The club is owned by the Agnelli family, who also happen to own FIAT, Italy's biggest company. In short, it oozes power, the kind of power that comes from being part of the Establishment.

But times had changed and, despite winning the UEFA Cup in 1990, the club was far from happy. New blood was needed at every level. Luca Cordero di Montezemolo, the man who had successfully organized the 1990 World Cup (and now runs Ferrari) was named as Executive Vice Chairman, with virtual carte blanche to rebuild the club. His first move was to call in the flamboyant Gigi Maifredi as manager.

Maifredi was a character, in every way. A former

champagne salesman, he was seen as a footballing vision-
ary. He had shaken up Italian football by taking Bologna
to Serie A and then leading them to two seasons of mid-
table respectability. More than his results, what impressed
people was the way his teams played. With him, it was
constant excitement: he played a pure zonal defence, where
everybody was encouraged to storm forward. He didn't
believe in holding midfielders, everybody had to join in
the attack.

It was highly entertaining, but most of all it was
anathema to the Italian football mentality. The traditional
Italian view of football is that results come before everything. It's always better to play badly and win 1–0 on a 93rd
minute penalty because your centre-forward took a dive,
than to play brilliantly and draw 3–3. Maifredi didn't view it
that way. He thought teams should attack from beginning to
end, that they should play attractive, offensive football, first
and foremost.

I still missed Lazio; deep down there was a part of me that
wondered if somehow I could have worked something out
with them. But I realized that things had gone too far, that
there was still too much poison in the air in Rome.

I remember a humid evening in August, in Turin. I
hadn't found a flat yet, so I was staying in a hotel and Betta
had come up to see me for a few days. We ordered room service, turned on the television and watched Lazio play Milan
in a pre-season friendly. The fan inside me got all excited, I
was cheering them on, when something stopped me dead in
my tracks.

I thought I was hearing things. But sure enough, even

through the television, I could tell what the fans were singing.

'*Pezzo di merda! Di Canio, pezzo di merda! Pezzo di merda!*'

They were singing 'Piece of shit! Di Canio, piece of shit! Piece of shit!' to the tune of 'Guantanamera'.

Those were my fans. My fans! My mates, my people, if it hadn't been for my footballing ability, I would have been right there among them!

And they were slagging me off. Calleri had convinced them that I was a traitor, that I had turned my back on them.

I broke down, completely. I just started crying and crying, I could not stop. If they only knew the truth, if they only knew how badly I wanted to be there.

I was hysterical. Betta tried to comfort me; if she hadn't been there, I'm not sure what I would have done. It was one of the darkest moments of my life. Almost every other time when I have felt pain, I felt anger right alongside it. However bad the pain was, the anger was greater and I found a way of channelling it. Here, it was just pain. Pure unadulterated pain.

The next day I called the leaders of the Lazio Ultras, the heads of the Irriducibili and Eagles. They told me it had been a minority, albeit a vocal one, of people who had accepted Calleri's words at face value. They said they would make sure it didn't happen again.

I was still upset, but in my mind I knew I had to press on. I was about to start a new season at Italy's biggest club and I couldn't let my chance go to waste.

Juventus were desperate for a change and, as changes go, it was the most radical available. Maifredi was given free rein to rebuild the club and to do this he went on a wild shopping spree.

In addition to buying me, that same summer he acquired Roberto Baggio, fresh from a sterling performance at the 1990 World Cup; Massimo Orlando, an Under-21 international who was compared by many to the legendary Brazilian Zico; and German World Cup star Thomas Hassler. Basically we were all offensive players, joining a strike force which already included Italian internationals Totò Schillaci, the top scorer from the previous summer's World Cup, and Pierluigi Casiraghi.

Casiraghi was my roommate and one of the most genuinely kind-hearted people I have met in football. That first year, we were inseparable. What happened to him, it sends shivers down my spine. He had just moved to London, he was ready to start a new career in English football and, after just two months, it all ended. Just like that.

The possibility of injury is always hanging over you, it is just something you must accept as a professional. The most obvious trauma is that you can no longer do what you did. Think about it. Footballers do not lead the same lives as normal people. We spend our entire existence from the age of fourteen (and sometimes even earlier) with just one objective: to become a professional footballer. We make so many sacrifices, we often have to turn our backs on friends, on an education, on our family, just to make it. Then, we achieve our dream, only to have it taken away from us.

Beyond the psychological blow, there is the financial

blow. It may seem ludicrous to say this when there are players who earn millions of pounds a year. But the reality is that they are the extreme minority. Many of us left school early to pursue a career in football. Very few have any kind of school qualification and you can count on one hand those who have university degrees. Once we give up football, there is very little we can do.

In spite of everything, Casiraghi was fortunate. He had a successful career, he has a wonderful family, he probably never needs to worry about taking care of his loved ones ever again. But what about all the others? What about all the footballers in the lower divisions who are forced to leave the game at age 23 or 24? What happens to them?

I think that, given where I come from, I know the value of money. I know that footballers, by the mere fact that they can earn a living by playing the game they love, are incredibly fortunate. But the fact remains that not being able to provide for your family is one of the worst things that can happen to a man. And it happens to footballers as well.

This is a material world. We are defined by what we have, what we own. It may not be right, but that is the way it is. Why else does a nurse who works twelve-hour shifts six nights a week make less in a year than a pop star or fashion model makes in a day?

Material possessions therefore become important. They become a way for society to measure your worth as a human being. If you are a man, your most basic instinct is to have a family. How well you provide for your family becomes a benchmark of how well you do your job as a father. Maybe it's not the only benchmark, but it is an important one. A father who sees his children go hungry, or simply not have as much as their neighbours, is a broken man. Dignity and respect, values which should be a hundred times more important, inevitably pale in comparison. And for a footballer whose career is cut short in his early twenties, it is the most fatal of blows.

Of course, the flipside is that the money you earn can make your life incredibly comfortable. It opens doors, gives you opportunities, it allows you to surround yourself with beautiful things.

It would be hypocritical of me to say that footballers earn too much money. We earn what people are willing to pay us. I'm the first to say that a perfect world would be one where we all got along, we all were happy, we all shared everything and worked equally hard for the common good. But that would be a Communist world and, beyond the fact that history proved that it doesn't work, we certainly don't live in a Communist society. Instead, we live in a capitalist world and I think it's only fair that those who have ability, those who work harder, those who produce results are rewarded. If you want to quibble about what's wrong with society, well, if anything it's the fact that many never get a chance to show what they're worth, they never get a chance to succeed. But that is a different argument and it has little to do with footballers' salaries.

Of course, there are many who get used to a certain lifestyle and sometimes lose sight of reality. I know of a foreign footballer in the Premiership whose car was held up at customs when he moved to England. I'm not going to mention his name because there is no need to embarrass him, but he found himself needing a car, since his own vehicle wouldn't be available for three months. A mutual friend offered to lend him his VW Golf in the interim. He flatly refused.

'What the hell am I going to do?' he told me. 'Drive around in a little Golf? You've got to be having a laugh. I can't be seen in a Golf, I'm a professional footballer!'

So the guy went out and spent thousands of pounds a month to lease a Mercedes. To me, that's utterly ludicrous. It's a slap in the face to the average man.

I own a Jaguar and maybe to some that is excessive, but I own it because I like it, not because I like to be seen in it. If I wanted to be flash, I could have bought a Ferrari. I could afford a Lamborghini, too. But those cars don't grab me the way the Jaguar did. I bought it because to me a car is something to be admired, like a woman, a work of art or a monument. Cars are monuments too, monuments built by men.

Of course, all of this was far from my mind in my first season at Juventus. I was just worrying about how we would fare in Serie A. The squad was totally top-heavy, way too attack-minded, but we knew it was going to be fun. Even our defenders loved to attack. To shore up the backline, Maifredi brought in Brazilian international Julio Cesar and two guys from his old Bologna team, Marco De Marchi and Gianluca Luppi. All of them were perfect for his system, because they liked to get forward and pass, and that's what Maifredi was all about.

He was a big, jolly bear of a man to whom fun was paramount. Football was a game; treating it as a game was, in his opinion, the road to success. He had no qualms about playing Casiraghi, Baggio, Schillaci, Hassler and myself, all at the same time. It was show time. Imagine Kevin Keegan's Newcastle to the nth degree.

There were times when we would tear the opposition apart, when they would simply never see the ball. The problems occurred when we had to defend. It just wasn't part of the manager's mentality. I was playing on the right wing. In theory, all the front players had to share defensive duties; in practice, since I was the youngest, guess who had to do all the running and tackling back?

Still, I didn't mind, because Maifredi managed to make everything fun. We steamrollered the opposition in the first half of the season and were in first place as late as December. No top Italian club had ever played that way and, simply put, nobody knew how to deal with us.

Halfway through the season, I also became an unwilling protagonist in one of the most chilling and widely publicized incidents in Italian football. We were playing Bologna, Maifredi's old club and Totò Schillaci had had more than a few run-ins with the Bologna midfielder, Fabio Poli. It wasn't anything out of the ordinary, just the usual niggly tackles, but Schillaci was unusually tense that day. Just before half-time, there was another incident, as both went for a loose ball.

Schillaci got up and insulted Poli, who yelled something back at him. As we walked off the pitch for the interval, the two of them carried on, threatening and needling each other.

All of a sudden, Schillaci whirled around and shouted: 'I've had it with you! I'm going to have you killed!

Understand? I'll have you shot! I'll have you shot right there on the pitch!'

Poli froze in his tracks. He was stunned. I was right next to Schillaci. I grabbed him and dragged him away.

'What the f**k did you say?' I yelled. 'Shut the f**k up, do you realize what you just said?'

Poli spilled the beans after the match. He was genuinely upset.

'If he simply said he was going to kill me, I could live with it,' he told the media. 'But he said he was going to have me *shot*. That is something entirely different! I couldn't believe my ears!'

Indeed, coming from Schillaci it was a loaded phrase. It may not have been fair to him, but everybody knew he was from Palermo, the capital of Sicily and, sadly, of the Mafia. His words came at a time when two prominent anti-Mafia judges had been assassinated, when tensions were running high. Opposing fans would routinely call him a mafioso, which wasn't right, but incidents such as these didn't do him any favours.

The media went wild. I, too was shocked and saddened. God knows, I've probably threatened to kill more than a few people in my day, but Poli was right, there's a big difference between saying you're going to kill somebody and saying you'll have them taken out. It saddened me that even in the 1990s a guy like Schillaci would say something like that. It saddened me that he would be unable to escape from his roots, to grow out of that mafioso mentality.

In Italy, there is a lot of tension between North and South. The North views the South as lazy and corrupt, the

South thinks of the North as arrogant and mean-spirited. As a Roman, I'm caught in the middle. I can see both points of view, though perhaps I have a little more allegiance to the South, simply by virtue of the fact that it is weaker. Maybe that's why Schillaci's threat hurt so much. What he was really saying was: 'I'm from the South of Italy, I'm a mafioso, you'd better watch it.'

Anyway, with Maifredi we were part of one of the greatest tactical experiments Serie A had ever seen and we felt like innovators, pioneers. Alas, it all fell apart. Perhaps it was inevitable that sooner or later clubs were going to find a way to stop us. You can't play a virtual 4–1–5 (or actually 2–3–5, since our full-backs were essentially wing-backs) system forever and we began paying the price.

We went into a tailspin and never recovered. Maifredi tinkered with the side late in the season, but it was too late. It all just unravelled. Juventus finished tied for seventh. It was the club's fourth worst finish in history and, more importantly, it was the first time in 29 years that it had failed to qualify for Europe.

To most other clubs it would simply have been a terrible season. To Juventus it was abject and total failure, utter tragedy. The great Maifredi experiment had fallen flat on its face. Rather than looking ahead, the club did a 180 degree turn and looked to its past.

The legendary Giovanni Trapattoni was recalled as manager. Trapattoni isn't just a successful coach, he is a national institution. As a player, he had a long and glorious career with AC Milan, becoming famous for his encounters with Pele. But it was as a manager that he achieved immortality.

His first spell at Juventus lasted ten years, until 1986. In those ten seasons, he won the scudetto six times and finished second twice. He also won a Cup Winners' Cup, a European Cup, a UEFA Cup, a World Club Championship and two Italian Cups. After leaving Juventus, he had a five-year spell at Inter, finishing in the top-three four times, winning another UEFA Cup and the 1988–89 Italian title with a record points total.

Today he manages the Italian national team. Simply put, he was a living legend and remains one to this day. Only Jock Stein and Sir Alex Ferguson have won more trophies than he has and, with all due respect, both won many of those titles in Scotland, which isn't quite the same as Serie A.

I knew I would have to make an adjustment to play under Trapattoni. In many ways, he and Maifredi were polar opposites. Trapattoni was old-school, he believed in defending, in exploiting your opponent's weaknesses, in sitting back and waiting for him to make an escape. If Maifredi was a streetfighter, jumping straight in and going for the jugular, Trapattoni was more of a Judo competitor, turning the force of the opponent's blows against him.

Trapattoni scrapped Maifredi's offensive style. He only made two signings, and typically they were both defenders and both German internationals: Jurgen Kohler and Stefan Reuter. That said a lot about him.

There was little room for me in his lineup, since he already had to accommodate his three star strikers; Baggio, Casiraghi and Schillaci, all of them Italian internationals. I started on the bench for 23 out of the 34 matches. Trapattoni couldn't fathom the idea of having an extra talented player in the midfield, when he already had three forwards on the pitch. So my job was basically to come on for one of the strikers, usually at half-time. It happened sixteen times that year.

What was frustrating was that when I did come on, he would have a laundry list of tactical duties for me. Essentially, he wanted me to be a full-back in midfield. This was pretty typical of Italian managers; they believe technical ability and tactical discipline are everything. Only later, when I joined Celtic, did I truly understand the value of passion and commitment. I had always been passionate and committed, but in Italy, those were often seen as negative traits, and only once I arrived in Britain, did I understand how crucial they can be.

It wasn't like that in Italy. At Juve, Trapattoni would send me onto the pitch with very specific instructions. I was assigned a small rectangle to the right of midfield. That was my responsibility, God forbid I should ever step outside it. Trapattoni's assistants would monitor my every move; the moment I strayed from my position, even if the ball was clear on the other side of the pitch, they would alert the boss. Trapattoni would then call me back, usually by whistling. It's one of his trademarks, he has this ability to whistle shrilly and loudly. You can't miss it. He'd catch your attention and gesticulate furiously and, when he did, you knew you had better get back. It made you feel rather like a dog.

I don't mind tackling back, helping out the defence. In fact, it gives me a rush. I've noticed that fans in this country, especially West Ham fans, love it when a striker like myself loses the ball and then runs back the entire length of the pitch to win it back. It sends them into a frenzy and it has the exact same effect on me. I don't mind hard work and defending, but what Juventus and, later, AC Milan, did to me was a different matter. I was constrained, shackled and straitjacketed by tactical dogmas. Looking back, I don't understand how any sane manager can take a genuine talent like myself and treat him that way. I was sacrificed on the altar to the God of Tactics and, if it hadn't been for my move abroad, it might have ruined my career.

We finished the season in second place, but were a full eight points behind AC Milan. Still, at least we had improved five places on the previous season and would be back in Europe. Not to mention the fact that we had advanced to the final of the Coppa Italia.

The Trapattoni regime was starting to yield its first dividends, but there was still a long way to go. He told me there would be more opportunities for me the following season, but I had to get stronger.

'Son, there will be no holiday for you this summer,' Trapattoni said. 'You're going to work your butt off and come back bigger and stronger.'

He sent me to work with a specialist, Professor Bergamo, for three weeks. It was very intense, the man was brutal. I would train in the morning by myself, come back for a high-protein lunch (always steak and eggs) and then lock myself in a gym and lift weights for four or five hours. It was very tough, but I didn't mind. I knew I had to get stronger and I could see the results. Before, a shove would send me flying, I was thin and spindly. Now, I'm still thin, but I'm all nerves and muscles. I can be a much more physical player. I am not sure if the old Di Canio could have cut it in the Premiership, but the new Di Canio loves the physical aspects of the English game.

My new physique wasn't the only talking point at Juve's training camp that summer. Encouraged by our success the previous season, the club had gone on a summer shopping spree, buying players such as Dino Baggio, David Platt, Fabrizio Ravanelli, Andy Moller and, above all, Gianluca Vialli.

All told, there were twelve current or future Italian internationals in the squad, plus the two German World Cup winners, Kohler and Andy Moller, plus Platt, plus Julio Cesar, plus myself. Competition for places was sure to be intense, but I was pumped up and ready.

Vialli and I hit it off right away. We could not have been more different. He was the rich kid from the wealthy northern town of Cremona, I was the working-class boy from the Quarticciolo. He was 28 years old and a world-renowned footballer, I was 24 and still trying to live up to my potential. He had led little Sampdoria to the scudetto and was just coming off an emotional extra-time loss to Barcelona in the European Cup final. I had yet to win a major trophy, my greatest footballing moment to date having been the goal in the Rome derby.

Yet we also had many things in common, not least our birthday, 9 July (he was born in 1964, I was born in 1968). We were both fanatical about training and we both hated to lose. We both retained strong emotional ties to our previous clubs, he at Sampdoria, I at Lazio.

We spent a lot of time together, probably because most of

our teammates were married, whereas we were both single.

He needed a place to stay while house-hunting, so, since there was plenty of room at my flat and he never liked hotels, he stayed with me. It was only supposed to be for a few days, but it ended up lasting more than a month.

It only made sense that it would take him forever to find the right type of home. That's just the way Luca is; he's a perfectionist, nothing is ever good enough. He couldn't just settle for a nice, comfortable home, he had to find the perfect home.

Luca is one of those people who has to do everything right. If he can't do it perfectly, he will practice obsessively until he gets it bang-on, 100 per cent correct. Throw in the fact that he is one of the fiercest competitors I know, a guy who absolutely hates losing, and you've got quite a mix.

I remember endless table-tennis matches in Juve's training camp that year. We had our regular doubles quartet: Angelo Peruzzi, Ravanelli, Vialli and myself. The interesting thing is that each of us had his own style: Peruzzi relied on sheer power, Ravanelli on consistency, while I was all flair and athleticism. As for Luca, his style was technically perfect. It looked like he had taken lessons or spent all night practising by himself. His style, his posture, his execution, they were all flawless.

He couldn't stand losing to us and we usually had to keep playing until he beat us. Which, to be honest, didn't take that long. We were pretty evenly matched, but the bottom line was that he wanted it more than we did.

I think that without his ultra-competitiveness and perfectionist nature, he wouldn't have had the same type of career he enjoyed. Sure, he is a tremendous natural athlete with outstanding footballing skills, but that would only have got him so far. What got him to the top was his desire, his love of hard work and hatred of losing.

In many ways, he confounds the old stereotype by which people who come from the gutter are always willing to work harder to achieve their goals, because they have nothing else to aspire to. There is a lot of truth in it; when you only have one way out you are generally willing to make that many more sacrifices to reach your goal. Simply put, you have nothing to lose.

Most professional footballers are that way. You need to put in so much work to have any chance of making it that only a certain type of person is willing to do it. Most others, faced with the slim odds and enormous commitment, simply choose a different path, and I don't blame them. It's no coincidence that virtually all footballers come from lower-class or working-class backgrounds. The few exceptions, the ones who were relatively comfortable growing up, are the children of former professionals, guys like Jamie Redknapp, Paolo Maldini or Frank Lampard. But there again it's different. These guys grew up in a sporting environment, they had a role model right there at home, so in some ways it was easier for them to accept the sacrifices that were required.

A guy like Vialli, however, always had everything. Everything always seemed to come easy to him. He was a star at 17 and has lived in a goldfish bowl ever since. Yet he always fought tooth and nail; he always had a snarl on his face, the expression which said: 'I'm working as hard as I possibly can. I couldn't give an ounce more than what I am giving now.' And it was true. He was a beast, an example to all of us.

In his first season at Juventus, Trapattoni had the bright idea of moving Vialli from striker to central midfield. The manager reckoned that with his strength, vision and intelligence, he could turn into an excellent playmaker. Most of all, it would allow Trapattoni to accommodate his three other world-class strikers, Baggio, Ravanelli and Casiraghi. It was a huge transition and a tremendous amount to ask of a guy in mid-career who had been bought as a centre-forward. Imagine Bobby Robson asking Alan Shearer to play in the middle of the park. How would he react? Would he do it? *Could* he do it?

The rest of us were astounded. I was among those leading the rebellion, trying to talk some sense into Trapattoni. Vialli was a striker, he belonged up front. You wouldn't ask Diego Maradona to play in goal, would you?

Yet Luca simply put his head down and tried to learn his new role. He didn't whinge, he didn't complain, he didn't say: 'I am Gianluca Vialli. I am the greatest striker in Italy, I've won important trophies in my career and I have nothing to prove to anyone. I am a striker and if you won't play me in my position, then go ahead and sell me.'

He adapted. He bared his teeth and dug deep inside him. Eventually, Trapattoni recognized his mistake and Vialli went on to enjoy three spectacular seasons at Juventus, winning the scudetto and the European Cup. Would another player, a lesser man, have been able to bounce back the way Luca did? I don't think so.

Of course, I knew nothing of this when Vialli first moved in with me. I soon began to realize that I was living with a quirky guy, to say the least.

For example, the first day he moved his belongings in, I left the flat for a few hours so that he could have time to settle in. When I returned, I noticed that his clothes were all neatly stacked in the kitchen. I mean all over the kitchen: on the table, on the counter, on top of the cooker, everywhere.

It struck me as rather strange, but I figured he simply didn't have the time to put everything away. A day passed and then another. Luca's clothes were all still happily residing in my kitchen.

It didn't really make a difference to us, we always ate out and hardly ever went in there, but still, I reckoned there must be a good reason.

'Luca,' I asked him one day. 'Is something wrong with your room?'

'No,' he replied calmly.

'What about your closets? Do you not have enough closet space? Do you need more room for your clothes?'

'Not at all. There are plenty of closets in my room.'

I looked at him strangely.

'Then why are your clothes all over my kitchen?'

'I hate closets. I don't like putting my clothes in there. In the kitchen, they get air and since we don't ever cook, it's a nice, clean environment for them. Why, is that a problem for you?'

He said it like it was the most natural thing in the world, putting your designer shirts and trousers on your gas cooker.

But then, Luca has always been obsessive about his clothes. He spends hours in front of the mirror, mixing and matching them. Do the grey slacks go with the cashmere sweater? Can I wear the pinstripe shirt with the yellow pullover or does it go better with the teal cardigan?

He doesn't do this because he's vain, he does it because he's a perfectionist. I've always enjoyed fashion, I think I have an excellent sense of style and dress very well.

I became very involved in fashion however in 1990, when I bought a boutique in Terni. It was my friend Gianluca Munzi (who, at the time, was dating Betta's sister, Stefania) who first floated the idea. It seemed like a smart investment; even though I was young and hadn't made a lot of money yet, I knew that I had to start thinking about the future. Gianluca taught me a lot about how a man must take care of himself and his family, though since then our relationship has developed beyond that and we are now almost like brothers. The boutique is called 'Il Conte', 'The Count', and I play a part in selecting the styles we sell. I like the classical, English, Savile Row designs, I guess it foreshadowed my move to London. Perhaps that's why Luca counted on me so much to help him dress. That, and the fact that he is rather obsessive about it.

It's funny, he's actually somewhat insecure about it. We get together about once a week and he always talks about clothes. Where did I get those cufflinks? Can he get a blazer like mine, but in navy blue rather than a powder blue?

I think that without me, Luca would be a fashion victim. But you won't hear me complain. He does a lot of shopping at my boutique in Terni (as do other footballers), so from a business perspective, he's a very lucrative friend to have.

The other unusual side to Luca is his fondness for being naked. Maybe if I had a body like his, I'd be the same way, I don't know, but I do know that it took a while to get used to it. He walks around the house naked all the time, like it was the most natural thing in the world.

After training, we'd all shower and get dressed, while he would sit there in his birthday suit, reading the newspaper, as if he was wearing a double-breasted suit and lounging in the reading room of a gentleman's club.

They say he's become more serious since becoming a manager. I remember him as an unreconstructed prankster, always wreaking havoc around the clubhouse. He had started shaving his head a few years earlier and I remember, one day, he offered to do mine as well.

'Are you mad?' I told him. 'I'd look like a freak with a shaved head!'

'Come on,' he insisted. 'I'm not going to shave your head, I'll just give you a little trim around the sides. Your hair is getting a little unkempt, you know.'

I should have known better. I should have seen that devilish glint in his eye and the mischievous, up-to-no-good grin that accompanied it. Foolishly, I trusted him.

He took the clippers, fixed the maximum setting, and cut a deep channel squarely through the top of my head. Hair cascaded all around me, the sight of my locks on the ground drove me wild.

I whirled around and yelled: 'What the hell did you do?'

'Oops!' he said. 'I slipped.'

He convinced me that at that point it was best just to shave off the rest of my hair, otherwise it would look even worse. I had no choice and let him do it. I was horrified later when I looked in the mirror. I didn't recognize myself. Some guys look good with their heads shaved. Not me. My head is long and bony, without hair it looks disgusting. I mean, I looked like one of those poor bastards you see in refugee camps.

Vialli was also responsible for me getting my first tattoo. We went together, naturally he agonized over it, doing everything possible to ensure that his would be perfect. He got an eagle, I got a warrior. It's an old, battle-weary warrior, a guy who looks like he's seen it all.

I guess I got hooked on tattoos, because it was the first of many. In Naples, I got an eagle, but unlike Luca's, it was the Lazio eagle. I also got another warrior, this time on horseback. I like to think that the old warrior is looking back on his life, seeing himself when he was younger and reflecting on his battles.

In Milan, after winning the Italian title, I got a tattoo of the scudetto. Later, in Sheffield, the letters 'L' and 'E', for Ludovica and Elisabetta. When Lucrezia was born, I added another 'L'. Don't worry, there's still room for more on my arm, in case we have more kids. I had the artist surround the three letters with flames. To me, the fire makes them indelible, irremovable.

I know they are just symbols, but they are important to me. After all, a symbol is only as important as the importance you attach to it. And in my case, they are everything.

The extra work I did over the summer paid off. Even with

all the competition for places in the side, I started 19 games that year and came on as a substitute in another 12. We finished the season in fourth place, as Milan once again took the title, but we did win the UEFA Cup, beating Borussia Dortmund in the final. All told, I played 45 matches in all competitions that season and felt like a key player in the team.

When I returned for pre-season training after summer however, I felt as if something had changed in my relationship with Trapattoni. He had acquired another right midfielder, Angelo Di Livio. I didn't mind healthy competition, God knows, I had enough of it at Juventus, but all of a sudden he made me feel like I was surplus to requirements.

He didn't say anything, he just began ignoring me. It was still the summer, it was only pre-season friendlies, but with every match that passed, it got worse and worse. One day we were playing a friendly in Palermo. It was one of those meaningless matches, where the boss simply wants to give everybody a run-out.

I started on the bench, knowing my time wouldn't come until the second half. The half-time interval came and went and Trapattoni started sending on the substitutes. One by one, all the first-team squad members came on, except me. There were maybe twenty minutes left, when he signalled for another substitution. I was all ready to come on, but instead he sent on one of the kids from the youth team. Then another, then a third.

Now I can understand that we were on a summer tour and it was a meaningless game. I can also understand that seniority shouldn't count, we are all equal. But I was a professional, these guys were spotty kids! I had paid my dues and still, they got on before I did.

I was furious, steaming inside. He finally put me on with five minutes to go and I barely broke sweat. I was so angry at the way he had humiliated me, I couldn't think straight, I just wandered around the pitch, unable to concentrate.

When I walked off he said something to me, something about my poor performance that day. I snapped.

'What?' I said. 'What did you say? You have the balls to talk to me after the way you treated me? You have the nerve to come out and tell me I played badly for five minutes after the way you took the piss out of me?'

I was harsh, but I felt totally humiliated by what he had done.

He couldn't believe that anybody would stand up to him. After all, he was Giovanni Trapattoni, the most successful manager in Italian history.

'Young man, you need to learn some manners!' he hissed. 'Obviously, your parents never taught you how a civilized person behaves. What kind of people were you raised by?'

That did it. Nobody, and I mean NOBODY, insults my parents like that. Nobody. To me, they were everything, they taught me what life was, gave me a blueprint to follow. Without them, I might never have got out of the Quarticciolo, I might be dead or in jail. I wasn't going to allow anybody to speak that way.

'Why don't you go f**k yourself?' I shouted back at him. 'I don't need to take this shit from you. Who the f**k are you to talk to me like that? How dare you talk about my parents, people who you don't even know! All you're good for is taking the piss out of others.'

He looked at me with a mixture of confusion and anger. He didn't know how to react. He got closer and closer to me, like he was trying to challenge me. I just took a step towards him and shoved him away as hard as I could. He flew backwards, landing on the physio's bags next to the bench.

He was in shock.

'You're finished, Di Canio!' he blurted out. 'You're gone! Done! Finished!'

I stood over him and glared.

'No,' I said, sounding unusually calm. 'I'm not finished. You can't fire me. I have a contract. I decide if I stay or if I go. And I'm leaving. I'm finished with your bullshit!'

My teammates rushed to hold me back, I had Vialli hanging on to one arm and Julio Cesar, the giant Brazilian, holding the other. Even then, even though they were twice my size, they had a hell of a time restraining me. When you get mad, and believe me, I was furious, your adrenalin starts pumping and your strength virtually triples. I could have killed him, whereas I think he was just stunned with disbelief.

I stormed off and didn't see Trapattoni for several days. When we did run into each other again, it was as if nothing had happened. In the end, no irreparable damage was done, Trapattoni was intelligent enough to understand that we each have our own personalities and sometimes there will be a clash. He was wrong to say what he did, but I tried to look past that.

Juventus kept the incident under wraps, but it was obvious to both me and the club that it was best if I moved on. There were a number of teams eager to buy me, but Juve wanted to retain my rights. So they shipped me out on loan to Napoli.

The fans were furious. They had always loved me, always appreciated me. They didn't know the whole story, until now. To them it was simply a case of Trapattoni preferring Di Livio to Di Canio and it made no sense to them.

But again, the old rule held fast. Players come and go, clubs endure. I accepted my fate; at Napoli I would have more playing time, a greater chance to show what I could do.

I vowed never to return to Juventus.

CHAPTER SIX

STANDING UP TO JUVENTUS

Napoli was a club which had gone into rapid decline following the departure of Diego Maradona. The 'Pibe de Oro', or Foot of Gold (rather than the Hand of God) as he's known in Italy and around the world, had brought the club two scudetti, a Coppa Italia and a UEFA Cup, but most of all he had shown the world that the south of Italy could indeed excel in football.

He was a source of pride to the entire region and the fans regularly sold out the San Paolo stadium, Italy's largest at over 86,000 capacity. People kept shrines of Maradona in their homes and with good reason.

But after he left in 1991, Naples found that it couldn't sustain the team's success. The team was teetering on the edge of bankruptcy, new judicial inquiries revealed that it had been doing so for a long time. The banks and other creditors gave the chairman an ultimatum: sell players to raise cash or the club would be wound up.

Napoli had finished eleventh the previous season, the club's worst finish since the pre-Maradona era. It should have been going in the opposite direction, strengthening the side to get back into Europe. Instead, it had no choice but to turn into a veritable car boot sale, with most of the last relics, the guys who had triumphed alongside Maradona, being let go that summer. Gianfranco Zola and Massimo Crippa went to Parma, Giovanni Galli to Torino, Antonio Careca back to Brazil. The only veterans who remained were defenders Giovanni Francini, Ciro Ferrara and Giancarlo Corradini.

It was a complete wipe-out. But because the club had no cash, the rebuilding was done on the cheap. They took players on loan (like myself), promoted others from the youth team, poked around in the lower divisions. Rarely has the term 'motley crew' ever been so appropriate.

Our defensive backbone of goalkeeper Pino Taglialatela and central defenders Fabio Cannavaro and Giovanni Bia had a combined total of four Serie A appearances at the start of the 1993–94 season. Then there were guys like me who for some reason or another were hungry for a second chance. There was former Under-21 star Eugenio Corini, who joined Juventus when I did, but never settled in the side, Ezio Gambaro, much-hyped when he was bought by AC Milan, then left to rot in the reserves and Sergio Buso, a striker who scored a goal on his debut as a 16-year-old for Juventus, but who then disappeared in the lower divisions. We did have two quality foreign players in the Iceman, Jonas Thern, captain of Sweden, and the Uruguayan striker Daniel Fonseca, who would score sixteen goals that season.

Beyond that, we were a mixed bag of wily veterans, eager youngsters and misfits all under the command of an up-and-coming manager, a guy named Marcello Lippi, who had led unheralded Atalanta to a seventh place Serie A finish the previous season. Of course, Lippi would go on to manage Juventus, where he would win Italian titles and Champions Leagues and establish himself as one of the top managers in Europe. At the time however, like us, he was a young manager trying to make a name for himself.

We knew that it was going to be a struggle, better yet, a streetfight, every step of the way. We would have to be totally committed and totally united if we were going to get anywhere.

The pre-season was less than three weeks old when we received an early indication that, in terms of unity and team spirit, we would have absolutely nothing to fear.

Our skipper, Ciro Ferrara, Napoli born and bred, took us out for a team dinner a few miles out of town along the coast. The dismantling of his club affected him a lot, but he knew that he would have to play a big part in turning a random bunch of players into a cohesive unit.

After dinner, we moved on to a bar, some ten kilometres away. We were all in different cars, so we all got there within five minutes of each other. Ferrara, Corradini, myself and others had just ordered drinks when Ezio Gambaro walked in.

He had an angry scowl on his face and looked genuinely upset.

'What's wrong, Ezio?' Ferrara asked him.

Gambaro was reluctant to answer at first, he kept saying 'Nothing, nothing's wrong', but we could tell something was up. Ferrara kept pressing him and eventually Gambaro told us. He had been the last one to leave the restaurant and, as he was walking out, the staff started making fun of his nose.

Indeed, Gambaro does have a rather large nose and his ears tend to stick out. He's not exactly a movie star and he is fairly self-conscious of his looks. It probably wasn't a big deal, but nobody likes having the piss taken out of him by total strangers.

'Right, that's it!' Ferrara said. 'Nobody is going to make fun of my teammate. Nobody is going to mock a Napoli player and get away with it. Not as long as I am captain of this club. We need to go back and teach them a lesson. Who's with me?'

Naturally, I was one of the first to jump on board. Team spirit is everything. Mutual trust and respect, knowing that your teammate is going to be behind you 100 per cent, makes all the difference. Normally, you only build that kind of unity over time. Yet here we were, a bunch of guys who had only been together for a few weeks, and we were ready to stand up and fight for each other. It was wonderful.

Ferrara got up and headed for the door. One by one, we all followed him. All of us, even the most mild-mannered, went along. We had become a team, ready for our punitive mission.

We got to the restaurant just as it was closing. The waiters were putting everything away for the night, the manager had the cash register open and was counting the evening's take.

Ferrara strode in purposefully, while we all followed, close behind. Immediately, the staff rushed up to him, showering him with greetings and generally sucking up to him. After all, while he wasn't quite a god in Naples (only Maradona had reached that status), he was at least a saint.

'You guys see me and you treat me like a prince,' Ferrara told them. 'But then, behind my back, you harass one of my teammates. You make fun of him, you mock the way he looks.'

The waiters all shifted uncomfortably. They knew they had just crossed the wrong group of people.

Ferrara grabbed Gambaro's arm and pulled him close.

'This is my teammate,' he continued. 'Does he make you laugh? Is he funny? Come on, go ahead and laugh at him. You were all eager to do so before.'

'Why are you all silent? What are you afraid of?'

The staff were all petrified. Even the manager had stopped counting his money. He just stared at Ferrara, mouth open, cigarette burning down to the filter.

'These are my teammates. This is my team. This is Napoli. And you had better respect each and every one of us. You call yourself Neapolitans. Tonight you were a disgrace to my city. It had better not happen again.'

With that, we all walked out together.

It may seem now like a silly, mundane incident, nothing more than male bravado on a hot August night. To me, however, it set the tone for the entire season, it proved to all of us that whatever lay ahead, we would be facing it together. We were like a clan, ready to defend our turf.

And it also showed me another kind of leadership. Ciro Ferrara had to deal with seeing his club dismembered, driven into the ground by greedy and incompetent people. He had plenty of offers to join bigger, wealthier clubs. He was an Italian international and one of the top defenders in Europe, he could have gone anywhere. Yet he chose to stick around, he chose to fight another day. You could not help but be inspired by somebody like that.

Lippi and I hit it off immediately. He understood me, he understood what I could contribute and he understood what I needed. What more could a player ask for? He played me up front, from the start of the season. I was a second striker, deployed just behind the centre-forward, Fonseca. I was free to roam, to create, to invent. Rarely had I ever felt so free, so confident, so sure of the manager's total backing.

One day, after training, he took me aside. I'll never forget what he said.

'Paolo, I have to compliment you,' he told me. 'I was very sceptical when the club signed you. Everybody told me to watch out, that Di Canio was a troublemaker, that Di Canio was undisciplined and lazy. Instead, you are the most serious and committed professional I have ever worked with. I have never met anybody quite like you.'

I was pleased to hear this from Lippi, but it also saddened me that by now I was stuck with this reputation. Whoever was spreading those lies about me either didn't know me or was blinded by jealousy. I don't know where it comes from. If people want to say I'm stubborn or edgy, that's fine, it's probably true. But when it comes to training, when it comes to working hard every day, I think few players can match me.

Part of the problem is that in Italy, clubs want their players to behave like robots, never questioning, never expressing their personality. If you don't immediately fit into their little cubbyhole, you become a troublemaker. It's a backward, medieval attitude.

It was obvious we weren't going to compete for any titles,

there simply wasn't enough quality in the side, but we turned more than a few heads as the season progressed. The fans were wonderful, magic had returned to the San Paolo. It wasn't like in the Maradona days, (there could never be another one like him, of course) but there was definitely a sense that things were happening, that we were moving in the right direction.

By the spring, we were seventh and still in with a shot at grabbing a place in the UEFA Cup the following season. On 27 March, we entertained AC Milan. They had lost just one game until then, taking 46 out of a possible 56 points, and were nursing a nine-point lead over Juventus. A Milan win would guarantee the title, with five matches to spare; even a draw would guarantee them at least a playoff for the scudetto (championships are not decided by goal difference in Serie A, if two teams finish level, they stage a one-game playoff).

It was a huge game, in every sense. There was still a lot of resentment between Napoli and Milan. In the late 1980s, Serie A was all about the rivalry between Milan's Dutchmen (Ruud Gullit, Marco Van Basten and Frank Rijkaard) and the Napoli of Maradona and Careca.

To this day, many believe that Milan's 1987–88 scudetto, its first in nine years and the one which set off the brilliant Capello-Sacchi cycle of triumphs, was tainted. That year, Napoli were pipped by Milan in the final days of the season, throwing away a lead they had held for much of the year. Many Neapolitans are convinced that the Camorra, the Neapolitan Mafia, simply sold the scudetto to Milan and its billionaire chairman, Silvio Berlusconi. A few years back, the theory resurfaced in a bestselling collection of essays by elementary school children in Naples entitled 'Io Speriamo Che Me La Cavo' ('I Hope I Will Make It'). One of the children wrote that Berlusconi had paid 'one thousand billion dollars' to the Camorra in exchange for the scudetto. It's all ludicrous, of course. There isn't a shred of evidence to support this.

Yet it is significant because it is ingrained in the mentality of Neapolitans. The ten-year-old boy who wrote the essay was simply reflecting the views of those around him. To this day, many Neapolitans are convinced that if Milan hadn't 'bought' the title, history would have been re-written. Milan would have never won the European Cup the following year (or the year after that), manager Arrigo Sacchi would have been fired, Gullit and Van Basten would not have become living legends. At the same time, the pain of losing the scudetto wouldn't have driven Maradona to drugs, Napoli would have won several more titles (including some European Cups for good measure) and Diego would still be the King of Naples (God knows, he might even still be playing).

This may all seem ridiculous, but it is significant in illustrating the prevailing mentality in much of Naples and why beating Milan was (and still is) so important.

Everybody expected Milan to have their way with us. We were missing key players such as Ferrara and Thern, yet we managed to hold our own for much of the game. Then, with about ten minutes to go, the unthinkable happened.

Buso won the ball inside our own half and hit a long pass forward. I was the only Napoli player in Milan's half of the field, so I chased it down, controlled it and ran up the left flank. I beat Christian Panucci and cut inside, where I was faced by Franco Baresi and Stefano Eranio, who had tracked back from midfield. I faked one way and dragged the ball back with my heel. It was the biggest dummy I had ever sold. Not only did it leave Baresi and Eranio (both Italian internationals, as was Panucci) for dead, it also fooled the goalkeeper, Sebastiano Rossi. He was convinced I was going to cross the ball, my drag-back completely fooled him. I struck the ball crisply and watched it slip just underneath the crossbar.

It was one of the greatest goals I have ever scored and it was also one of the most important. It delayed Milan's scudetto celebration by a week and it virtually guaranteed us a spot in the UEFA Cup.

It was a triumph, a complete and utter triumph, for me personally and the club. I had started the year demoralized and eager to prove people wrong. I had finished it on a high. The Italian press voted me on to the team of the season and there was talk of my being capped for the first time.

Around this time, Lippi told me that he had accepted the Juventus job for the following year. He asked me to come with him back to Turin. He had big plans for me, he wanted to build on my success at Napoli.

'Paolo, you and I make a great team together,' he told me. 'Come with me to Juventus. It will be different this time.'

I was very tempted by his offer, despite my reservations about going back to Juve. Technically, I was still a Juventus player since my loan spell at Napoli would end that summer. To further complicate matters, my contract expired that June. Alas, this was in the days before the Bosman ruling.

Out-of-contract players couldn't be signed for free as they are now. Back then, you had to pay the player's club a certain amount based on parameters fixed by UEFA, which reflected the player's age and wages. In my case, the parameter was set at around £3 million.

Napoli had also told me that they wanted to keep me. The chairman, Ellenio Gallo, assured me that he would pay Juventus the £3 million fee, turn my loan into a permanent move and offer me a five-year deal. I was torn.

On the one hand, I had the chance to continue working with Lippi and to return to Juventus as a winner. It would be sweet revenge on those who had doubted me.

On the other hand, I was a hero in Naples. I loved the town, the fans, Betta and Ludovica were happy there, we had everything we could ask for.

Betta and I talked it over and I told Lippi that I wasn't going with him. I was going to stay and help rebuild Napoli. He was disappointed, but I think he understood my position.

Looking back, that was one of the pivotal moments of my career. Had I chosen a different path, had I followed Lippi to Turin, it could well have changed not just my life, but the course of Italian football.

Lippi had told me that if I joined Juve, I would play in a three-man strike force with Vialli and Ravanelli. Alex Del Piero, who had emerged from the youth team the previous year and was still just 19 years old, would have been sent out on loan. My decision changed both our careers. Instead of going to some smaller Serie A club, Del Piero stayed at Juve and enjoyed a breakout season, one which turned him into a star. It would have been me in his position. Juventus won three of the next four Serie A titles, as well as the Champions League in 1995–96. I could have played a key role in those triumphs, who knows, I might have become an Italian international as well. After all, guys like Di Livio and Gianluca Pessotto, players who were no better than I was, enjoyed long international careers, thanks largely to Lippi.

But I don't like to ask myself 'What if?' I don't believe in looking back and having regrets. Things might have turned out better, but they might also have turned out worse. You have no way of knowing. And since I am happy with my life today, I can honestly say that I would not change a thing in my past. If I had joined Juventus then, I might never have gone abroad, I might never have experienced Scottish football and the Premiership, I simply would not be the person I am today.

Having said that, I paid dearly for my decision. As the season wound down, I waited and waited for Napoli to buy me from Juve and offer me a new contract. Weeks passed and nothing happened. Napoli fans sent a petition to the club, signed by 15,000 supporters, demanding that Gallo keep me.

It emerged, however, that the club was virtually bankrupt. Gallo, the chairman, had made me promises in good faith, but he simply did not have the means to follow through. I should have seen it coming; after all, we went six months without receiving our paychecks. But deep down, I wanted to believe that everything was going to work out. I wanted to believe that somehow Napoli would find the money to keep me.

Had I known that the club had no money, I would have probably taken Lippi's offer. As it turned out, my situation got very complicated.

After the season ended, I started getting calls from Luciano Moggi, Juventus' general manager. He told me that they couldn't wait on Napoli any longer, that they would sell me to Genoa. I spoke to them but soon made up my mind that there was no way I was going there. For starters, Genoa wanted to cut my salary. I was on good wages on my old Juventus contract and had just enjoyed a stellar season at Napoli. It simply didn't seem fair to me that I should take a pay cut, just because I was going to a smaller club.

Moggi insisted that I had to take their deal, that they couldn't afford to pay me any more, since they had to pay the UEFA parameter of £3 million to sign me. I told him that wasn't my problem, if anything, that was their problem.

He got very angry. He told me I had better take what Genoa was offering or I would be in big trouble.

In the pre-Bosman days, out-of-contract players actually had very little power. Your old club retained your rights, anybody who wanted to sign you needed to pay the fee set by UEFA. If, like me, you were stuck with a high parameter, it became very difficult to find a club, especially since your old club could veto any move.

Moggi told me that Genoa was the only club interested in me and that if I didn't take their deal, I might as well hang up my boots for good, because I wouldn't have a team to play for. The transfer window would close and I would be stuck at home, out of football completely.

'Fine,' I said. 'I don't really mind.'

Under UEFA rules, the parameter fee was only valid for twelve months. After a year, it got reduced by 50 per cent (which meant I would only cost £1.5 million). If another year passed, it would be lifted entirely and I would be available on a free transfer.

'What do you mean?' Moggi said. 'Are you crazy?'

'Not at all,' I replied. 'I just won't play for a year. That will cost you money, my parameter will be halved. You don't like that do you?'

'What are you saying? You can't sit out a season!'

'Why not? I don't care. I'm just not going to let you push me around and decide my future for me.'

Moggi could not believe what he was hearing. He is the most powerful executive in Italian football, his son is a major agent, between the two of them, they pull most of the strings in the Italian transfer market. Most of Italian football fears him, because he can be shrewd and ruthless. Not many have stood up to him and survived to tell the tale.

But I wasn't afraid. I was tired of being ordered around. Nobody was going to decide the future of me and my family but us. If it meant being sidelined for a year, if it meant training on my own with no club and no salary, so be it. I was determined not to give in.

'How dare you talk to me like that!' Moggi was furious. 'Do you know who I am? Do you know who you're dealing with? You'd better watch it, I can ruin you, I can make sure you never play football again!'

My agent, Moreno Roggi, tried to calm things down.

He turned to Moggi and said, 'Look, don't listen to what

Paolo is saying, he's just a little on edge, it's just his personality, he doesn't mean to offend . . .'

'Shut up, Moreno!' I snapped. 'I know exactly what I'm saying. I'm not on edge, I'm perfectly calm! I am going to decide my future, not Juventus, not Moggi, not anybody! I will not be pushed around!'

I meant what I said. I had made my decision and I was ready to stick with it and face the consequences. It was a matter of principle. I know that word, 'principle', gets thrown around a lot. The difference in this case is that I was willing to back it up. I was ready to suffer first hand, to not get paid for one or two years, in the name of my values.

I trained by myself the entire month of August. I had no idea what would become of me. Had I jeopardized my future? Perhaps. But when you know that you are right, when you know that you are standing by your values and personal integrity, it becomes easier to accept even the most difficult situations.

I don't know what would have happened to me if it had not been for Moreno Roggi. To me, he is much more than an agent, he is like an older brother, and his son, Matteo, who works with him, is like a younger brother. He has had to put up with a lot throughout my career and I know that in some cases he suffered personally and professionally as a result. He could have left me, he could have abandoned me to my own fate at that point. If he had done so, it would have made things a whole lot easier for him. Few agents would dare stand up to a club like Juventus and a man like Moggi. But he was at my side, every step of the way.

He was a man of his word. He worked tirelessly to find me a club that was willing to pay the £3 million asking price. Eventually, he worked out a deal with AC Milan, who offered £1.5 million, plus full-back Alessandro Orlando. Moggi took the deal, even though he would have preferred the £3 million in cash that Genoa were offering. It was a personal victory for me and for Moreno.

Joining Milan meant joining the most successful club in Europe. In the previous seven years, they had won the Italian title four times, finished second twice and third once. In that same time period, they had also won three European Cups and two World Club Championships. Simply put, nobody was better.

The facilities and organization at the club were out of this world. Every aspect of AC Milan, from the groundkeeper to the catering staff, from the weight room to the woman who brought us our mail after training, oozed professionalism. I don't think that there is another club like it, anywhere.

They were also one of the first clubs to operate a genuine squad system. The basic principle was that there would be two or three world-class players for every position on the pitch. That way, no matter how many injuries or suspensions you had, you would always be able to field a first-class side.

Today, it's not a big deal, but at the time it was a revolutionary concept. It also meant competition for places was cut-throat. The year I joined, Milan had five other players who could play on the right of midfield. Of those five, four were capped for Italy: Gigi Lentini (who was Milan's record signing), Giovanni Stroppa, Stefano Eranio and Roberto

Donadoni. Between them, those four would win 100 caps for the azzurri. The one guy who hadn't been capped for Italy, was a pretty decent player himself. You might have heard of him. Does the name Ruud Gullit ring any bells?

With that kind of competition, you would be happy just to get on the bench. But I didn't mind. I wanted to test myself at the highest level. Besides, the club actively encouraged competition among the players. You were given the feeling that nobody was sacred, that if you were good enough, you would get your chance.

In that sense, Fabio Capello, the manager, was brilliant. He knew how to motivate us, how to pit us against each other in a healthy way. This does not mean that I liked him, because I didn't. It just meant that he was a winner and a successful manager.

I have come to realize that, with a few very rare exceptions, to be a successful manager you have to be mean, tough and often a little unfair. That is how Capello was, and probably still is, today. He would tease me, coax me, tell me that I'd play the following week and then leave me out. I think he used it as a way of motivating both me and the players against whom I was competing. That's what intelligent managers have to do. They can't be friends with the players, they can't always be good people.

Look at Vialli. Before, he was everybody's mate, laughing and joking along with the others. After he became manager, he became a boss in terms of mentality as well. Many times it meant he had to be the bad guy. It's ironic, Luca hates Arrigo Sacchi but he had to become like him to become a successful manager. He had to develop a rigid, nasty side to his personality, one which would lead him to leave players out without explaining why.

It's a sign of intelligence. You're not there to be a friend or even to be a good person. You're there to win and if it means that you have to lose some of that basic honesty, then so be it. I can understand that. I should stress that it hasn't affected Luca in his private life. His attitude towards me hasn't changed one bit, but then, he isn't my boss. I think it's a transformation he underwent to make himself a better manager, it's not a permanent personality change.

That first year I contracted mononucleosis, a nervous disorder, and missed four months of the season. It was very frustrating. Being sidelined is bad enough, but when you have a physical injury at least you can work on it, it's real, it's tangible. With mononucleosis, however, I couldn't do anything. I just felt weak and sick, I had to sit there and wait for it to pass.

At least it gave me a chance to settle into the Milan environment. It was there that I met two of the greatest professionals I have ever known: Franco Baresi and Mauro Tassotti.

Those two were the elder statesmen of Milan's legendary backline: from right to left, Tassotti, Baresi, Alessandro Costacurta and Paolo Maldini. Those guys played together for nine seasons, at club and country level. Between them they have some 260 caps (and Maldini is still going strong); they were genuine icons.

Baresi was the captain and he always had this image as the strong, dour, silent type. And it was true. He never said a word in the dressing room or around the clubhouse. Even on the pitch, it was just the bare minimum of communication between defenders. He didn't need to speak, his mere presence was communication enough. Perhaps it was the fact that I'm the exact opposite which fascinated me so much. I'm a big believer in yelling and shouting to psyche up yourself and your teammates before a match. On the pitch, I'm always talking, spurring others on, warning them of danger.

Away from football, Baresi would open up. We became close, he was like an older brother to me. I think in many ways I brought out the kid in him. He was always so serious, I think he enjoyed having me around. And I discovered he was not just this severe, unsmiling football machine, he was a good bloke who enjoyed a laugh just like everybody else.

It's funny how some people have radically different personalities on and off the pitch. Peter Grant, our skipper at Celtic, was the same way. Outside of matches he was sweet and mild-mannered, he couldn't hurt a fly. Lace up his boots, however, and he turned into a wild man, a tough, committed fighter who would scrap for every inch of turf.

Watching Baresi play, seeing him up close was a treat to anybody who loves football. Simply put, he was as close to perfect as any footballer I have ever seen. You simply did not beat him one-on-one. I pride myself on my dribbling ability, but I don't remember ever beating him, not even in training. He could be nasty, sometimes even dirty, but never in a stupid way. I know defenders have to be like that, the trick is doing it intelligently. He would always let you know he was there, you could feel his presence and, as an opponent, it was very intimidating.

But it was his movements on the pitch which really set him apart. He was like a virtual footballer, it was as if he wasn't real, like there was a computer controlling him, shifting him around the pitch with mathematical precision. His timing was exceptional, he never made a mistake, he always made everything look effortless. I think he was to defenders what Maradona was to forwards, the standard against which everybody else was to be judged.

Tassotti on the other hand was living evidence that you can always evolve, you can always improve. When he first arrived at Milan, he was the typical rough-and-tumble full-back, a guy who was all strength and heart, but with little skill. He spent 16 years at Milan and in that period he became a totally different player. He had the intelligence to learn from those around him and the work ethic to use what he learned to better himself. By the time I got to Milan, he was nearing the end of his career and had become one of the most refined and sophisticated defenders I had ever seen.

He learned to pass and move with frightening accuracy. He could dribble like a forward, he had the confidence and elegance to pull off just about anything. And he did this while keeping his toughness, his meanness (you may remember him from the 1994 World Cup when he punched Spain's Luis Enrique in the face, breaking his nose and receiving an eight-match ban).

We called him 'Maestro', or 'Teacher', because you never stopped learning from him. There are few former teammates I keep in touch with but he is one of them. He taught me the importance of family, how to face your problems with serenity and tranquility and, most of all, how a balanced life off the pitch can help you on the pitch as well.

Indirectly, I also learned from people like Gullit. When I got there, he was still a Milan legend and I think he spent a lot of time basking in his former glory. He is a difficult person to understand, to me he seemed very full of himself. He had problems adjusting to Capello and I think part of it might have been that he felt as if his past was sufficient to guarantee him a place in the side. Seeing Gullit left out reinforced the notion that you could not rest on your laurels, you had to continue giving, pushing yourself to new limits. In football, the past is irrelevant, it's about what you can do right then, at that precise moment.

I'm not sure Gullit understood that. At Chelsea, his managerial career got off to an excellent start. Everybody seemed to love him and then he threw it all away by making crazy wage demands (£2 million was the figure quoted in some papers). I never understood that.

He should have thanked God that Chelsea had given him a chance to manage a top-flight club at 35 years of age and with no track record to speak of. Maybe I could understand his demands if he had been dirt poor, but he wasn't. He made millions as a player and he could look forward to another thirty years as a manager. Instead, he threw it all away.

If I were ever to find myself in his position, I would jump at the opportunity. Even if someone paid me just £150,000 a year, plus a house, I would kneel down and kiss his feet. That's one-fifth of what I make now, but I would have no right to expect more. What other field can offer a guy with zero experience the chance to make hundreds of thousands of pounds a year?

It's no coincidence that Vialli, who is an intelligent man, took the offer and was grateful. He went from being a reserve player at Chelsea to running the whole club, all in the space of a week. And he was smart about it. He didn't go to the chairman and say, 'Hey, now that I'm player-coach I'm doing two jobs, so I should really earn two salaries.' He took the same money he made before (which, granted, was a lot) and simply got on with the job, because he knew had been given a huge opportunity and he was grateful for it.

We finished fourth in Serie A that season, but managed to reach the Champions League final, where Ajax beat us with a late goal from Patrick Kluivert. My illness limited me to just eighteen appearances in total that year, but I was becoming a key member of the squad.

The following season we stormed to our fourth Serie A title in five years. Our squad was as impressive as ever. We had just signed Roberto Baggio, who teamed up with Dejan Savicevic and George Weah up front. Marcel Desailly and Demetrio Albertini ruled the midfield (with a young Patrick Vieira waiting in the wings) and the defence was as impregnable as ever.

I got more playing time that season, scoring some important goals and appearing regularly in our UEFA Cup run (we reached the quarter-finals). Still, it was clear to me that my future at Milan was going to be limited. I started looking around, thinking about other opportunities.

Just before Christmas, on 22 December, Moreno Roggi and I went to have a dinner in a Brazilian restaurant in

Milan. It was called Picanhas and they served up these huge platters of Brazilian-style barbecue. We chatted openly about my future, about what I wanted out of life, out of my career.

Suddenly Roggi said: 'There's someone you should speak to.'

He dialled a number on his mobile phone and passed it over to me. The voice on the other end spoke a strange mixture of English and Italian. It was Joe Jordan. He told me Celtic were genuinely interested in me, that Glasgow was all abuzz.

Maybe it was the Caipirinhas (I had more than a few) but I started getting very excited. He told me a little about Celtic and its fans and I got really pumped up. It was Roggi (as usual) who restrained me.

We told Jordan that we would talk about it at the end of the season.

I was still totally excited however and could not stop thinking about it. I knew very little about Celtic, but it had a certain mystique. I remember being very young and my father telling me about this strange and wonderful team from Scotland with this amazing forward, Jimmy Johnstone, who could dribble past anybody and anything. Still, I tried to put it out of my mind until the end of the season.

I didn't want to leave Italy without first winning the scudetto and our triumph that year helped seal things in my mind: I was going to leave Milan. As it happened, the choice was partly made for me.

At the end of the season, the club went on tour to the Far East. Because many players had international commitments,

Capello took along some guys from other clubs, simply as a way of strengthening the squad and padding out the numbers. Typically, Capello had picked guys like Stefano Desideri and Marco Giandebiaggi, defensive midfielders, since Desailly and Albertini were at Euro 96.

I wouldn't have cared, I was enjoying the sightseeing, but eventually it began to annoy me. These guys weren't Milan players, they were here on a month's loan and yet they were playing ahead of me. The fans didn't want to see them, they wanted to see the stars, the players who had won the title. It was just a series of exhibitions, Milan were getting paid a lot of money to be there (around £400,000 per appearance), why couldn't we just sit back and put on a show? I raised the issue with Capello.

'We're on tour here, boss,' I said. 'Why can't you just let me play the entire game? These Chinese fans want to see the star players, they don't want to see Giandebiaggi!'

'Because, Paolo, you've got to understand that we have to maintain a certain tactical equilibrium,' he replied. 'We can't just treat this as a game, we have to ensure that we stay balanced as a team.'

'What equilibrium? Against a bunch of Chinese who can't even play proper football? This isn't the Champions League, this is just an exhibition. We're here to entertain!'

Capello just gave me a dirty look. I don't think it was a personal thing. He was leaving Milan in a few weeks' time anyway, he had already agreed to take over at Real Madrid. That's why I didn't understand why he had to be so stubborn. Looking back, it's probably typical of Italian managers. They are so tactically obsessed, they think that formations

and systems win matches, not players. And he probably genuinely thought that the 60,000 Chinese who had paid to see
us had forked over their cash to see his 4–3–2–1 system
in action, not to watch the likes of Roberto Baggio and Paolo
Di Canio.

The next night, we played in Beijing. Baggio, Lentini and
I were up front. We took a 1–0 lead, but all three of us played
poorly. Naturally, Capello decided to take off a forward and
send on a defender to protect the lead, even though it was
only an irrelevant exhibition and he was leaving in two weeks
anyway. And naturally, I was the one he picked on.

I got angry. Once again, I felt I had been singled out for
speaking my mind.

'What the f**k are you doing?' I asked him at half-time,
when he announced that I would be coming off.

'F**k off,' he replied. Capello wasn't the kind of man who
minced words. 'You're coming off, because you're holding
back, you're not trying.'

'You're crazy, you're sick in the head,' I shouted back.
'You go f**k off!'

Capello lunged at me, he always had a quick temper. I
shoved him, we took a few swings at each other. I was
furious. Fabio Capello is a big, strong man, but I was not
afraid of him. Milan's coaching staff steamed in and tore us
apart.

I was still livid.

'You can't treat me like this!' I yelled. 'You already signed
for Madrid, you're a nobody here! I still have my contract,
you'd better learn to respect me!'

Capello must have had four people holding him back.

'GET THE F**K OUT OF MY SIGHT!!!' he bellowed. 'GO BACK TO THE F**KING HOTEL!!!'

I looked him straight in the eye and replied: 'You're not going to tell me what to do. Whether I go back to the hotel or not, it's up to me, it's my decision. You're going to stop deciding things for me! One thing is sure, I'm not going to hang around here and look at your ugly penis face any longer!'

He got his wish. I walked straight out of the stadium, grabbed a cab and returned to our hotel. I packed my bags in fifteen minutes and called Roggi. He was surprised, but handled it well.

'Don't worry about it, get the next plane back,' he said. 'Celtic are still interested, it's time we gave them a ring.'

I went straight to the airport, even though I had no clue when the next flight was. I bought a ticket for Hong Kong. From there I flew to Frankfurt and on to Rome. It took fifteen hours and at least it gave me time to cool down.

At that point, the further away I got from Fabio Capello, the better.

CHAPTER SEVEN

CELTIC PASSIONS

Moreno Roggi went to work immediately, trying to secure my transfer to Celtic. In the meantime, I prepared Betta for the possibility. I bought a map of Europe, took it home and laid it out on the kitchen table. I wanted to get a clear idea of where Glasgow was, but I also wanted to break it gently to my wife.

'It looks kind of interesting up here in the top part of the map,' I said, peering down intently. 'What would you say if we went to live up there for a little while?'

She looked at me.

'Up there?' she replied with a smile. 'Paolo, even if you took us off the map it wouldn't matter. We are your family and we will always stay with you.'

I knew she would take it well. I have been so lucky to have a supportive family. I always put them first, but then Betta has always been 100 per cent behind my decisions. I think she knew how excited I was to try a new experience, how important it was for me to get out of Milan and find a place where I could be happy.

On the one hand, honesty is crucial to any relationship.

You don't want to keep things inside, to keep your anger hidden away, because one day it might explode and, even if it doesn't, you'll probably be miserable in the long term. But there is a certain skill in knowing when to voice your disagreement and when to keep your mouth shut. Betta always knew how to do that. I don't know if she was truly enthusiastic about going to Glasgow right away or if she only grew to love it later. Either way, I always felt as if we were in total agreement.

I knew very little about Scottish football. I was familiar with Celtic's famous green and white hoops from my days playing Subbuteo as a kid. I loved those shirts, the way they looked more like rugby jerseys and didn't have numbers on the back. Just the idea of wearing something so different, so unusual, got me excited.

The other aspect of Scottish football I was familiar with was the existence of Ally McCoist. If you lived in Italy and loved football, you would have had to be brain dead not to have heard of McCoist. Nobody had actually ever seen him play, but you always heard about this phenomenal player, scoring 30-plus goals every season and winning the Golden Boot.

To me he seemed exotic and wonderful. I would think to myself: 'This guy has scored 3000 goals in Scotland, he must be awesome!' Of course, later, after I moved to Scotland and actually played in the Scottish Premiership, I began to understand exactly why McCoist scored so much.

The fact that Scottish football isn't exactly top quality, however, didn't in any way diminish my view of McCoist. It wasn't his fault the opposition was so poor. Some people, particularly in Italy, believe that unless you prove yourself at the highest level (i.e. in Serie A), you'll always be something of a flop. Not only is this an incredibly arrogant attitude (based on the opinion that Serie A is far better than any other league), it's patently unfair. McCoist was happy staying where he was. He was, and still is, a national hero. Why should he have moved?

Milan chairman Silvio Berlusconi let us use one of his private jets to fly up to meet the Celtic officials. My agent Moreno Roggi, the Milan general manager Ariedo Braida and I, came up to Glasgow for the day. The city didn't make much of a first impression. It was cold and rainy, the streets were empty, it looked almost post-nuclear.

But then we arrived at Celtic Park and everything changed.

It looked like the kind of ground you might dream about as a kid. It was beautiful, you could smell the history and tradition. They gave me a scarf and a few videos to show Betta and Ludovica. We flew back that same afternoon and that evening, I stayed up late watching the Celtic videos. I was enchanted. I couldn't believe how intense the passion was, how fired up the crowd got.

A week later I returned to Glasgow and met the manager, Tommy Burns. We spent the whole day together; Tommy showed me every last corner of Celtic Park and I soaked in every second. I saw the picture of Brother Wilfrid, the priest who started the club in 1888, the portraits of the club captains, the dressing rooms and the stands.

Tommy would speak really fast in this strong Glaswegian accent and, while I didn't understand a word he said, I realized I knew exactly what he was saying. It's strange, sometimes you can strike up a rapport with somebody and completely understand them, even if you don't speak the same language. It was like that with Tommy; I felt as if we were brothers, as if we had grown up together in the Quarticciolo. In reality, I had known him for twenty minutes.

What struck me most was how excited Tommy got while speaking to me. He would be showing me the most mundane thing, a scoreboard or some director's office and he'd be waving and gesticulating and speaking at a million miles per hour. I knew exactly how he felt. I'm the same way, when I get passionate about something. I begin talking very quickly and descend into a sharp, Roman inflection.

Rarely had I felt such a connection with another person. He would point to the stands and bang his hand on his chest, while repeating 'Heart! Heart!' I guess it was his way of telling me that Celtic fans had a lot of heart. I responded by pointing to myself and banging my chest as well, trying to make him understand that I had heart as well.

While this was going on, Moreno was meeting with Celtic officials to discuss the terms of my contract. Celtic had acquired me for just £800,000, but they told me they couldn't spend too much on wages. They felt like they were taking a chance on me, but if things worked out, I would be rewarded.

'Don't worry, Paolo,' the chairman, Fergus McCann told me. 'We will take another look at your contract at the end of the season. If you do well, you will be rewarded. I promise you.'

'I promise you.' Those three words eventually ruined my

Celtic career. I was foolish enough to believe McCann was a man of his word. To me, a promise is worth more than a thousand contracts.

I had no idea that in ten months' time, I would discover that to Fergus McCann a promise was meaningless.

They took me out for the official introduction to the fans. It was incredible, something unlike anything I had ever experienced. The sun was shining, it felt like Naples. I was on the steps of Celtic Park and all around me, as far as the eye could see, were Celtic supporters wearing green and white strips. There must have been dozens of photographers and television cameras, while a massive security cordon kept people back.

For a second, I told myself 'This can't all be for me. They must have signed somebody else, some big-name star.'

Then I began to make out what the low roar coming from the crowd was: *'Paolo, Paolo! Paolo, Paolo!'* They were singing my name, to the tune of the Pompey chimes!

I was stunned, it was like Naples when Diego Maradona was signed. I loved every minute of it.

The Celtic press officer told me to say to the crowd: 'Celtic are a grand team to play for.' I didn't really under-stand what I was saying, but when the words came out of my mouth, the crowd went crazy. I mean, they were in a frenzy. At that point, I too had fallen in love, just as I had fallen for Tommy Burns.

I still spoke almost no English, but a pre-season tour to Holland was a golden opportunity to pick up some of the lingo. My roommate was Peter Grant, our skipper. He was one of the kindest and nicest people I've ever met, in some ways he was too nice. To liven things up, I decided to mess around with him.

By sheer chance I discovered that he had a phobia about fish. It didn't make much sense to me, I guess it was just one of those weird conditions that nobody can explain, but every time they served fish at dinner he would leave the table or, at the very least, look away in disgust.

Anyway, I decided to exploit it for my own amusement. One night I sneaked down into the kitchen of the hotel and found a huge salmon head. It was still fresh and rather creepy. The salmon had one of those eyes that seemed to follow you around the room. Even I was a little freaked out by it, and I love fish.

I placed the salmon head in a clear plastic bag and went back up to our room. Peter was lying on the bed.

'For you!' I said cheerfully, tossing the fish head on his bed.

Peter must have jumped three feet into the air. I've never seen him move so fast. He ran to the other side of the room and started yelling. I couldn't quite make out what he was saying, but it was clearly to do with the fish.

He was staring at the salmon's head in absolute terror, like it was some monster, on its way to gobbling him up.

Naturally, I played dumb.

'What? You want fish?' I said, picking up the salmon's head and taking a few steps towards him.

'No! No!' he yelled.

He was truly frightened. At first, I thought he was joking around with me, pretending to be scared, but pretty soon I realized he was completely terrified. So I chased him around the room with the fish. He was going mental, running into furniture, knocking down lamps, trying to get away from me. I was running after him, laughing my head off.

He eventually locked himself in the bathroom. I could hear him screaming at the top of his lungs.

'You madman, Di Canio! You're a f**king madman! Get that fish away! Get it out of here!'

I was laughing so hard, there were tears in my eyes. I hadn't laughed this much in years. I rattled the bathroom doorknob, just to scare him even further, and whispered: 'Peter! Oh, Peter! Time for dinner! Time for fish!'

I harassed him like this for a good ten minutes. I could hear him thrashing around in the bathroom and occasionally telling me I was crazy.

Eventually, I chose a different tactic. I hid the fish head in his bed, just under the duvet. He went silent in the bathroom, so I knocked on the door.

'Peter? It's OK, no fish! Come Peter, come Peter come. No fish for you. Fish finish, no more fish!'

I could hear him cursing, but for the life of me, I had no idea what he was saying. After a while, he opened the door and peered out. I was lying on my bed watching television, looking as innocent as I possibly could.

He gave me a dirty look and scanned the room. Satisfied that the fish head was gone, he walked back to his bed.

'You're f**king mad, Di Canio!' he burbled as he got undressed for bed.

'Sorry, no more fish, Peter,' I said as sweetly as I could.

He shook his head and pulled back the duvet. I'll never forget the look on his face when he discovered the salmon head staring right back at him. He let out a blood-curdling cry and ran to the opposite corner of the room. He was yelling and screaming, making no sense. His features were all contorted, he was hyperventilating. I was doubled over with laughter.

He was shocked, he couldn't even yell at me. He just lay there, breathing really fast. Eventually I got rid of the fish, but it was a while before Peter spoke to me again.

Despite this incident we became very good mates. As I said, he was a great lad and, together with Tommy, Billy Stark and Paddy Bonner made Celtic feel like a big family. I think that was a large part of Tommy's ability as a manager. He made us all feel like we were part of something special.

Nobody seemed to care that I was foreign, or that I made more money or that I was different. I felt accepted right away, like I had known these guys all my life. One night, after a pre-season friendly, we went up to Loch Lomond to see Oasis in concert. It was a different world from AC Milan or Juventus!

We played loud music and drank beer on the bus ride up. Pierre Van Hooijdonk got me to sing an Eros Ramazzotti song, 'Se Cantassi Una Bella Canzone'. Singing is most definitely something which isn't part of my repertoire, which explains why after a few seconds they all told me to shut up.

'F**k off, everybody!' I said. Swear words are always the first things you pick up when learning a foreign language.

I'll never forget the only time Tommy got mad at me. It was about a month into the season and I became frustrated in training one morning. Going from AC Milan, where I was surrounded by talented players, to Celtic was a big adjustment. I don't mean that as a knock to Celtic, but, in terms of technique, there was no comparison.

We were playing a practice match and I was getting more and more frustrated because I never seemed to receive a proper pass. It was always overhit or underhit or at waist level. I meant to tell my teammates to just relax and focus on hitting the ball cleanly and properly, rather than trying to hurry it along.

Instead, because my English was limited, I just shouted out in anger: 'These are shit passes! It's all shit!'

I really hadn't learned to say much else. Peter Grant told me to calm down and not talk that way. I lost control for a minute.

'No! I talk like this because this is shit!' I shouted. 'You are shit! We lose to Rangers forever because you are shit! You make shit passes, you are shit players! It's all shit!'

I didn't mean to insult my teammates, but that was the only way to express myself. I was trying to say that we needed to work harder and concentrate, because we weren't good enough to challenge Rangers yet. Instead, it came out all wrong.

Tommy rushed over.

'Paolo, be quiet!' he yelled. 'Calm down! Don't you dare talk like that!'

'No, Tommy, this is all shit!' I replied. 'Look at these shit players!'

'Paolo, stop it!'

I could not stand being yelled at. I was frustrated, nobody seemed to understand what I was trying to say.

'No, I don't stop!' I shouted. 'These are all shit players! This is a shit club!'

Tommy's expression changed.

'Get out!' he said. 'Get out now.'

I could tell he was furious. But I was angry too. Angry that nobody understood me. It was no one's fault, of course, but that did not make my frustration any less.

I walked straight out of the ground and made my way back to Celtic Park. It's a good two miles from Celtic's training ground, Barrow Field, to Parkhead, but I covered the distance in my boots and training attire. People looked at me in a strange way, maybe they even recognized me as I walked through the housing estates, but it did not matter.

My mind was racing, trying to make sense of what happened. By the time Celtic Park came into view, I began deeply regretting the bust-up with Tommy. I knew it was a misunderstanding, I knew that we had both fallen victim to our tempers. But I also thought that this was it, that I would never play for Celtic again.

I walked through the gate and saw Tommy standing there. Right after I'd left, he had jumped in his car and driven to the ground. He did not want it to end this way.

'Paolo!' he called out.

I just stared at him. I didn't know what to do.

'Paolo, don't go! Don't leave us!'

I would have never expected him to do this. Managers are arrogant, they are full of pride, they simply don't come up to players and apologize. I was lost for words.

'Paolo, it's okay!' Tommy's voice cracked with emotion.

'Just don't leave us, don't go away for something stupid like this!'

I got really emotional. I'm not sure what I did next, but I think I remember hugging him. The fact that Tommy cared so much about me and about Celtic to put aside his pride was astounding. That is when he became like a brother to me.

Betta and Ludovica joined me in Glasgow in mid-August. At first I was concerned that they might not like it, but they too fell in love with Scotland almost as soon as they arrived. We had a gorgeous house, just outside Glasgow. It had a garden with a little brook bubbling through it. Best of all, there were ducks, squirrels and foxes. Ludovica went nuts. To her, it was like something out of a Disney film, I think she had only ever seen wild animals on television. I remember many a night when she and I would sit and stare out at the garden, waiting for a fox or a squirrel to trip our motion detector and activate the lights.

We had never lived abroad, but we soon developed our own circle of friends. 'Il Pavone', an Italian restaurant in Glasgow's Prince's Square Shopping Centre, became like a second home to us. We still keep in touch with the owners, Guerino and Marco.

I started taking English lessons right away, though I really wasn't much of a student, especially compared to Betta. She seemed to soak up the language immediately. I felt like a bit of a dunce, but I quickly got used to the fact that people didn't always understand what I was saying. I know I could and should speak better English. I look at somebody like Vialli and I'm a little envious. He's lived here as long as I have, yet his English is ten times better.

I know part of it is that his English teacher is a real drill sergeant who forces him to study. I think the trick is that to be comfortable in a foreign language, you need to think in that language. Most people simply translate the concepts they want to convey from their own language into English. Vialli, on the other hand, actually thinks in English and that is the key to speaking foreign languages.

I made my league debut away to Kilmarnock. It was the third game of the season and I was still suffering from a twisted ankle, so Tommy started me on the bench. We were 1–0 down with 30 minutes to go, when he sent me on.

I could hear the roar rising from the visiting Celtic supporters. I was not going to let them down.

I scored right away, then I set up Andy Thom for the second and Jorge Cadete for the third. At the final whistle I ran over to our fans to thank them. They were all singing my name, I couldn't believe their passion. I had found a home.

By that point, the importance of the rivalry with Rangers had become obvious, but I had no idea what was in store for me at my very first Old Firm game.

It was 28 September 1996, we were about to take on Rangers at Ibrox and I was about to step into another world. There is nothing like it. I am a full-blooded Roman who grew up breathing, eating and drinking our rivalry with Roma. I sincerely thought the Rome derby was the greatest match in the world.

That was until I moved to Celtic and experienced the Old Firm derby.

You could take all the derby matches in the world, add

them all together and they still wouldn't equal one-millionth of the Old Firm. There is nothing like it.

I could tell the mood was different right away, in the players' tunnel. Normally, you'll shake hands, have a chat, at least acknowledge your opponent. That day however, nobody said a word. We just stared at each other. Nobody was actually growling, but that's what it felt like. We were like rabid dogs, sizing up our opponents, ready to be unleashed.

On the pitch, the din bordered on the unbearable. I know many players, especially foreigners, might lose themselves in the intensity and hostility of such a game. It can be intimidating, and I don't just mean the opposing fans. You look up at your own fans and you see their passion, their anger, their faces contorted with emotion and it can be scary.

But not to me.

To me the pressure was my lifeblood. I would feed on it. I could seriously feel myself getting stronger, physically and mentally as I heard the fans singing. I felt like I could just about hear them all individually, one by one, separate voices uniting to cheer me on.

I wrapped myself up in their passion and let it flow through my body.

I had to be the Pride of Celtic. I had to, with fans such as those. Nothing less than my best would be acceptable.

I knew how important it was to stop Rangers. They had won eight consecutive titles, if they beat us that year they would equal the legendary Celtic teams of the late 1960s and early 1970s who had won nine in a row.

We could not let it happen.

Beyond that, I was getting sucked into age-old rivalry.

I know people say that you have to be Scottish, or, better yet, Glaswegian to understand the Old Firm rivalry. Perhaps it's true, I can only speak about my experience and what it meant to me.

The word 'hate' is not a nice term, but hatred does have a place in sport.

Not only that, a certain dose of anger, of meanness, of rage is healthy, because it spurs you on to push yourself, to excel. Of course, it is a temporary hatred which disappears after the event, but during the competition and before, while you are preparing, it is essential.

You need rage in your daily life. I have it in abundance, it is what helped me get where I am today. And in sport, coupled with hatred, it can help you achieve great things. Often, it is what differentiates a great player from a good one and is what allows mediocre players to compete regularly at the highest level.

There was hatred in the Old Firm and I soaked it up. I used it to my advantage. I knew perfectly well that it was about religion and, while I did not understand or wish to get involved in the dispute, I would feed off it.

I am Catholic, they were Protestant. It was very clear to me.

This didn't mean that I ran around the pitch shouting (or even thinking): 'I am Catholic! You are Protestant! I shall destroy you!'

I did, however, know what I represented to the Celtic fans and, more importantly, I know what beating Rangers meant. It was a chance to gain a victory, albeit a small one, against an enemy who for decades had oppressed them, on the pitch and off it.

Their hatred wasn't only about football, but it was in football that it came into my sphere. And it was in football that I could make it my own and use it to make me stronger.

It gave me that extra rage, because I desperately wanted to enter into Celtic history. Their enemies became my enemies and, until the final whistle, I hated the enemy as much as they did.

As for the reasons behind the fans' hatred for each other, well, to me it seems absurd. I have read about the history, the roots of the problem going back to Northern Ireland and the discrimination Irish immigrants experienced in Scotland.

My rational mind tells me that continuing to hate makes no sense. It is the year 2000, why carry this with you into the realm of sports?

As I said, there is nothing wrong with hatred. There is nothing wrong with loathing Rangers with every ounce of your body. But to do so because they are Protestant, because of events that happened far away and a long time ago is ludicrous.

You have a right to protest, you have a right to fight back, sometimes you even have a duty to do so. But when people die because of a conflict dating back centuries, a war which neither they, nor their fathers, nor their grandfathers began, there is something profoundly wrong going on.

When the IRA or the loyalist paramilitaries kill women and children, there can be no justification. When a 14-year-old kid in Belfast says, 'This is my land, I was born here and I'm going to die here,' there can be no justification.

What saddens me most is that kids are raised to hate, without understanding the reasons for that hatred. These children have no choice in the matter. They have been robbed of their free will.

I imagine a young Protestant boy in Glasgow just discovering his love of football. He might see me or Henrik Larsson or Tom Boyd and admire our skill or our passion. In a normal world, that is how children become fans, they remain enchanted by one specific footballer and then fall in love with his team.

But that young Protestant boy could never become a Celtic fan. He could never fall in love with us. And that is wrong. That is evil.

Even when you don't teach somebody to hate, even when you just teach him not to love, it's wrong, it's perverted.

And yet, having said all that, I cannot condemn Rangers and Celtic fans, Protestants and Catholics, for hating each other.

I am mindful of the fact that I come from a different culture. My background informs and affects my opinions, it could not be otherwise. And so, in my mind, in my culture, this hatred makes no sense.

But precisely because I am not from Glasgow, because I wasn't raised in that context, I have no right to tell them that what they are doing is wrong. I never had to face the issues they did, I never grew up in that environment.

I don't believe it has to be this way. I think things can change, if people are willing to make it happen.

But I am not convinced they are. If they were, they would

do something about it. Take the schools, for example. Ludovica went to one of the few mixed schools in Glasgow. All the others are either Catholic or state schools, which basically means they are Protestant, since the Catholics all go to Catholic schools.

These kids grow up seeing others as different. They grow up not knowing any better, unable to make up their own minds.

I think if people really wanted to change, they would allow their children to think for themselves. They would say, 'Okay, we're too different now, we can't make peace, but maybe one day our kids will be able to.'

But they don't. They simply pass on their own ignorance, their own hatred. Probably because deep down they fear that if one day their children or grandchildren do manage to achieve peace, it will simply render meaningless all the hatred they poured into their own lives.

Anyway, we lost that Old Firm match, 2–0, just as we lost the next two.

We were pretty much murdering everybody else in the league, but Rangers were our bogey team. We spent much of the season playing catch up, but we always felt that we were close, that with a little bit extra we could overhaul them.

But I felt that the referees weren't doing us any favours.

And I said as much in an interview with an Italian magazine which was picked up by the Scottish press. My words were twisted, so it came out as if I had said that the referees were anti-Celtic because most referees were Protestant.

I didn't say that. I simply pointed out that if Protestants

make up 80 per cent of the population, it stands to reason that 80 per cent of the referees would be Protestants too. That's all I was saying, you can draw whatever inferences you want from it. Naturally, it was all blown out of proportion, which probably made me even less popular with referees.

Having said that, it's a well-known fact that referees naturally tend to favour big clubs. In Italy we have a word for it, we call it 'sudditanza psicologica', which literally translates as 'psychological subjection'.

What it basically means is that you have a natural and perhaps involuntary allegiance to the stronger, bigger club. If, for example, Manchester United play Scunthorpe at Old Trafford, it is very difficult for the referee to award Scunthorpe a penalty.

This is not necessarily because the referee is biased or evil. It has to do with the fact that the referee's basic mandate is to ensure that the laws of the game are enforced. If he does this properly, the better team will win. And, the better team, in our example, is invariably going to be Manchester United. If he gives the penalty and Scunthorpe go on to win the match, it becomes more difficult to say that the better team won, because clearly it did not. Therefore, if the better team didn't win, the referee did not do his job properly.

It is this fear of failure, fear of doing wrong, which creeps into referees' minds and influences their decisions. If Michael Owen runs at a Wimbledon defender and there is contact, the penalty will probably be given. Why? Partly because Owen is a fast, skilful forward and Wimbledon defenders are seen as clumsy players who give away penalties. The fact that Liverpool are a big club while Wimbledon are a small club also plays a part.

But if Neil Ruddock runs at, say, Gareth Southgate, and the two make contact, odds are the penalty won't be given. Why? Partly because Aston Villa are a bigger club than Crystal Palace and partly because Ruddock is viewed by many as a rough, slow player while Southgate is considered an elegant central defender with impeccable timing.

I am not suggesting that referees follow a script and that they intentionally favour certain teams or players. But they do allow themselves to be influenced. Hence the psychological subjection.

It goes further than that. In some cases there is simply a fear of hurting powerful and influential clubs, clubs which could then exact revenge by damaging a referee's career. After all, the league assigns referees and decides which referees get promoted and which referees get left out.

And the league is made up of clubs, and within the league structure certain clubs are more powerful than others. Why? Because they are bigger and generate more money. At the end of the day, football leagues aren't charitable organizations. They exist to make money. Manchester United winning the Premiership generates more money for the league than, say, Bradford winning the title.

These are facts; this isn't Paolo Di Canio talking, this is history talking. Go back and look at the percentages, study the videos, talk to the players. To get a penalty at Old Trafford, Jaap Stam needs to take out a machine gun and riddle you full of bullets, and even then there will probably be much debate over whether you were shot in the penalty box or just outside.

This isn't just a British problem, this psychological subjection exists in every country, in every sport. In Italy, it's just as bad, if not worse.

Funnily enough, Celtic are probably the only big club which do not benefit from psychological subjection. That's because everything in Scotland is geared towards Rangers. Everything: the league, the media, the referees.

Even when we played the likes of Raith Rovers or Dunfermline, the referees would be against us. That's because in Scotland it's always only a two-horse race and by hurting us, they were helping Rangers.

Again, I don't know if this is conscious or not. I would hope that for most referees this is something they do involuntarily. But I know for a fact that there are others who are simply biased.

There are some who, if you question them in the first minute, it won't matter if your opponent kicks lumps out of you for the entire game, you just won't get anything called in your favour. Referees like that are a joke, in my view.

In my own personal case, now that I play for West Ham, it's even worse, for three reasons. First, we aren't a big club, we've had a number of controversial players and we have a certain image; second, I'm a foreigner, which never helps; and third, I'm Paolo Di Canio and I have a reputation.

Even before the Paul Alcock incident at Hillsborough, I was considered a troublemaker, a guy who would dive and complain. The reality is that I do speak out, because I cannot stand injustice. But as for diving, and I've said this many times, I haven't done it since coming to this country.

I will admit that in Italy you're encouraged to go down when you feel contact. Since coming to Britain however, I've adopted the British mentality, the idea that it's always better to stay on your feet. I can't stand diving, I abhor it. And yet I'm always accused of it. Funny, though, that every single time people have gone back and looked at the video replay, they have never found any conclusive evidence that I took a tumble. That's because it simply doesn't happen.

It's a fact that I'm quicker and more skilful than most defenders. I'll show them the ball, they'll swing their leg to take it away but by the time it gets there, the ball is gone, I've shifted it to my other foot or to the side or whatever. And they hit my leg instead. And because most defenders are bigger and heavier than I am, I lose my balance and go to the ground. It's physics, pure and simple. But nobody wants to recognize that.

I don't recollect having had any good referees in matches I've played in this country. Honestly. Nobody has ever refereed me well. It is a constant battle, I'm not just playing against my opponent, I'm playing against the referees as well. In 1999/2000 I must have had eight clear-cut penalties which were not given by match officials.

It has got to the point where I don't even expect a call. At Upton Park, referees won't grant penalties; on the road, it's even worse, they just book me for diving. There are times when I get so frustrated that I tell my teammates to have a go themselves rather than passing me the ball in the box, because if they do, I'll just get fouled and the referee won't do anything about it.

If you happen to be a Premiership defender and you want to stop Di Canio in the penalty area, there are times when you're better off just kicking me or pushing me over than trying to defend against me legally. If you try to defend against me without breaking the rules, I might go past you and score. But if you just foul me, you'll be alright, because the referee will never, ever grant the penalty.

All joking aside, this is a serious problem.

There are hundreds of thousands of fans who don't support Arsenal, Manchester United or Rangers and they are having the mickey taken week in, week out.

Referees are there to make sure that the laws of the game are obeyed, but also to guarantee that the game is played in an open, honest way. This means providing fairness, making sure that rules are applied equally. This does not mean blowing the whistle instinctively to protect certain clubs.

The Football Association should open a public dialogue with the clubs about the quality of referees. Instead, all they do is simply defend match officials, always and everywhere, no matter what the circumstances, like they did with Paul Durkin, who booked Trevor Sinclair twice in the space of a minute last season during the West Ham–Arsenal derby. They view referees as a sacred institution, something which cannot be touched or criticized.

And yet referees are part of the game, just like corner flags, goalposts and, indeed, players. They are human, they make mistakes, we all know that. Yet they rarely, if ever, admit to their errors. Why not? Admitting you were wrong isn't a sign of weakness, it's a sign of humanity.

I don't think anybody expects or even wants infallible

referees. I certainly don't. I just want honest referees whose work can be scrutinized, just like mine is. The Football Association should evaluate referees publicly, explaining just why Referee 'A' was sacked and Referee 'B' promoted. That would make everything clearer for everyone.

I know some referees wouldn't like it, but I think most would. I think most would understand that doing everything behind closed doors simply raises suspicions and actually makes their job more difficult.

It wasn't until 6 March, the Scottish Cup quarter-final, that I finally tasted the joy of beating Rangers. The fact that it was at Celtic Park made it that much sweeter. We took the lead after 11 minutes through Malky Mackay and I added a second, from the penalty spot, in the 19th minute. When the ball hit the back of the net, I heard 50,000 voices singing my name. It was unreal.

We played well, created more chances and hung on for the victory. By the end, every time we touched the ball, even if it was just to retrieve a throw-in, there was a roar so loud, I felt the ground tremble. It was deafening, the loudest sound I have ever heard and each time it seemed to get louder and louder.

That was by far my fondest Old Firm memory, partly because it was the only one I actually won.

Ten days later we faced Rangers again. We were five points adrift, with seven matches to go. A win in front of our own fans would bring us within two and give us a legitimate shot at the title. A loss would extend their lead to eight points and virtually hand them the all-important ninth championship in a row.

We were fired up and the match got nasty from the beginning. Studs, elbows, head butts, we were throwing everything we had at each other. Brian Laudrup scored for Rangers in the 44th minute, then Mark Hateley and Mackay were sent off, leaving both clubs with ten men.

I did what I could, struggling up front with Jorge Cadete. Pierre Van Hooijdonk had been sold the week before, following a contract dispute with McCann. We sorely missed him.

At the final whistle, the Rangers fans went wild in their corner of the ground and started singing *'Ten in a row! Ten in a row!'*

I was gutted. I sank to my knees. It hurt terribly. We had given Rangers twelve points in our four encounters. Even if we had just split those matches, two wins each, we would be nursing a four-point lead at the top of the table. Instead, they had triumphed. Again.

I was walking off the pitch, head down, when Ian Ferguson ran up to me. He had spent a good part of the game picking off our players one by one with vicious tackles. I'm all for strong players and a degree of nastiness is sometimes necessary, but Ferguson had gone well past that. He wasn't mean and committed like, say Roy Keane, he was just a brute on the pitch.

Still, from my point of view, everything had ended at the final whistle. I never carry over bad feelings from one match to the next. When it's over, it's over, regardless of what happened on the pitch.

But then Ferguson leaned over and yelled in my ear: 'F*** off, you bastard!'

At that point, I just lost it. It took a few seconds to register what he had said.

We had just lost the game and the title in front of our own fans at Celtic Park, our temple, and this guy Ian Ferguson, this nobody, had the gall to come up and insult me for no reason.

That is called kicking an opponent when he's down. If he had just said something sarcastic, like 'Good job winning the title' or something like that, it would have been different. I would have simply told him where to go and that would have been the end of it.

But he didn't. He purposely said what he said to hurt me, to humiliate Celtic even further.

I was not going to stand for that.

I turned and chased him across the pitch. He had run over to where his teammates were celebrating. But I wasn't going to let him get away.

He kept backing away, it was obvious that he was terrified. I grabbed him but the struggle didn't last long. Other players swarmed in to separate us.

It's a good thing they did. I would have beaten him to a pulp. I don't think I have ever been that angry in my life. Ever. There is no question in my mind that I would have hurt him severely.

Shortly thereafter Tommy Burns was sacked. It was a severe blow for me. We had become very close and his firing made no sense. The club could have waited a few weeks, let him finish the season with some dignity. Instead, they simply dumped him. That gave me some indication of the kind of people the Celtic directors were.

The season ended on a high note for me. I was voted Player of the Year by the Scottish Professional Footballers' Association. Being recognized by my peers was a tremendous honour. The Football Writers' Award went to Brian Laudrup, the sixth consecutive Rangers player to win the award. But I didn't care. Winning the players' award was much more important to me.

I wore a kilt to the awards ceremony. It seemed like an appropriate way to show my respect to Scotland, the country I had grown to love. I actually did some research. I bought a book on clans and chose the St Andrews' kilt. It was a wonderful night out.

I was ready to renegotiate my deal with Celtic. I was hoping for a long-term contract, maybe one that would allow me to end my career at Celtic Park. Betta and Ludovica loved Glasgow and, I, well, I had genuinely found a second home, a fantastic place where I could be truly happy.

Just before the summer, Moreno Roggi came up and we went to see McCann.

'We need to talk about some of the promises that were made,' Moreno said. 'You asked us to sign for less money when we came over, but promised that if Paolo had a good season we could talk about a better deal. Well, I think Paolo has had a good season, don't you?'

McCann had a puzzled expression on his face.

'No, I don't remember making any promises,' he said.

He was stonewalling us, playing dumb, taking advantage of the contract I had signed in good faith almost a year earlier.

I turned to Roggi and said in Italian: 'Fine, if he doesn't

remember the promises he made, then I won't remember that I have to play for this idiot.'

We went back to Italy for the summer, still hoping that the situation could be resolved. After all, I was Player of the Year and, relatively speaking, I was earning very little money. Plus, McCann had given me his word.

McCann is a businessman, I guess he figured that Celtic would sell out, regardless of whether Paolo Di Canio suited up or not. It was all about money for him, he didn't care if we won the title or not.

When I compare him and, say, Peter Storrie at West Ham, I almost have to laugh. When I first arrived at Upton Park, Storrie made me sit in his office for two hours, telling me all about the club, it's history, it's traditions. He showed me pictures of Trevor Brooking and Bobby Moore, he told me about the Academy, he went on and on. In short, he got all excited and shared his passion with me. I loved that. I love a man who loves football.

McCann, on the other hand, must have spoken to me three times in all the time I was there. The first was when I arrived at Celtic Park after my transfer. That day he popped out of nowhere, said, 'Nice to meet you', shook my hand and disappeared. I could have been the new tea lady, for all he cared.

The second was when he promised my contract would be renegotiated and the third was when he decided he didn't remember that promise. That was it. Apart from that, I don't think I ever saw him.

When I returned that summer, I was called in to meet Jock Brown. Now Jock was brought in by McCann as

General Manager. In reality, his role was to play the tough guy who would take on the prickly issues that McCann didn't want to deal with.

I figured him out immediately. He would be all smiles one second, cold and calculated the next. He greeted me like I was one of his long-lost brothers. After a few minutes of small talk, he suggested we go to his office.

The second I sat down his eyes narrowed and got really hard and mean.

'Paolo, you have to do exactly what I say,' he said. 'You are under contract which means I decide what's best for you. You need to forget about these promises you keep talking about. You need to do what Celtic Football Club tells you to do.'

I realized he was trying to intimidate me. It was written all over his face. He had no intention of offering me a new contract. McCann had sent him over to be the hatchet man and now he was trying to scare me into playing sweet.

I wasn't going to let this clown push me around. I gave him a way out.

'Are you joking?' I asked, lowering my voice.

He looked me straight in the eye, his jaw set. He looked like a cartoon character.

'You're not joking, are you?' I said. 'You're serious. Are you sure of what you're saying? Do you really want to do this?'

He smiled broadly. He was challenging me, being smug. Then the smile melted into a frown. Not a puzzled frown but a mean, aggressive frown.

I shook my head: 'You are wrong, you are so wrong and you don't even know it.'

He showed no reaction.

'I go,' I said, my voice now little more than a whisper. 'I go back to Italy. See you later!'

I got up to leave. He wasn't expecting this.

'No, Paolo, you need to stay,' he protested. 'You can't do that, you are wrong . . .'

'No! YOU are wrong!' I leaned forward. 'You just made a really, really big mistake.'

'You, you can't do this!' he said, raising his voice as I was walking out of his office.

I turned around.

'I don't think you know what you are dealing with,' I said. 'I go back to Italy. You can fine me forever if you like, I don't care.'

With that, I returned home.

To me, it was an issue of principle. I wasn't going to let these guys push me around. If they had approached it differently, if they had explained that they needed the money to strengthen the squad or bring in a new player, I would have understood. All they had to do was be civil and reasonable.

Instead, they tried to bully me in the most crass and naive manner. I wasn't intimidated by Luciano Moggi at Juventus, so there was no way Fergus McCann and his buddy, Jock Brown, were going to scare me.

Still, I felt awful. I felt poisoned by what had happened and disappointed that these people who cared nothing for football were running Celtic Football Club.

I went with the club on their pre-season tour to Ireland

and met the new manager, Wim Jansen. He was a great guy, he asked for advice on how to rebuild the team. It was going to be quite a task: Van Hooijdonk had left, Cadete was on the way out and, as for me, my future was in limbo. I think he would have wanted me to stay, but it was pretty much out of his hands.

While in Ireland I kept getting calls from one of the Celtic directors. He kept assuring me that he had enough support to oust McCann. He said he was going to bring in new investors, people who had a genuine love for the club and that I would get a five-year deal. Nothing came of it, but it was nice to know that not all Celtic directors were cut from the same cloth as McCann.

I only stayed in Ireland for a few days before going back to Italy. The pressure had become too much. I felt betrayed, humiliated. I loved the club so much and yet I was being slapped in the face.

There was no way I could continue. Even back in Terni, I felt sick to my stomach. I was hoping something would change, but it didn't, the situation just got worse and worse.

Celtic agreed to put me up for sale. I had offers from Serie A, Bologna and Napoli were eager to sign me, but by this stage of my career I was loving playing abroad. I would have stayed in Scotland, but obviously, playing for Rangers was not an option. So I looked to the Premiership.

CHAPTER EIGHT

WHEN THE PUNCHES STARTED FLYING

I did not want to leave Celtic, but I knew I had to try to make the most of the next chapter in my career at Sheffield Wednesday. You can't live your life with regrets or with too many 'ifs'. If I had stayed in Glasgow, things might have worked out well or they might not have. As it happened, I'm happy with my life now, so I can't go back and wonder if it might have been better elsewhere.

Besides, joining Wednesday meant playing in the Premiership. I was leaving a huge club in Celtic for a mid-sized club in Sheffield Wednesday, but the prospect of playing in a high-profile league was very tempting.

Apart from the Old Firm, Scottish football simply doesn't register on anybody's radar screen. The Premiership is another matter. Games are screened live in Italy, there are weekly review programmes, it gets a lot of coverage. After a year in relative obscurity I was back on the big stage. As much as I loved Scotland and Scottish football, it was something I had to consider.

Then there was the competitive factor. In Scotland, Celtic had only one real opponent in the league. In the

Premiership, I would be facing clubs like Manchester United, Arsenal and Liverpool, legendary, historic teams I would hear about as a boy. I was anxious to measure myself against them.

Moreno Roggi, his son Matteo and I flew into Manchester airport, where Sheffield Wednesday had sent a car to pick us up. It was August, we left 30-degree weather and glaring sunshine in Italy only to find cold, wet, drudgery in England. The drive to Hillsborough took an hour and a half and the further we went, the worse it got. Perhaps it was just an illusion, but as the Yorkshire countryside sped by outside my car window, it seemed as if we were descending into Siberia.

We drove through Sheffield city centre, past boarded-up stores and kebab shops. It looked like something out of Eastern Europe, before the iron curtain came down.

I turned to Moreno and said: 'My God, where the hell are we? What kind of a place is this?'

He smiled.

'Don't worry,' he said. 'It can't get any worse. It will only get better.'

To be fair, Sheffield wasn't the prettiest place I had ever visited. It won't be winning any beauty contests anytime soon. But when you're a professional footballer, that's not what is truly important. What matters is finding some kind of serenity, for you and your family.

Once we had settled, we were very happy with our life in Sheffield. We bought a beautiful house in the countryside, it was calm and quiet, ideal for a young couple with small children.

You always hear stories of foreigners who are unhappy in certain places, particularly in the north of England. It tends to be a hot topic in the press; but hearing some of these complaints makes my blood boil. In Italy, the press write that pretty much all Italians who live outside of London are miserable, that every place is a dreary, ugly dump. They are convinced that we would all rush back to Italy at the drop of a coin.

Says who? Not me, I'm happy at West Ham, I was happy in Sheffield and in Glasgow. I don't want to go back, hell, maybe I'll never go back to Italy. Who knows?

The point is that for an Italian footballer, playing in the Premiership is a privilege. It's a chance to experience a different way of life, another culture, learn a new language and play in an exciting, fast-paced, high-profile league. Not to mention the money. Yes, the very best players make a lot more in Serie A than they do over here. But most, if not all, Premiership-based Italians earn a lot of money, certainly more than we could make back home.

It saddens me when I hear certain comments. I don't want people to think that we would all rather be sitting in Rome or Naples, drinking our cappuccinos and watching the world go by. I'm not like that. I love it here.

I know it works both ways. Guys like Ian Rush and Hakan Sukur were miserable in Italy. But I think they are the exceptions.

Look at the Italians in the Premiership. Almost to a man, they have settled very well and love their life off the pitch.

Roberto Di Matteo is happy. He has his restaurant, he is

now a father, he has his friends. Gianfranco Zola is happy. He plays golf, he bought a nice house, his kids go to the same primary school that Prince Charles attended and soon will probably speak better English than Italian. And, of course, Gianluca Vialli loved it here, and why shouldn't he have? He had the opportunity to manage a top-notch club, to walk through Hyde Park without getting hassled, to basically do whatever he liked, whenever he liked.

And it's not just those of us who live in London.

Gianluca Festa lives in Middlesbrough, the ugliest place in the world, but he's happy too, as is Stefano Eranio. They wouldn't have stuck around this long if they didn't enjoy it.

People ask me: 'Paolo, does it take a special kind of person to adapt to living in a foreign country?'

Well, all it takes is somebody who isn't ignorant. Somebody who understands that when you move abroad you are a guest and you can't expect everything to be the way it is back home. You can't expect people to speak the same language or eat the same food or enjoy the same things you enjoy back home.

To me, it's sheer common sense. We foreigners have to accept the fact that this is not our country. We are guests and we must be respectful of the local customs.

It is we who have to learn how to speak English. It is we who have to adapt to the English way of doing things. I wouldn't want foreigners coming to Italy and acting as if they owned the place. If they come to my country, they have to play by my rules. And by the same token, we foreigners in England must accept the English way.

It goes well beyond that. We are not just guests, we must

remember that we have been given a great opportunity. England is not just where I live, it is the country that gives me opportunities, that gives me work, that allows me to earn a living and play professional football – which is the greatest job in the world.

As I said, unless you're ignorant, you will be able to adapt. You just need to get your priorities right, understand what is truly important.

OK, so I'm not in Italy and that means I need to change my routine. I can't wake up in the morning, wander into my local bar, have a cappuccino and a pastry and shoot the breeze with the *barista* about last night's television, just as Ian Rush probably struggled to find half a dozen teammates who would go drinking down the pub with him.

So what? Are you going to let yourself get fossilized in your habits? Are you going to tell me that your morning cappuccino is worth more than the tremendous opportunity you have as a foreign player in England? Is that cappuccino really going to change your life?

Not to mention the fact that nobody is holding a gun to your head, it's not like you have to live here the rest of your life. If you don't like it, if you really can't stand not having your cappuccino and not eating real pizza on Sunday night, then you can always move back in a couple of years.

If you can't adapt when you're a professional footballer in your mid-twenties and make more in a month than most people make in a year, when are you going to adapt?

Especially when you're in London, which is an absolutely wonderful city where everything you could ever want is at your fingertips. People complain that English cities are ugly.

And yes, many of them are. But that doesn't mean they are bad places to live. Granted, if you live in places like Sheffield or Middlesbrough, you won't be visiting beautiful historic churches or museums or monuments. But so what? It's not as if people in Rome spend their entire lives wandering around the Collosseum or staring at the Pantheon.

More than anything else, a city is made up of the people who live there. I found some wonderful people in Sheffield, Gianluca Festa found them in Middlesbrough and so on. If you are open-minded and manage to shed your preconceptions, you can fit in just about everywhere.

When you reach the right balance between your work and your family life, you will be happy anywhere. I really believe that and it doesn't only apply to footballers.

Of course, having the right kind of wife or girlfriend is crucial. I'll be the first to admit that if I wasn't married to Betta, if I had a different partner, perhaps it would not have worked out and I would have gone back to Italy.

Think about it. As a footballer, I am the breadwinner. I go to training, I go to matches, my daily routine is very similar to what it would be back home. My work is essentially the same. Inevitably, I'll make friends with my teammates, I'll have something to talk about, we'll share experiences. But it's totally different for wives and girlfriends. They have to stay home and adapt to a whole new world. It's more difficult for them to meet people, they not only have to learn a new language but discover where to go grocery shopping, where to drop off the dry cleaning, how to drive into the city centre. These may seem like silly, mundane things, but they have to start entirely from scratch. Wives don't have the same familiar reference points that we footballers, or indeed any man who moves abroad, might have.

I was fortunate. Betta and I made the decision to move abroad together and we agreed 100 per cent that it was the right thing to do. We were certain and it wasn't just a financial decision, though that is important as well.

At the heart of our choice was a deep conviction that we wanted to have a new experience, that it would be beneficial to the growth of our family. We weighed up all the factors, good and bad, and made our decision. And we were very clear on the opportunities it offered.

I, for one, have always been fascinated by English football, it's history and traditions. For my daughters, it was a chance not only to discover, but become a part of, an entirely different culture. Ludovica is eight years old and she is perfectly bilingual. Her English is just as good as her Italian, she slides in and out of both languages with the utmost of ease. In fact, she loves calling Betta from friends' houses, speaking in English and fooling her into thinking she's talking to somebody else!

Imagine that. Betta can't even recognize her own daughter over the phone. That's how good Ludovica's English is. Her accent is perfect. I wonder if people realize just how great a gift that is.

I have friends in Italy who will spend £5000 to send their kids to those full-immersion summer programmes in Britain and their children return speaking less English than before. That's because they don't even go to school, they just hang out with other Italian kids in pubs and discotheques and get absolutely nothing out of it.

I don't understand it. There are foreign footballers in this country who would return to their own countries for a third of the salary they earn here. To me, that's crazy. You come here, you make a lot of money, your family has this wonderful foreign experience in a new culture, there is a lot less stress and it's not something you're going to do for the rest of your life. How can you not fit in?

So maybe it wasn't too surprising that, in spite of the horrible conditions on my very first visit, we settled quickly in Sheffield. I was very enthusiastic, very eager to start over once again.

That first night we met the club secretary, Graham Mackrell (little did I know that our paths would cross again, albeit briefly, at West Ham) and the chairman, Dave Richards. They were charming, they told me manager David Pleat really wanted me at Hillsborough.

Sure enough, the next morning Pleat himself came to my hotel and drove me to the training ground. When we arrived, I got a bit of a surprise.

The players all started singing: *'There will never be nine in a row! Singing, Paolo Di Canio, there will never be nine in a row!'* The song, sung to the tune of the theme from *The Sting*, was a Celtic favourite from the previous season, when we were trying to prevent Rangers from winning their ninth consecutive title.

I wasn't quite sure if they were taking the mickey. Obviously, in spite of me, Rangers had won nine in a row, so it was badly dated. Still, they were all laughing and cheering, so I guess they were trying to make me welcome.

I wasn't match-fit when the season began (I had only

arrived a few days earlier), so Pleat left out me out at Newcastle. We lost 2–1, with Tino Asprilla netting two great goals, but I came on to play the last twenty minutes and got a great response from our travelling fans.

It was a disappointing start, but it only got worse. We lost against Leeds in our home opener, drew at Wimbledon (I got the equalizer fifteen minutes from time, but it was scant consolation) and then got absolutely hammered at Blackburn. The final score was 7–2, we were 5–1 down at half-time. We were awful, but what struck me most was the way our fans kept singing in the driving rain, even after they scored their seventh.

I didn't start too well; after a season at Celtic it was difficult adjusting once again to facing competitive opponents. The fact that Pleat insisted on playing me in midfield on the right flank didn't help things. It was the position I used to play in Italy, but things were totally different at Wednesday. In Serie A, we always played the ball through the midfield, I got a lot of possession and felt like I could actually make a contribution.

In Pleat's system, the defenders simply belted the ball up the pitch for the forwards to chase. The midfielders had just one job: winning the ball back from the opposition. It wasn't quite Wimbledon's kick-and-rush, but not too far off either. I felt I had to tell him I wasn't being used properly.

'Look, you've got to play me up front,' I told him one day after training. 'This is silly, I'm no use in midfield.'

He scrunched up his face and had this very uncomfortable look.

'Well, we don't really have a choice,' he said. 'We have to

use you in midfield, because I've got Andy Booth and Benny Carbone. If you play as a forward, what am I going to do with them?'

'That's not my problem,' I replied. 'You're the manager. Look, if I had known you were going to stick me out on the right of midfield, I would have gone to another club. This is silly. Play me up front.'

Pleat didn't say anything, but in the next match, against Leicester City, he played me as a striker alongside Carbone. We won, 1–0, and I think he began to see the light.

I never really got along with Pleat. I know that in England he's regarded as some kind of sophisticated footballing genius, but that's not the impression I got. He seemed incredibly detached. He never explained anything to me, we just never had any kind of relationship.

I know he changed his game plan to accommodate me and I suppose I should be grateful, though it was obviously for the good of the team. But I never really understood him, there was never any real substance to him.

Maybe I've been spoiled in terms of managers. I've had some truly great ones like Marcello Lippi, Giovanni Trapattoni and Fabio Capello. I've had others who, while perhaps not as successful, at least had a winning attitude and knew how to fire up the players and build team spirit, like Tommy Burns or Ron Atkinson. Perhaps it's not fair to compare a guy like Pleat to people like that. But he was just a blank sheet of paper. He didn't have any real emotions and was almost entirely devoid of spirit.

Anyway, with Benny and me up front, things improved. We became more creative, at times Sheffield Wednesday were actually attractive to watch, which is saying a lot given the resources we had. However, without a natural centre-forward like Andy Booth in the lineup, we found it difficult to put the ball in the back of the net on a regular basis.

We lost two games on the trot (including a home shocker against Crystal Palace) and went to Old Trafford on 1 November in 19th place. We were annihilated, simply blown away. By half-time, we were 4–0 down and had been played off the park.

Pleat's solution was typical. We're 4–0 down at half-time? Take off the two Italians, it must be their fault!

I might have understood his logic in taking off both forwards if he had Pele and Diego Maradona on the bench. But even Andy Booth was unavailable, so instead we were substituted by Richie Humphreys, our fifth-choice striker, and Steve Nicol, who not only was a defender but was also thirty-five years old at the time.

Hardly surprising, then, that Pleat's brilliant tactical masterstroke backfired. He was sacked two days later, leaving behind a team which had collected just nine points in thirteen matches and was propping up the Premiership.

Ron Atkinson took over and we bounced back immediately, winning four games in a row, including a 2–0 victory over Arsenal. Suddenly, things were starting to look up again.

I didn't really know what to expect with Big Ron. He is a man of extremes. One moment he is jovial and calm, the next he is a raving maniac. He was always running around, appearing on television or opening some supermarket. He wasn't always around for coaching duties. Sometimes, we wouldn't see him for days at a time. In his absence, Peter Shreeves, a true gentleman in every sense of the word, would run the training sessions.

Then Atkinson would show up, usually on a Thursday or Friday, with a case of champagne and bellow: 'Hello, lads! Let's all scrimmage today! I've got champagne for the winners!'

It was rather bizarre, but it worked. Atkinson knew what he was doing tactically and he had a knack for getting the team fired up. The jokes and image are just an act. He is a sharp guy.

Having said that, he also has an incredibly nasty temper. When he explodes, he really blows up, as I experienced first hand.

We had just lost away to Bolton, 2–3. I had a bad game, as did the rest of the team. Atkinson stormed into the dressing room after the final whistle and got right up into my face.

'Paolo, you're f**king shit when you play away from home!' he roared. His face was bright red and his eyes seemed to bulge out of their sockets. 'You f**king p****, you were so scared out there, you didn't touch the f**king ball once!'

Now, there are many different kinds of manager. Some are quiet, others curse and yell from morning to night. If Atkinson had been the latter kind, I would not have really cared. Yes, it would have annoyed me, because I hate it when people say I play badly away from home. Performing on the road is very difficult, I don't see Dennis Bergkamp tearing it up away from Highbury. That was especially true at Sheffield Wednesday. We weren't exactly Manchester

United, but Atkinson expected me to do everything. I had to be a defender, holding midfielder, winger and centre-forward rolled into one.

Still, I would have taken it. Some managers are just that way. They have to assert themselves by ranting and raving and spewing all sorts of obscenities. But that wasn't the case with Atkinson. He had never raised his voice with me and I had rarely heard him yell at other players.

Even then, I would have let it pass if it hadn't been for what he did next. I remember the scene like it was yesterday. I had just taken off my boots and was sitting on the bench, when he came barrelling forward.

'You are a f**king p****!' he screamed. 'And next time you go to collect your wages, why don't you take a long, hard look in the mirror! You ought to be ashamed of yourself!'

That drove me over the edge. I jumped up on to the bench and lay into him. Our faces were centimetres apart.

'What are you f**king saying?' I whispered.

'What are you f**king saying to me?'

For a moment, we were frozen in time, staring at each other. He had the face of a crazy man.

'Who the f**k do you think you are, talking to me like that?' I screamed. 'You're the one who should be ashamed! You come to training once a week! Once a week! You, of all people, should be silent! Even if they paid you one pound a week, you would still be a thief, because you don't do anything at this club! You are nothing but a thief! You steal money from the club, from the supporters!'

By now, his face had gone from red to purple. He

was shaking, hyperventilating. I could see foam and saliva drooling out of his mouth.

'We've got a shit team and a shit manager!' I roared. 'All of us, we are shit! Today, we were all shit and you dare come here and single me out?'

I could see that he was about to completely lose control.

'I put my ass on the line every single day!' I screamed, pounding my chest. 'I saved your ass all season! I work my ass off every day in training! I earn my wages every day! You come here and you steal, you steal money from the club! You can say I'm shit, you can say I'm a bad person, but don't you ever, ever, dare talk about my wages and my professionalism! I am a professional, you are a thief!'

Atkinson's hands balled up into fists.

He was shaking, his whole face was deformed into a furious scowl. He just kept repeating, over and over, in a hoarse whisper: 'You p****! You f**king p****!'

I leaned towards him and said, as calmly as I could: 'Come on, come here, I'm right here, who's f**king scared now?'

It went off immediately. I was still standing on the bench when the punches started flying. He looked like a man possessed.

Shreeves, Des Walker, Andy Hinchcliffe and others stepped in to separate us. It took several minutes to calm everything down. People can say whatever they like about me, but nobody, nobody, can ever question my value as a professional. I take great pride in my training, I work as hard as anybody I know and I will not allow anybody to question my integrity as a professional.

In retrospect, I don't think either of us meant what we said that day. I certainly didn't. I think perhaps Ron and I are the same way. When we get angry, when we are pushed far enough, we say things we don't mean, certainly not to that degree.

You explode and it just comes out, it's a visceral reaction and it has little to do with your true feelings. In those situations, you want to hurt the other guy as much as possible. He hurt me by saying I was useless away from home, I hurt him by saying he didn't do his job around the club.

What happened next speaks volumes about the kind of man Ron Atkinson is. I know some people view him as a self-promoting joke. Whatever the truth may be, he is an intelligent man, a fair man, a guy who knows how to get the job done. I wish people could judge others by what they do, by the results they obtain, rather than how they appear.

The next time I saw him, everything was forgotten. Everything. It was as if the incident at Bolton had never happened. With another manager it could well have been a different story. I might have been fined or transfer-listed or both. But Atkinson realized that he had a job to do. He had to find a way to keep Sheffield Wednesday in the Premiership, by any means necessary. And he knew that the team's chances of avoiding relegation were that much higher if I was in the side. I am not saying I am indispensable, no one player is bigger than the team. But Atkinson knew that my contribution to the team far outweighed what happened after the Bolton match.

Not only did he not take any action against me, but a few weeks later he gave me the captain's armband. Our skipper,

Peter Atherton, was unavailable for our trip to Barnsley and he chose me to lead the team out. It was something which meant a lot to me. There were plenty of other guys he could have chosen, people like Des Walker for example, who had been at the club for four years and was a former international. Instead, he picked me, a foreigner who had been at Hillsborough for eight months and with whom he had been involved in a fistfight just two weeks before.

I think that says a lot about both of us. On my part, I've had the honour of wearing the captain's armband at Celtic, Sheffield Wednesday and West Ham. People criticize me for all sorts of reasons, but I think it shows that those who work with me every day, that is, the managers and the club staff, know that I am a natural leader who can inspire by example. In the press, I'm always described as 'temperamental' or 'controversial' or 'unreliable', as if I were some kind of raving lunatic. The reality is quite different. Three different British managers have trusted me with the captain's armband in my first full season at their clubs. Would that have happened if I were nothing more than a selfish prima donna? I think not.

More than anything, Atkinson's actions reveal that deep down he and I are very similar. We lost our cool, we blew up, but there was no lingering feeling afterwards, neither of us held a grudge. In those situations when you lose control, your deepest feelings come to the surface, but you don't necessarily express them in the way you would like. Looking back, I think we both believed part of what we were saying. He thought, for whatever reason, that I underperformed away from home. I thought that he should have run the club differently. Perhaps we both still held those views, but that did not mean that we could not get along. We were being honest and that caused us to clash, verbally and physically. But bringing things out into the open is always the best solution, because once your concerns have been aired, you can begin to heal and move on.

Ultimately, it doesn't matter if either one of us was right. The reality is that he and I got the job done, we saved Sheffield Wednesday. Whatever people say about him, his record speaks for itself. He is a winner and one of the better managers I have had in my career.

I am pure inside. There is no hatred in my soul. It is very difficult for me to stay angry at somebody. And I think Atkinson is the same way, as was Tommy Burns at Celtic. We had our fight and that was it. We both had a greater priority: keeping Sheffield Wednesday in the Premiership. Both of us could have walked out at that point. I know many players who would refuse to play for a manager who had physically attacked them. And I know many managers who would never accept working with a player who had questioned their authority and even come to blows with them (don't forget, I experienced that directly with Trapattoni at Juventus and Capello at Milan).

But above all, we both wanted to save Sheffield Wednesday, which is why we stuck around. I will always respect Atkinson for what he did, for being big enough to put the incident aside and do what's best for the team. I haven't seen much of him since he left Wednesday. He goes on television, acts like a caricature of himself, but so what? I don't mind. He's a showman, he's very popular, and he's happy that way.

This does not mean he is not a great football man at the same time. It's not my place to judge or criticize him. What I will say is that it's strange that when people think of him they think of a character, a guy not to be taken too seriously, whereas when they think of Pleat they think of a serious footballing brain. And yet Pleat brought Sheffield Wednesday to the brink of oblivion, while Atkinson took over a last-placed club and kept them in the Premiership, beating clubs like Manchester United and Arsenal along the way.

I finished the season with fourteen goals, twelve in the league, two in the Worthington Cup, all of them from open play. It was a good start to my Premiership career and when I returned from Italy after the summer break, I was looking forward to the new campaign.

CHAPTER NINE

'MY GOD, WHAT'S GOING TO HAPPEN TO YOU?'

We began the 1998/99 Premiership campaign without Ron Atkinson, whose short-term contract as manager was not renewed by the board despite having helped save the club from relegation the previous season. Danny Wilson, fresh from relegation at Barnsley, was our new boss. He was considered a rising young star among managers, but I could tell right away he lacked something. He didn't carry himself with any kind of confidence. When I first met him, he sort of skulked up to me with his tail between his legs and introduced himself. After telling me how happy he was to have me in the team, he put his arm around me.

'Paolo,' he said. 'You've got to help me out. We need to buy some players or we're going to be in big trouble. You are the star of the team here, you have a lot more power than me. You need to talk to the chairman, convince him to spend some money. Will you do that for me, please? Please?'

I just looked at him and said I would do my best, but I knew right away that it wasn't a good sign. I don't mind talking to the chairman or sharing my views with teammates and coaches, but putting pressure on the club to buy players is not part of my job description. It was an absurd situation.

I spoke to chairman Dave Richards a few times, but I wasn't really comfortable doing it. I felt like the pain-in-the-ass foreign star who demands new signings from the chairman. And, to some degree, I felt used by Wilson. It was obvious to all that we desperately needed new players, but it should have been his job to approach the chairman, not mine. He was the manager, he should have had the guts to go up to Richards and say: 'Listen, you hired me to keep you in the Premiership. But I can't do the job with the players at my disposal. You need to give me some cash so that I can bring some other guys in.'

Instead, I think he couldn't bear the thought of facing Richards. He was the new guy, the young manager trying to make a name for himself, and he was terrified of making waves. I think he was also annoyed because Richards would always pay attention to me while not caring about what Wilson had to say. He definitely had some kind of inferiority complex, which in some ways is understandable. He was no Ron Atkinson, a guy who was confident enough to get what he wanted. When Atkinson needed a left-back, he got the club to buy him Andy Hinchcliffe; when he saw a dearth of quality in midfield, he made them buy Niclas Alexandersson. That's how a manager operates.

Of course, it's not really fair to compare a guy like Wilson to Big Ron, a man who was very streetwise and had twenty years of managerial experience. Still, the transition from Atkinson to Wilson was far from easy.

I think I intimidated Wilson. You could tell it was a total learning experience for him and in many ways he wasn't sure what he was doing. One day he came up to me to talk about plans for the new season.

'Listen, Paolo, I know we're having a difficult time getting new players in, but don't worry. I'm on to a very good one. If all goes according to plan, I'll soon be able to buy a top-notch midfielder to give you and Booth some good service.'

'Really?' I replied. 'That's excellent, Danny. Who's coming?'

'Simon Donnelly!' he grinned.

The sad fact is that he wasn't taking the mickey, he was truly excited. I know he was only trying to reassure me, but what kind of a man thinks Simon Donnelly is going to be the saviour of Sheffield Wednesday?

We had a shaky start to the season. We opened with a home loss to West Ham (1–0), then trounced Spurs away (3–0, I scored the second) and then were beaten again at Hillsborough, this time by Aston Villa, 1–0. I twisted my ankle badly in that game and the team doctor told me to take two weeks off. But Wilson, for some reason, insisted I return in our next match, away to Derby County.

He walked up to me and said: 'You're playing at Derby and that's final.'

'Excuse me?' I replied.

'You heard me. I said you have to play against Derby. No discussions.'

This was the new Danny Wilson, or rather, Danny Wilson impersonating a tough guy. The smiles had disappeared, all of a sudden he was very serious.

I looked at him and said: 'No. I'm injured. My ankle is in

bad shape. I know my own body, I know what I can and cannot do. And besides, the doctor agrees with me.'

He took a few deep breaths and his eyes narrowed.

'You're doing this on purpose, aren't you?' he hissed, halfway between pleading and anger. 'You're doing this just to spite me, aren't you?'

He stormed off in a huff. I just shook my head. Did he really think I was doing this to spite him? Why would I? He was an absolute nobody to me. He was just another Sheffield Wednesday employee, just like I was. I felt he was beginning to lose it.

Anyway, we lost at Derby (1–0), but followed it up with a good win over Blackburn (3–0, I got the third). But there were storm clouds looming.

We were knocked out of the Worthington Cup by Cambridge United. We somehow lost the first leg at home (1–0) and could only draw the return leg (1–1). Simply put, they were up for it and we were terrible.

Wilson obviously thought that reading out the riot act was the right way to handle the situation and after the match he tore into us. He went on for a while, criticizing our performance. He was very harsh, but then he had a right to be, because we were awful. I sat there and took it, like the rest of my teammates, until he said: 'We need to show more commitment! And as for those two Italians . . .'

I jumped up and interrupted him right away.

'What's this bullshit about *the two Italians*?' I said. 'What the hell are you saying? My name is Paolo. His name is Benny. We are not *the two Italians*! We play for Sheffield Wednesday just like everybody else. If you want to talk about me, you call me Paolo, if you want to talk about him you call him Benny. You don't call us *the two Italians*. What the hell are you trying to say?'

Wilson fell silent, but I could see he was still very angry. I didn't care. I was angry too. I can accept my responsibilities if I play badly, what I can't accept is sheer xenophobia from a frustrated nobody. If he had said 'Benny and Paolo were shit' I could have accepted that. Everybody is entitled to their opinion. But why did he have to say *the two Italians*?

He decided to punish me by leaving me on the substitutes' bench in our next fixture, away to Wimbledon. Big mistake. We lost 2–1 and we were awful once again, though I came on in the second half and pulled a goal back.

By this point in the season, I had started five games, come on as a sub in another, and scored three goals. I wasn't having a bad season and, in spite of Wilson, we could have at least aimed for a mid-table finish. Carbone was in fine form, as was Alexandersson, and Wim Jonk gave us some shape and experience in the middle of the park.

I don't think anybody could have predicted what would happen next.

Sheffield Wednesday versus Arsenal, 26 September 1998, Hillsborough. The Push Heard Around the World.

To think that it had started so calmly. In the tunnel before the game, I chatted amiably with Patrick Vieira. He and I had been teammates at AC Milan in the spring of 1996. At the time, he was a 19-year-old prodigy, trying to earn a spot in an impossibly large squad. I was a veteran in mid-career who, in the back of his mind, had already decided to move on. He was a hard man, a ball-winner. I was a winger, a dribbler. He was born in Dakar. I was born in Rome. We had little in common, but we had still developed a friendship. Now, we were face to face again and as I waited in that tunnel the last thing on my mind was that Patrick could become the flashpoint of my nightmare.

It was a physical affair from the start. That's just the way Arsenal play, but we were not to be intimidated. We held our own quite well and it didn't look like spilling over into anything nasty until a minute from the half-time whistle. Vieira had the ball in the Arsenal half, facing his own goal. He was being pressurized by Jonk and Richie Humphreys but did well to turn between the two of them. It looked like he was going to get away, when Jonk tugged his shirt, bringing him to his knees. Frustrated and angry, Vieira lost his cool, got up, and shoved Jonk to the ground.

I've been criticized many times for what I did next, usually by people who refuse to believe that I was acting in good faith. I ran some twenty yards to where Vieira was standing, but I did it to calm him down. We were laughing together less than an hour earlier, all I wanted to do was tell him to cool it.

Of course, nobody gave me the benefit of the doubt. All I heard was 'That Di Canio, he's a right troublemaker. Look at him running across the pitch to get involved!' Which is rubbish. I did it for a reason, I did it because Patrick and I were friends, because I did not want things to boil over. If it hadn't been Vieira, if it had been some guy I didn't know, I would not have done it. But of course nobody bothered to find out the truth. Nobody bothered to ask Patrick what happened. They were all too preoccupied with crucifying me.

I grabbed Vieira and said: 'Patrick, come on. There's no need for that. Cut it out!'

He didn't have time to reply. Martin Keown, who had also sprinted over, stepped between us and elbowed me in the face. Maybe Keown thought I had run over to attack Vieira and he felt the need to protect his teammate. Whatever the case may be, Keown smashed his elbow into my nose. Immediately I felt a sharp, hollow pain shooting up into my brain. I felt something crack and all of a sudden I was blinded by pain.

My instinctive reaction was to grab hold of him, to hurt him back somehow. I kicked him in the shin. He whipped around and we grabbed each other's throats. It just happened so fast. It was all over in twenty, twenty-five seconds.

Petter Rudi dragged me away. I was livid. The pain in my nose had spread across my skull, I had no clue what was going on. But as Petter held me back, I slowly regained control.

Paul Alcock strode purposefully towards me. My first reaction was: 'Damn, he's going to send both of us off! What a time to get a red card!' But then I saw that he wasn't even looking at Keown. He made a beeline straight for me, as if Keown didn't even exist. I realized that I was going to be the only one punished even before he called me over. But that was the final straw. Incidents like this happen all the time and the referee, even the most incompetent, inexperienced referee, usually calls both players over.

That's not what Alcock did. I was the only one singled out. And that's what pushed me over the edge. It was the sheer injustice of it. I can accept that I should have been sent off for reacting to Keown's elbow, regardless of whether it was intentional or not (and to this day, I don't know if he hit me on purpose or not). I can also accept that when I ran over to talk to Vieira, nobody was going to give me the benefit of the doubt. They were always going to assume the worst, that's just how people are when it comes to me.

What I don't understand is why Alcock did not reprimand us both. If we had both been called over, none of this would have happened. Instead, I felt like I was the only one who was going to be punished. He didn't consult the linesman, he didn't think twice about it. He just showed me that red card.

Later, after I had left the pitch, the linesman came over and told him that Keown needed to be sent off as well. There is little doubt in my mind that if the linesman hadn't taken the initiative of sorting out Alcock, Keown would have stayed on the pitch.

Of course, I didn't know any of this at the time. All I knew was that I was the only one being punished. So I pushed Alcock away. It wasn't a violent gesture, it was a gesture of disappointment, that's all it was. I was turning my body away from him at the time, as if to say: 'Forget it, get out of here!' I didn't insult him, I didn't say anything to him, I was just angry and disappointed that I was being sent off.

People described it as an 'assault'. Believe me, if I had wanted to assault Alcock, if I had wanted to do something violent, it would have been totally different.

And then he fell over. I've watched the video a million times and to this day I still don't understand how he managed to fall over like that. I could push my eight-year-old daughter Ludovica that way and she wouldn't fall over. She might take a step or two backwards, but that would be it. Instead Alcock kept going backwards, dragging his leg along the ground before collapsing on his buttocks. It certainly looked bizarre. When I saw him fall I was as surprised as anyone. My first reaction was that somebody must have been crouching behind him, like in one of those old slapstick comedies. That is the only way it is humanly possible to fall over like that. There simply is no other way.

By the time he had picked himself up I was already walking off the pitch. It was utter chaos around me. On the sidelines, I could see Danny Wilson's grim and somewhat confused expression. The fans were going nuts. They knew they had seen something very unusual. I was holding my nose, I could feel blood. I had been trying to show Alcock, trying to explain what happened, but to no avail.

As often happens in these situations, tragedy spilled into farce. As I strode up the sidelines towards the tunnel, Nigel Winterburn was right next to me. He had taken the trouble of running clear across from the other side of the pitch with the sole purpose of insulting me. At first, I didn't even notice him amidst the chaos and confusion, but then I heard his raspy voice bellowing in my ear above the din.

'You f**king bastard!' he was screaming. 'You're done! You f**king Italian bastard! You're finished!'

On and on he went. When I watched videos of it later I realized he must have been yelling in my ear for a good thirty or forty seconds. I looked up at him and the funniest thing happened: he jumped back and cowered in terror. Watch a video of the incident if you get the chance. It's hilarious. One second Winterburn is yapping away like one of those hyperactive dogs and the next he's retreating, wetting his pants in fear. And to think that all I did was look at him. At the time it obviously didn't strike me as funny, but now, two years later, when I watch the tape, it's genuinely hysterical.

I'm not the only who noticed. Indeed, when I arrived at West Ham one of the first thing the lads did was bring up the incident with Winterburn. They were in stitches, laughing themselves silly: 'Look at Winterburn! He looks like a scared little puppy!'

And they were right. At that moment, Winterburn did look terrified. In situations such as those, men regress to their primal instincts. I wasn't going to be bullied by Winterburn's insults. My reaction was a street reaction, it's the kind of thing you grow up with, not the kind of thing you learn. It was the kind of look that said: 'Are you sure you want a piece of me?' And it was enough to make him look silly.

It's ironic that now he's my teammate at West Ham. I don't hold grudges, to me what is in the past stays in the past. I think he's the same. We have both put the incident behind us, if anything having him as a teammate taught me that in football, as in life, you never know when you might run into somebody again. I don't know if we're going to be friends. What I do know is that I can count on him one hundred percent, and I think he knows he can expect the same from me. Winterburn was backing up a teammate, Keown, that day. He may have been wrong in his actions, but it shows what he's made of. I know we can work well together.

Wilson didn't say anything as I walked past him and entered the tunnel. The blood was racing through my veins, my mind was all over the place. The stewards became a blur as I flew past them into the dressing room. Benny Carbone stormed in right after me. He was suspended that day and had been watching from the director's box.

'Are you okay, Paolo?' he asked. He looked like he had seen a ghost.

I didn't answer. All I wanted to do was talk to Betta. She was in Italy at the time and I thought she might be watching the game on television. I wanted to reassure her. As it turned out, she was unaware of what had happened.

'Don't worry, something bad happened today, but it's alright, everything is going to be alright,' I told her over the phone. 'I got sent off, I got angry and pushed the referee. I think I'm in trouble, but everything is going to be OK.'

My main priority was that she hear it from me first. Her immediate reaction wasn't good.

'No, no. Paolo, what did you do?' she sobbed. 'Why? Why? What are they going to do to you? My God, Paolo, you're always the same, when will you learn? God, Paolo, what's going to happen to you?'

I reassured her as best I could and then went straight to the showers. Betta is the centre of my world. She keeps me calm and balanced. I couldn't let her worry.

When I got out of the showers, Matteo Roggi was waiting for me. He was in Sheffield by sheer coincidence and, in retrospect, I'm glad he was there. He told me a car was waiting to take me home and that the club had instructed me to go back to Italy until things cooled down. By the time I had finished dressing, it was half-time and the team was back in the dressing room.

My teammate and club captain Peter Atherton came up to me. He had a strange expression, halfway between a smirk and a smile.

'So, what are they going to do to you, now?' he wanted to know, entirely oblivious of the situation. 'I reckon it's pretty serious, mate. I think you'll get at least eight weeks.'

He was basically grinning and I remember not understanding why. At the time, I had more important things to worry about than what went on in Peter Atherton's mind, but looking back it did seem rather strange that he seemed to enjoy my misfortune.

Matteo and I drove home. The next few hours are a blur. The club told me I had been suspended indefinitely and confirmed that I should return to Italy. Tommy Burns rang me up almost right away. It was good to hear his voice. He reassured me, told me everything was going to be alright, though at the time there wasn't going to be anything that would make me feel better.

We were able to book the very last flight out of Heathrow. I went direct to Terni and the waiting began.

I knew I was going to be punished, I knew it was going to be serious, but I had no concept of the kind of venom and xenophobia that was in store for me. I don't like to talk about the media and the views expressed, but in this case I think it's important. The initial coverage set the tone for everything that was to follow.

There is reality and then there are different versions of reality. Sometimes, if you repeat something often enough, it becomes the truth or, at least, the accepted truth. Watch the video of the Alcock incident again, and you'll see what I mean.

Certain things were never questioned, nobody took the time to think about Keown's part in the incident or why I decided to get involved or, indeed, Winterburn's behaviour.

That night, on BBC's *Match of the Day*, while describing the incident, the commentator said: 'It seems to me Keown was only protecting himself . . . Winterburn sees it as his job to protect Martin Keown from Di Canio . . . He [Di Canio] has no reason whatsoever to get involved . . . He has flattened the referee and I think his Premiership career may well be at an end.'

Those comments laid down the agenda for the media's treatment. They made certain assumptions, i.e. that Keown was totally innocent, that Winterburn was only protecting a teammate (as if a guy like Martin Keown needs Nigel Winterburn to protect him), that I had no business getting involved and that my career in England was over.

As a result of all this, the basic premise was that I was some raving lunatic who had destroyed his own Premiership future without any kind of provocation. There was little critical, objective analysis of what happened. Many took it as a given that I would be banned for life: anything less than that and I should consider myself lucky.

There was little mention of the fact that Keown hit me.

And yet, on *Match of the Day*, Danny Wilson himself said in a post-match interview: 'There's one or two things that went on off the ball. I know for a fact that Paolo was punched.'

Nobody picked up on that. And the strange thing is that Wilson seemed to forget that minor detail in the following weeks. It never came up again. Ever.

I didn't expect Wilson to defend my actions. He suspended me immediately, which made sense. The best way to ingratiate the club with the Football Association was to show that they were taking the incident very seriously. From that standpoint it was the logical thing to do.

What is more difficult to explain is why, apart from that post-match BBC interview, he never mentioned the fact that I was hit. It wouldn't have justified my actions, but it would certainly have helped to explain them. It could have been a mitigating factor. But no, all we got from Wilson was silence.

A few weeks later, the Football Association quietly overturned Keown's red card. A direct sending off equals an automatic three-game ban. In Keown's case, the red card was simply wiped off. It was as if it had never, ever happened. Just like that. Whatever responsibility Keown might have had was removed in one fell swoop.

I bear no grudge against Martin Keown. He is a very hard, committed defender; in my view, he's the best central defender in the Premiership. He is strong and fast and does whatever it takes to win. I respect him a lot as a professional. In my opinion, he could have easily been a star in Serie A. I know he doesn't have that many caps for England, and I think that's surprising. Maybe he only improved over the last few years or perhaps he just wasn't rated until recently. Either way, he is an exceptional player.

I would not have expected Keown to come out and say,

'Yes, I smashed my elbow into Di Canio's face and I think that's why he reacted the way he did.' But then, nobody bothered to ask him directly. It was just assumed that he was a victim and nothing more.

We barricaded ourselves in my home in Terni. Betta was a rock by my side, calming me down, helping me deal with the situation. After the initial shock, she actually took it quite well, especially when you consider that she had just given birth to Lucrezia. With Ludovica it was more difficult. Even at six years of age, she knew things weren't quite right.

She didn't understand why we hadn't gone back to Sheffield. The phone would ring constantly, journalists ringing us up at all hours of the day and night. We would sit there, and let the answering machine pick up. If it was a friend or a family member we would answer, if it was a journalist we wouldn't. More often than not it was a hang-up. I can still hear the tone on the answering machine after the umpteenth hang-up.

Meanwhile, another media pack waited outside our front door. They came from everywhere, not just the tabloids. It seems I had become a cultural phenomenon, a symbol of all that was wrong with football and society. Every time I peeked out my window I would see them, waiting for me to come out. The guy from Sky, Rob McCaffrey, must have been out there for weeks.

All this made leaving the house very difficult and so we rarely did. Betta's family was our link to the outside world. The toughest part was explaining to Ludovica what had happened, why our lives had been turned upside down. I told her we were playing a game, hide-and-seek, and that nobody could know we were there. It's ironic, but it's just like that film *Life is Beautiful*, where the Roberto Benigni character tells his son that being in a concentration camp is really one gigantic game.

About a week later I saw Ian Wright and Neil Ruddock re-creating the Alcock incident as part of their goal celebration. Ruddock pushed over Wright and they all had a right giggle about it. To them it must have seemed like the funniest thing in the world. I can still see those two clowns laughing away. I suppose it was pretty funny, though at the time I didn't see it that way.

'Look at these two morons!' I said to Betta as we watched on television. 'These two jokers have just made everything worse for me! They think it's funny, but the FA won't see it that way. Now, I'm going to be banned for life and I'll have them to thank!'

Fortunately it didn't turn out that way. And when I walked into the West Ham dressing room four months later, who should be there but the two idiots, Ruddock and Wright. And what did they do? You guessed it, they performed an encore of the Alcock–Di Canio goal celebration. This time I laughed along. They're great guys and I know it was all in fun.

It seemed that everybody in the world wanted to get in touch with me. Everybody, that is, except Sheffield Wednesday. Nobody from the club called me. Not Wilson, not Richards, not even Graham Mackrell, the club secretary. Several weeks passed before I heard from the club. I felt totally abandoned.

My family was close to me of course, as were some

friends. It is in times like these that you discover who your true friends are. In fact, I don't even like to use that word 'friend'. To me it's a huge word, it gets thrown around a lot.

Apart from the non-stop barrage of journalists, I had plenty of people ringing me up to see how I was, but many were guys whom I had not spoken to in years. Acquaintances, former teammates, friends of friends, they seemed interested in knowing only one thing: whether or not I was finished with football.

'So, man, what are they going to do to you, now? You really screwed up, didn't you?'

I cannot tell you the number of times I heard that. These people cared more about whether my ban would break world records than whether or not me and my family were okay. It was morbid, like those people who drive by car wrecks after accidents, just to leer at the bloodshed.

It was the usual stuff. Crazy Paolo had messed up again. While the English press was busy creating a monster, a symbol for all the foreign evils in the world, in Italy they were shaking their heads knowingly.

'We told you so. For all his talent, that Di Canio is mentally unstable.'

It did not matter to them or to anyone that I was a human being, a father with a family and two daughters. No, it was Di Canio the beast, the animal, and that was it.

I knew I had to fight it, but it was difficult. Perhaps an insane man would have had an easier time. He could just go on thinking that he was totally in the right, that it was him against the world and that he would one day triumph.

But I am not crazy. I understood that the situation was

more complex, that while I was neither the monster the British said I was nor the lunatic the Italians were depicting, I was struggling, mentally and physically. I was a man who had erred and now lived with doubts. I felt that I had to be convinced that I could return. But when you don't know if you will ever be allowed to kick a ball again in your life, if you fear that your livelihood, your profession, the thing you have worked your entire life towards is about to be taken away from you, it becomes very difficult to go on.

I never believed I was insane, but I knew that I was unwell and it scared me. The cracks were beginning to appear, the first symptoms of the condition which would afflict me a few months later began to come to the surface. I had trouble sleeping, I was nauseous, I would awake shaking and frightened, short of breath.

Fortunately, my true friends rallied around me. One of those was Andrea Alciati. I had met him when I was at Juventus. I used to have fresh truffles delivered to my house, straight from the farmers. Andrea was the delivery boy who brought them over.

One day his Volkswagen broke down, and I ended up inviting him to dinner. We hit it off right away and our relationship grew from there. I think he was the younger brother I never had.

His father Guido ran a famous restaurant in Costigliole D'Asti, a few miles from Turin, called Da Guido. Year after year, it is ranked among the very best in Italy. It is one of those culinary paradises you only read about. When I go back there, I feel at home, whether I'm chatting with Andrea and his brothers, Ugo and Piero, or eating his mother Lidia's chocolate pear cake, which she makes especially for me.

I'll never forget the day Guido passed away and Andrea called me, in tears. I had just arrived in Sheffield and I remember Betta and I holding each other as we tried to console him over the phone. At that moment, I understood what fraternal love is and that it is not limited to blood relations. It is something which grows between two people, a man and a man, a woman and a woman, sometimes a man and a woman. That is why I asked him and his wife, Paola, to serve as godparents to Lucrezia.

Andrea was there for me when I was back in Terni. He gave himself up for me, he walked alongside me through my ordeal. No, he did not understand what I was going through because he was not in my shoes, just as I could not comprehend what it must be like to lose one's father. But it is not a question of understanding, it's a question of sharing. I shared my pain with Andrea and he shared his with me. We are brothers.

I tried to stay focused while in Terni. In the morning, I would sneak out of the house and go and train. Avoiding the press wasn't that difficult, since the city centre of Terni is made up of a series of narrow streets and alleyways. If you know your way around, it is not too hard to pass unnoticed.

I would train with Michele Palmieri, a personal trainer whom I knew from my days at Napoli. Every day we would go down to Ternana's ground, the Stadio Liberati and spend several hours doing sprints, runs and other exercises. I tried to push myself as hard as I could, I wanted to kill myself through training. In many ways, the physical pain was liberating. The workload Michele assigned me was very heavy, but I relished the struggle and asked for more. I trained as hard as I ever have. When you believe in your heart that you are alone against the rest of the world, you either shrivel up and die or become capable of achieving wonderful things.

Looking back, it's ironic that I had returned to where it all began. Twelve years earlier I was an 18-year-old kid, on loan to the lower divisions, trying to make it as a professional footballer. I was brimming with confidence, but deep down I had no clue what the future held. Now, I had returned to the beginning. I was thirty years old, I had a wife and two kids, I had played for some of the biggest clubs in the world. I was trying to salvage my career as a professional, but, like twelve years earlier, I had no idea whether I would ever play football again.

My hearing was scheduled for 23 October 1998. Sheffield Wednesday had given assurances that they would provide a solicitor to represent me. Until the eleventh hour however, I had no idea as to what the club's legal strategy would be. Given the witch-hunt climate at the time, their approach was tantamount to suicide. It made no sense at all, especially when *The Times* was saying that I was 'without a friend or supporter in English football' and another paper had compared my actions to the Hillsborough disaster. Only a twisted, demented mind can compare pushing a referee to a tragedy in which 98 innocent people lost their lives. But that is the kind of hysteria I was up against. There were many who wanted to ban me for life.

And yet there were plenty of mitigating factors and, more importantly, there were plenty of precedents, cases where players had pushed referees and received lesser punishments. David Batty had shoved a referee and received a two-match ban, while Emmanuel Petit was banned for one game for a similar offence. In those cases, the referee had not fallen to the ground, but anybody reviewing the videos would have seen that my push was no harder or more violent than Batty's or Petit's. The difference was that Alcock had lost his balance and the other referees hadn't.

Furthermore, it wasn't the first time that Alcock had collapsed theatrically after making contact with a player. In 1991, Frank Sinclair, then on loan at West Bromwich Albion, had appeared to headbutt Alcock and he went down just as easily. It was a lower division game, there were fewer cameras present and the incident received less attention, but even then there was speculation that Alcock's tumble seemed a little strange.

Moreno Roggi understood how serious the situation was. Without proper legal representation I would have been left out to dry. At first I did not understand why Sheffield Wednesday weren't doing everything they could to defend me, to ensure I got as light a ban as possible. After all, I had been their leading scorer the previous season and I was an integral part of the team. Without me, their prospects for avoiding relegation would have been very slim.

Then it dawned on me why we had not got round to discussing legal precedent and legal briefs before the hearing. The chairman, Dave Richards, couldn't care less whether I got banned forever or not. You see, the last thing he wanted to do was make waves. If he stood up to the judges at the disciplinary hearing, he risked upsetting the powers-that-be. From his perspective, it made much more sense to roll over and play dead, entrusting my future, my career, to the judges. That way he wouldn't run the risk of upsetting anybody at the FA.

However, this approach to the hearing would not just have sacrificed me, Paolo Di Canio. It would also have sacrificed the club, depriving the fans of their record signing and so hurting the very people who fork out their hard-earned cash to support the club, week in, week out.

It makes my blood boil that men who claim they love a football club can do things like that. There are plenty of Sheffield fans who pay good money, who make serious sacrifices, to support their team. Actions such as these are simply a slap in the face.

Think about how Sheffield Wednesday handled the situation. They turned me into a monster. They depicted me as a madman, a ticking time bomb which could go off at any time. They are entitled to their opinions, they can think whatever they like about me. I really don't care. But rubbishing me in public, trashing my reputation when I was still under contract to them was simply stupid. It made no sense.

Whether they liked it or not I was still an asset to the club. I had a certain value in the transfer market. And the first responsibility of management, as any economics textbook will tell you, is to increase shareholder value by protecting and exploiting the assets available. Instead of protecting me, instead of maximizing my value, they did everything they could to destroy me.

Let's think for a minute. Say the club had decided that after the Alcock incident they no longer felt I could be

Celtic and I hit it off right away, as I score one goal and set up another two on my debut.

Left: I go crazy as I'm hugged by a fan at Celtic Park. There is no such thing as too much passion at Celtic.

Below: My friend, skipper and fish-head phobic, Peter Grant.

Left: Celtic manager Tommy Burns – a fiery competitor, a genuine mate and a guy who deserved so much more.

Above: Martin Keown elbowing me in the face during *that* infamous fracas at Hillsborough in September 1998. I'll never know if it was intentional, but I do know it hurt like hell.

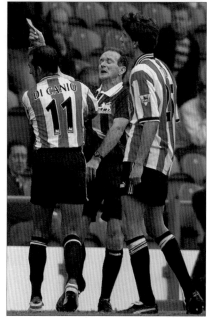

Right: Referee Paul Alcock just before his slow-motion tumble – the moment that changed my career in English football. But then, without it, I might never have joined West Ham…

Above: Celebrating with Benny Carbone during a league match against Southampton. I had many great times and fond memories at Wednesday.

Left: A new adventure. Harry Redknapp and I on the West Ham training pitch at Chadwell Heath. Harry isn't just a great bloke, he knows how to listen.

Above: Training properly is the key to a professional career. To me, every training session is like a World Cup Final.

Below: Referees and I still don't see eye to eye – and we never will if they refuse me penalties time and again.

Frank Lampard and I fighting over who gets to take the penalty against Bradford in the 5–4 thriller back in February 2000. There was no way I was going to let him have it.

Left: Great football is like great art. You have to be a connoisseur.

Right: Trevor Sinclair and I on the training pitch. Just one of the many great lads at Upton Park.

Below: My volleyed strike against Wimbledon that won the Goal of the Season in 1999/2000. As Harry said, I do this in training all the time…

Right: West Ham v Arsenal, Upton Park, 1999/2000, and I'm having a crack at goal before Tony Adams can intervene. And there's my old mate Martin Keown again!

Left: Here I am at the 1999 Ternana v Napoli game with Betta's sister, Stefania and our friends Betty, Vincenzo 'Vichingo', Davide 'Orsetto' Fabio 'La Maschia', Massimiliano 'Porcone' and Fulvio Biscione.

Below: The highlight of the 2000/01 season for me was my goal in West Ham's 1–0 triumph over Manchester United in the FA Cup 5th round back in January. I beat the offside trap (inset) and calmly passed the ball around keeper Barthez, and Old Trafford was in shock.

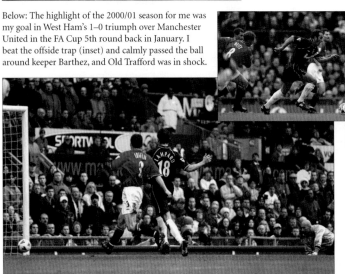

trusted and that I should be sold as soon as possible. Wouldn't it have made sense at that point to make sure I got as short a ban as possible? Wouldn't it have been better if they had kept talking about me in glowing terms? That way they could have received more money for me in a transfer situation. Are you more likely to buy an apple if the vendor tells you it is ripe, sweet and juicy or if he tells you that it is rotten to the core?

Sheffield Wednesday created a situation for themselves where they had no choice but to sell me. And every single club in Europe knew that. What's worse, along the way, they managed to tarnish my reputation as a footballer as well. Those are possibly the two worst things you can do when selling an asset. Which is why West Ham United were able to buy me for next to nothing.

The strange thing is that Danny Wilson was a victim of this as well, though he probably doesn't even realize it. I think at first he might have even been glad that I was banned. That way, he would have a perfect excuse if the club got relegated. After all, he could say that losing his top goalscorer and best player traumatized the club so much that staying in the Premiership became impossible. Of course, that scenario would have suited Richards just fine: he could then blame everything on me, because I would be gone by then.

In many ways, I feel sorry for Wilson. Everybody says what a nice guy he is. What I will say is that he was simply in way over his head at Hillsborough and his chairman did little to help him. In fact, by keeping Wilson around even as the club hurtled towards relegation, but not giving him any money to spend to strengthen the team, Richards wasn't doing Wilson any favours. Although the Chairman appeared to be supportive, in fact he was pushing the club towards relegation.

Wilson's reputation as a 'nice guy' may be intact, but so is his reputation as a guy who managed to get two clubs relegated in three Premiership seasons. And in the only season in which he did manage to survive, the team was terrible and only a super-human effort from Benny Carbone, after I was banned, helped him avoid the drop. It all came to light last year. If you run through the squads, player for player, Sheffield Wednesday were no worse than Southampton and certainly better than Wimbledon or Bradford City. The difference was that they all had good managers and team spirit. Paul Jewell did an excellent job at Bradford, Dave Jones and later Glenn Hoddle kept Southampton afloat. Even Wimbledon, despite all of their problems with Egil Olsen, managed to finish ahead of Wednesday because at least they had their 'Crazy Gang' ethos. But with Wilson, there was nothing. No personality, no guidance, no real strength.

Anyway, since we were heading into a hearing totally unprepared, we had no choice but to get our own lawyers. Naturally, guess who had to pay for them? Sheffield Wednesday wouldn't foot the bill; to them, their 'we throw ourselves to the mercy of the court' defence was more than enough.

Moreno Roggi called in Claudio Minghetti, an Italian lawyer who specializes in sports law. Except Minghetti was involved in a car accident in Germany, just one week before the hearing. At the last moment, we had to turn to his partner, a guy named Franco Censi. Now Censi knew absolutely nothing about sport. My daughter Lucrezia, who is two years old, can probably tell you more about football than Censi. What he lacked in background knowledge, however, he more than made up for in sheer hard work. The guy was a machine, a total egghead. We flew him to London, he locked himself in a library and, in three days, studied everything there was to study in FA disciplinary procedures and legal precedents. Simply put, he was amazing and I owe him a lot.

We drove up for the hearing, which was held at Bramall Lane, Sheffield United's ground. I went in, accompanied by Franco Censi, Howard Culley, a solicitor and director at the club and Gordon Taylor of the Professional Footballers' Association. Culley was telling me that I faced a twelve-month ban or worse. He was very negative about my prospects. Censi and Taylor were more cautious. Incidentally, I have to thank Taylor as well. Many foreign footballers say the PFA doesn't really care about overseas players, that it's a very insular organization. That was not my experience at all. I thought Taylor did his best to help me, even though in those circumstances he could only do so much.

I ended up with an eleven-match ban: three for the sending off and eight for the push. Culley told me I had been very fortunate. The sentence meant I could return on 26 December 1998. I told the media that I thought the ruling was fair and said goodbye to the fans, telling them I would see them all on Boxing Day. At the time, I really did believe both things. I thought I would be back and I thought I had received an appropriate sentence.

Looking back now, however, there was nothing fair about the punishment I received. It was way out of proportion with what other players had got. You punish the action, not the consequence. My push on Alcock was no different, no more violent, than what others had done. And they received one or two-match suspensions, plus the automatic three-game ban if they were also sent off. What made mine look worse was that the referee fell over. If he had been bigger and stronger, if he had been, say Uriah Rennie or Mike Reid, he probably wouldn't have collapsed to the ground. That's why I think a six-match ban would have been appropriate: three for the automatic red card and three for the push. I say three for the push, instead of one or two, because Alcock falling to the ground was not a nice image for the game of football. But *eleven* matches! That's three months. That's twice as long. That is just a ridiculous punishment! I became a scapegoat, I was sacrificed up as an example.

What I find truly humiliating was the way Sheffield Wednesday and others managed to convince me that I had got off lightly or, at least, had received a fair sentence. Simply put, they stitched me up. They fooled me into thinking that they had helped, whereas in reality they didn't lift a finger. The only ones who stood by my side at the time were the fans, Gordon Taylor, Moreno Roggi and our lawyer, Censi. Beyond that, I was alone.

They even had the gall to tell me I would have received a punishment worse than the eight months Eric Cantona got for attacking the Crystal Palace fan at Selhurst Park, three years earlier. Again, let's think about this. In the middle of the game, Cantona went and karate-kicked a spectator in the head. First of all, Cantona's was a premeditated gesture. He didn't just lash out, he ran over to the fan and attacked him. Secondly, it was a vicious, violent act. You can kill somebody by kicking him in the head, if you strike him in the temple. Finally, and most serious of all, his actions could have sparked a riot or a pitch invasion. There were no barriers at Selhurst Park. What if the fan he assaulted had twenty hooligan friends in the stands, all too eager to go and avenge their mate? What would have happened then?

And yet, after the initial outcry, Cantona was greeted as a hero upon his return. I don't know if it was because he played for Manchester United, a team loved by the media, rather than Sheffield Wednesday, a club entirely irrelevant to public opinion. Whatever the case may be, any attempt to compare our actions is ridiculous.

After the hearing, the club told me to return to Italy. I was scheduled to come back to Sheffield in early December to resume training with my teammates. The media pressure had relented a bit, but the club's handling of the hearing had left a bad aftertaste. I knew something was going on, but I did not know what. I had suspicions, fears gnawing away in my mind. It seemed like they were taking my absence a little too well.

The days slipped by and I followed my usual routine. Palmieri was with me and I trained as intensely as ever. I sought refuge in physical exertion, it was what kept me going during a very difficult time. It was tough because, as had happened before, there was no contact with the club. Only a wall of silence. Nobody called me to see how I was doing, it was as if I had died or disappeared.

I returned to Sheffield on 27 November, as agreed with Wilson. The atmosphere I found was terrible. I was angry that the club hadn't protected me. I felt like I couldn't trust anybody. They had let me down once before, they could do it again. Each night I would go home to an empty house – Betta and the girls were still in Italy – and lie awake all night. My mind was raging, thoughts and fears chased each other through my brain. Why had Sheffield Wednesday forsaken me?

I couldn't sleep. When I did wake up, the sheets were soaking wet and a jackhammer was pounding my brain. I'd look at the mirror and see a pale, empty figure staring back at me. In the morning, I was nauseous, I felt like I could be sick at any time. I told the club I needed to go home and flew back to Terni.

I am not the most relaxed person to begin with, but I had become a bundle of nerves. I was edgy, paranoid, crushed by layer upon layer of stress. After a couple of days, Sheffield Wednesday told me to return immediately. I simply couldn't. I wasn't fit to travel, I wasn't fit to do anything. The hardship of the previous months had taken its toll. I had bags under my eyes, I hadn't slept in days, everywhere I went the nausea and stress followed me.

Strangely enough, the only respite I could find was in training. Palmieri would take me down to the empty, ageing Liberati ground and I would pound my way up and down the stadium steps, sprinting until I felt like my lungs were going to explode. From a physical perspective, I pushed myself into extreme, uncharted waters. I punished my body, as if somehow I could transfer the pain and stress from my mind to my quadriceps and thighs, lungs and heart.

But the second I stopped running, it all came rushing back. Just as my heartbeat slowed after a series of wind sprints, my brain would begin pounding away again until I could barely stand. I needed help. Moreno Roggi sent me to a local doctor. He told me there was nothing wrong with me physically, apart from the lack of sleep. I was under extreme psychological stress however, and he advised me to see a psychologist for a psychiatric evaluation. I did, and was told that in my current state I was unfit to travel and work. I needed total rest in a stress-free environment. Otherwise, things would only get worse.

We explained this to Sheffield Wednesday and sent them a medical certificate. I was suffering from a medical condition, similar to that which had afflicted me at Lazio and at Celtic. Instead of supporting me, instead of trying to alleviate the situation, they reacted by fining me two weeks' wages.

What's worse, they communicated with me exclusively via Moreno. Nobody at Sheffield had the guts to pick up the phone and talk to me. Not Wilson, not Richards, nobody. It was as if they just didn't care about me.

At the same time, they played dumb with the media. They kept saying they didn't know where I was, that I had 'done a runner', that I had disappeared into thin air and they had no way of getting in contact with me. That was simply not the case. Every day I was getting dozens of calls from journalists. If they could find me, why couldn't Sheffield Wednesday? It seemed that the only people in all of England who did not have a way of getting in touch with me were employees of the club. Of course, the media never questioned this. They just lapped up the club's side of the story. There is this belief in England that once a foreign player crosses the Channel, he might as well be in outer space, far away and unreachable. The truth is that they knew exactly where to find me. They just didn't want to find me.

They also went out of their way to mock my medical condition. I was the 'dodgy foreigner' who got the 'dodgy doctor' to send them the 'dodgy sicknote'. And the tabloids simply ate it all up. I knew what was going on and with each day that passed my condition grew worse and worse. My psychological problem was no laughing matter. Think about it. I was not ashamed to say I was suffering psychologically, but it wasn't an easy thing to admit to. Football is a macho world, the mere suggestion that you have some kind of mental problem is usually greeted by howls of derision. And yet I faced up to it. I had to deal with it, while my club, my teammates, were treating it all as a big joke.

Again, as I mentioned before, in retrospect their attitude made no sense at all. I was an asset to the club; even if they had already decided to get rid of me, it would have made sense to help nurse me back to health and then sell me. This way, they simply smeared my reputation even further.

Another week passed and the situation didn't change. We sent them another medical certificate; if anything I was worse than before thanks to the club's insensitive and mean-spirited reaction. They fined me again, questioned the validity of the certificate and insisted I go to Sheffield for a psychiatric evaluation. Moreno Roggi fought them tooth and nail.

First, he threatened to get FIFA involved. You cannot fine a player who is sick and presents a medical certificate proving he is unwell. Naturally, Sheffield Wednesday were ignorant of this fact (but then, would you have expected otherwise?) and they had to back down. Second, he told them in no uncertain terms that there was no question of my flying to Sheffield to get evaluated. The whole point was that I was too unwell to travel. Again, their position was ludicrous, an inherent contradiction. They wanted me to travel to Sheffield so that I could prove to them that I was unfit to travel, which made absolutely no sense at all.

'If your doctors wish to examine Paolo, that's fine,' Moreno told them. 'But Paolo is unable to travel. If you want to see him, you're going to have to come to Terni.'

Eventually, that's what they did, but not before fining me another two weeks' wages. Sheffield Wednesday's team doctor came down, accompanied by a psychologist from the Football Association. They interviewed me separately, they examined me and they reached the exact same conclusion that my doctor in Terni had reached. I was suffering from stress, mental exhaustion and nausea. I simply could not return to Sheffield until my condition improved.

I don't know if the club had already decided that I was to be sold, or if the doctor's verdict was the deciding factor. All I know is that in early January 1999, Moreno got the green light to find me another club. The mere knowledge that I would be moving on, that I would be leaving Sheffield Wednesday behind, helped me face the new year with a modicum of serenity. I slowly started feeling better. Whatever was to happen, I would be ready.

CHAPTER TEN

HAPPY AS HARRY

Once Sheffield Wednesday made it clear they were releasing me, I had offers to join Bordeaux and AEK Athens – but I wanted to stay in the Premiership. Then West Ham began showing genuine interest and it wasn't long before personal terms were agreed and a deal was struck with Wednesday for £1.7 million.

Moreno Roggi and I flew up to London on 21 January to sign the contract, iron out the final details and undergo the medical. The West Ham doctor was checking out my knee when my mobile rang. Thinking it was Betta, I apologized and took the call.

It was Stefano Eranio, my old teammate at AC Milan. He was playing for Derby County and I hadn't spoken to him in months.

The minute he started speaking he was all agitated.

'Paolo, have you signed yet?' he asked.

'No. I can't really talk now, I'm in the middle of my medical . . .'

'Paolo, don't sign! DON'T SIGN!'

'What?'

'Listen, Paolo, I've got Jim Smith here, he's standing right next to me. We have the green light from Sheffield Wednesday, we really want you here at Derby!'

It was true. Derby County were offering me one-and-a-half-times more than what West Ham were prepared to put on the table. I hadn't signed anything, so I could have easily accepted their deal instead.

'I'm sorry, Stefano,' I said. 'But if you guys really wanted me that bad, you had three whole months in which to pick up the phone. If Jim Smith really thought I was so important, he could have called me at any time and made me an offer. It's just too late. I haven't signed anything, but I have given West Ham my word and to me that is a lot more important. I am not going to go back on my word.'

With that, I hung up.

There was no way I was going to turn my back on Harry Redknapp. He had the guts to sign me when everybody else in England wanted to crucify me. I trusted him immediately. It's funny, at that point, when I turned down Derby, I had known him no more than a couple of hours, but already I knew that he was on my side.

I have a sixth sense when it comes to people. I like to think I am a 'street psychologist'. Growing up on the streets, you learn right away what kind of people can be trusted and what kind of people it's best to steer clear of. Redknapp was one of the former.

I looked at his face and I saw somebody who had suffered tremendously. He was brought up the hard way and he survived a terrible tragedy ten years ago, barely walking away with his life after a horrific car accident. People like that either become mean and hard-hearted or they become gentle and kind. Redknapp's eyes told me all I needed to know. He is one of the good ones.

And he is a good manager. Year after year, West Ham do well, despite having very little money. Redknapp knows how to find players and turn them into stars. I mean, he not only managed to make John Hartson look good, he managed to sell him for £7.5 million. I say this with all due respect to Hartson. I'm not suggesting he's a bad footballer, but I think he'll be the first to admit that he's no Maradona.

Redknapp was also very good with the media. I knew I would have to give a press conference when I signed. It would be the very first time I had spoken in public to the British press since the Alcock incident and I feared it could get confrontational. But Redknapp was excellent. He managed to tone everything down. When they asked me about Wednesday I simply said: 'I'm lucky to move to a better club than Sheffield Wednesday.'

Which was the truth. There was no comparison between the two, on or off the pitch. One of the main differences was the atmosphere in the dressing room.

Sheffield Wednesday were a small-minded provincial club. Beyond the fact that nobody lifted a finger to defend me after the Alcock incident, even when I was there I could tell that some players were jealous of me. I think they had some kind of an inferiority complex and they reacted by turning on me.

These are people who did not understand that they had a chance to play alongside a guy whose talent and experience was so much greater than theirs. I could have taught them so much.

Instead, to them I was just someone who was there to take their paycheque or their place in the side. They didn't worry about becoming better players, they only worried about continuing to get paid and getting their contracts renewed.

I look at a guy like Andy Booth and it's so sad it's almost funny. After Benny Carbone left, he said: 'Without the two Italians, it's much better, they only ever passed the ball to each other. Now I'm going to score more goals.'

I couldn't believe he said something so ludicrous. After Carbone left, he scored a total of three goals all season. Yes, he's right. Without the Italians he sure turned into a scoring machine. He made a huge contribution to Sheffield Wednesday, didn't he?

People like Booth were the problem at Sheffield Wednesday. I used to think all English dressing rooms were like that, but after coming to West Ham I realized that Wednesday was an aberration, that fortunately it did not have to be that way.

At West Ham I found a perfect environment. There are plenty of talented players here, but even the most skilful understand that you are never too old to learn something. I think they understand that perhaps, in terms of experience and vision, I can give a little bit extra. Rather than resenting my presence, they try to learn from me and I, in turn, learn from them.

When I first walked into the West Ham dressing room, everybody was laughing, joking, carrying on. It was the polar opposite of Sheffield Wednesday. At first, I thought to myself 'My God, this is a lunatic asylum!' Then I understood. This was the way it should be. If this was an asylum, it was an asylum of sane people. Sheffield Wednesday was the real lunatic asylum.

I fell in love with that camaraderie right away. They weren't prejudiced against foreigners, they were pure, honest people. Each player was made to feel important, which is the way it should be in any team. I settled in quicker than I had anywhere else in my career.

We gave each other stick right away, but it was funny, it was good-natured. Guys like Neil Ruddock, Ian Wright and John Moncur were the heart and soul of the dressing room. For some reason, they became obsessed with the fact that I wore long socks. They thought it was a good reason to make fun of me.

'You guys are pathetic!' I said. 'The elegant man wears long socks. Not those little short ones. You have no sense of style, you dress like Germans! Look at you, with your disgusting, little white socks!'

They exacted their revenge by cutting my socks to shreds, or by hiding my shoes and putting spiders in them. That amused them no end.

'If I find out who did this, I put a big, nasty, hungry rat in your pocket!' I would yell as they all laughed like idiots.

Ruddock, Wright, Moncur, Hislop, everything I did seemed hilarious to that gang of idiots. I pretended to be upset, but I thought it was wonderful.

In every dressing room, in every club, there are always one or two guys who don't quite fit in, who for some reason aren't a part of the group. That's not what I saw at West Ham. I saw a genuine team, a real bunch of mates, led by Ian Wright, one of the greatest characters in the game.

Wrighty was so enthusiastic about everything, he was like a kid, always looking for a laugh. He was also a fine footballer. He told me he was disappointed that he never got to play a full 90 minutes alongside me. Coming from somebody like him, that is a huge compliment.

People say he's crazy, sick in the head. Well, in a world that has become so strange and twisted, perhaps the normal ones are the ones like Wright and myself, the ones everybody else calls insane. We take life as seriously as the next guy, but we know what really matters: being yourself, speaking out, not being afraid to be different.

Are we really the crazy ones? Does standing up for what we believe in make us insane? Is it crazy to not let others push you around even when it means that you will suffer the consequences?

If I had simply accepted everything rich and powerful people had asked me to do, today I might still be at Juventus or AC Milan. I might have become an Italian international. And I would certainly be wealthier than I am today (not that I am complaining).

But I don't have any regrets. I did what I believed was right at the time and, ultimately, I am happy with the way things turned out.

The only thing I never did which I would have liked to do is play international football. While I was capped at Under-21 level for Italy, I never got a chance with the first team. I would have loved to receive even just one call-up, just one token of recognition. But I didn't, even though I believe I fully deserved it.

I know that if I had been born in another country, any other country, I would have tasted international football. It's a cruel irony that I had to be born in the one nation that never fully appreciated players like me.

I am a nationalist and a patriot. I love my country and I can't say I would want to represent any other nation. Having said that, when I look at, say, Scotland, when I think of the warmth and passion of the Scottish people, there are times I wish I could play for them. They appreciated me, they understood the way I played football, they weren't puzzled by or suspicious of my passion for the game.

I made my debut for West Ham on 30 January, away to Wimbledon, 126 days after the Alcock incident. Redknapp sent me on as a substitute with 13 minutes to go. I was removing my tracksuit when I heard a loud chant rising from the West Ham end.

Our supporters were singing my name. I couldn't believe it.

'What the hell are they singing for?' I thought to myself. 'I haven't even done anything yet, the English press has been crucifying me for the past four months and yet they are all behind me already. This is incredible!'

The game finished 0–0, but the supporters were unbelievable. I thanked them after the final whistle and they just kept singing. It was wonderful.

Perhaps it's because I myself was a fan and therefore have an eye out for these things, but I think England has some of the best supporters in the world. In Italy, most of the support goes to the bigger clubs. You don't get, say, teams like Nottingham Forest or Manchester City drawing 30,000 fans in the lower divisions. Kids grow up supporting whichever club is strongest at the time. Now it might be Juventus, Milan or Parma, a few years ago it might have been Inter or Roma. Your father might be a Fiorentina fan because they won a few titles in the 1950s when he was a kid; you might support Juventus, because they dominated in the 1970s; and your son might be a Milan fan because they did well in the 1990s. It's all down to whoever was on top when you first discovered the joys of football.

From what I can tell however, in this country it's a more instinctive experience. Fathers take children to the ground and the kids end up supporting whatever club their fathers support. For example, I don't think there are many West Ham fans whose children support Arsenal and vice versa. It's like passing a trade from father to son, just like years ago if you were a butcher, your son would be a butcher.

English supporters have a passion that is like a disease – and I mean that in a positive way. It's a wonderful illness, supporting your club no matter what. When your club plays badly, you suffer along with them, but you still cheer them on. In Italy, when a team fails to perform, the fans lose interest. They'll boo for a while, eventually they stop going altogether. They are much more fickle. Italian fans love seeing their club win, English and Scottish fans love seeing their club, full stop.

That's why we footballers must never forget that we are the privileged ones. We are the ones who are blessed with the opportunity to wear a West Ham shirt and play football for a living. I look at our fans at Upton Park (but I'm sure it is the same for most other clubs) and I think to myself: 'Ninety-five per cent of the people here would give their right arm to be in my shoes.'

Our fans would trade places with us in an instant if they could. But they cannot, so they do the next best thing. They follow us everywhere, they make huge sacrifices, both financially and in terms of their spare time. I know what it's like, I followed Lazio every week, home and away, for six years.

On average, I receive sixty to seventy letters a week. Most are from West Ham fans scattered around the world, many are from Celtic and Sheffield Wednesday fans who have stayed in touch. I keep a picture in my living room of these twins from Sheffield, two 15-year-old girls. They have written me wonderful letters, thanking me for my time at Hillsborough, telling me that they miss me.

To me, fans like that are special and when I think of them, I become quite emotional. Their love for football, the football I played, was stronger than the Alcock incident, stronger than all the aggravation that followed between myself and the club. They refused to let themselves be influenced by the media or by propaganda from the club. Nor do they back me or admire me because they necessarily think I am a good person or that I acted properly, because they don't know me personally. I don't think they care about that. They loved me as a footballer, they loved the things I did on the pitch. And that is what matters. That is a big part of what being a fan, of loving the game, is all about.

One guy in Australia named his bar 'Di Canio's Hammer Bar and Grill'. Another wrote to me, telling me he had been a season ticket holder at Upton Park for 45 years. He told me I had taken the place of Bobby Moore in his heart.

'Bobby Moore was incredible, but I see you doing things with the ball that I did not even think were possible, things I could never even imagine,' he wrote. 'Those are things which have never been seen before at Upton Park.'

When I read that I began trembling and shivers shot down my spine. Anybody who knows anything at all about West Ham knows what Bobby Moore means to the club. He is sacred, he is a Hammer legend. I would never dream of comparing myself to Bobby Moore. Yet the fact that somebody would say something like that, not just anybody but someone who has been loyal to the club for a lifetime, well, I almost broke down when I read it. Of course, it's only one voice out of thousands, but nevertheless I was over-whelmed. I was able to connect with that supporter, I was able to give something back to him. And that is the greatest reward for a footballer.

When I see a fan wearing a West Ham jersey with my name on the back, I get a flurry of emotion. I think to myself: 'This guy specifically went out and chose to buy a Di Canio jersey. He could have picked anybody, but he chose me.'

It's not like they're pre-printed and he just wanted a West Ham shirt. He specifically went out and paid £50 for a shirt and then another £20 to get my name and my number on the back.

How can you not react to that? How can you not see that and say: 'Right! I've got to go out and bust a gut because somebody out there loves me and my club so much that they spent all this money and gave up all this time to support me.'

I draw strength from the fans. Each time I take a corner kick at West Ham, I see the same two guys by the corner flag. Every time I run over, I search for their faces in the crowd, I don't even know if they realize this. They're about my age, they have shaved heads, they yell out my name and do the 'We're not worthy!' gesture with their arms. I just think to myself that if I had been born in the East End of London and wasn't a professional footballer, that could be me there with my mates and one of them could be in my place on the pitch.

That's why we as footballers must give 110 per cent each and every time we're on the pitch. That's also why I have no qualms about criticizing my teammates if I think they could be doing better.

But doing better doesn't just refer to your effort during games, it means being totally professional in training, eating properly, and doing extra drills. Anything less than that is a smack in the face to our fans, it's a moral insult to them.

Those who know me know how hard I work in training. To me, it's a way of life. I always come in on days off during the week and I train on most Sundays as well. Too many times there are way too few of us doing extra training.

I don't understand this. I don't understand why you would choose not to work your hardest. After all, you are the first to benefit from it, because you become a fitter, better player. And it's not as if two-and-a-half hours of training on a day off (which is my usual routine) are going to kill you. You still have plenty of time to do whatever else you were going to do that day.

When we run laps around the field, I always run as far out as I can. Yes, it means I must cover a greater distance, but it also means my body is working harder and therefore getting fitter. Some of my teammates, however, choose to be clever, cutting corners and running along the inside. That's not being clever, that's being stupid. You're not getting away with anything, you're only cheating yourself.

It's about professionalism and understanding that if you act professionally, you will be the first to benefit.

Another example is when we do drills. If we're practising our shooting for example, and I make a mistake, I get mad. I curse and swear. And I concentrate that much harder on my next shot. Others will mess up, however, and start laughing. I can just see it now. One guy will shank a volley off the side of his leg and all the idiots start laughing. Why is that funny? Why laugh?

Is it really that funny that your teammate mishit a ball? What are you going to do when it happens in a match? Are you going to sit there and laugh when he squanders a chance at goal?

Too few people understand that there is a direct correlation between what you do in training and what you do in matches. You have to approach both in the exact same way.

I got a lot of praise for the volley I scored against Wimbledon in 1999/2000. Sure, it was a spectacular goal. What I did was extremely difficult, because it requires total body control, timing and balance. Compared to a bicycle kick or a scissors kick it is much more difficult, because in those situations your body weight is going backwards, which helps stabilize you. But when I struck the ball against Wimbledon, both feet were in the air, even just making contact was quite an achievement.

But goals like that don't come out of thin air. I was able to do it because it was something I had practised for hours and hours in training. I attempted it so many times that it became an instinctive gesture. As the cross came in, I didn't even think about what I was going to do. My brain just decided for me, it just happened. I wish my teammates and some of the younger footballers understood that without the hard work in training, I would not have pulled that off.

I'm not the only example. Look at David Beckham. People think he just has this natural gift for football, that he's a pretty boy who happens to be the best crosser of the ball in the world. Well, while there is no question that Beckham was born with some degree of talent, I can assure you that he would not be that good if he didn't spend hours practising his crosses. Yet he doesn't seem to get the credit for it. All you hear about is how wonderful and committed Roy Keane is, but Beckham's professionalism in training is rarely mentioned. Don't get me wrong, Keane is outstanding, but he has a reputation for being a hard worker so he is constantly being praised.

Alan Shearer has a similar reputation. He's supposed to be a workhorse, who spits blood and guts every time he plays. And, to be fair, most of the time, that's exactly what he does. But go back to his last three games before Ruud Gullit got sacked as Newcastle manager. Shearer walked around the pitch, rarely, if ever, putting his foot in. I don't know if it was because he was trying to contribute to Gullit's sacking or not, but I do know that wasn't the real Shearer.

Of course, nobody seemed to point this out. Why? Because in people's minds Shearer will always be the paragon of hard work. And Beckham will always be the pretty boy to whom everything in life comes easy.

CHAPTER ELEVEN

YOUNG HAMMERS

When I joined West Ham, we were ninth in the table. As the season progressed, we slowly worked our way up. I played twelve games, scoring four goals, and we finished fifth. Add in the games at Sheffield Wednesday, before the suspension, and the totals become seven goals in 18 matches. I had reason to be satisfied and to look forward to the 1999/2000 season, because our fifth-place finish won us a spot in the Intertoto Cup.

I know the Intertoto is not the Champions League, one newspaper even called it the 'InterTwoBob' Cup. I think that's silly. Prestige aside, it offered us a chance to play in the UEFA Cup, a goal we reached by winning the competition. They were all laughing when we entered the Intertoto, but I think they stopped once they saw we made it into Europe. Perhaps we didn't have the squad to go all the way in the UEFA Cup, but many of our youngsters gained experience playing against foreign clubs and, at their age, that can be invaluable.

We have an outstanding crop of young players at West Ham, from Michael Carrick to Joe Cole, from Steven Bywater to Rio Ferdinand. It's a testament to the ability of Harry Redknapp, Frank Lampard Sr and the rest of the staff that they have attracted and developed so many promising kids.

I enjoy being surrounded by kids. My old youth-team coach, Volfango Patarca keeps telling me that when I retire I should simply come and replace him as a Lazio youth coach. I don't know if that's going to happen, but I love teaching and setting an example for our youngsters.

Bywater has good goalkeeping skills and a good head on his shoulders. He had a nightmare debut against Bradford City, but he bounced back with some fine performances. As with all young keepers, he needs confidence and that will come in time. His work ethic is outstanding, he's sure to be around for a long time.

Carrick is another one of my favourite young players. I think originally he was considered a forward. I don't know why, because he is a natural leader in midfield. He is technically sound, very methodical and is a brilliant, creative decision-maker. Most of all however, he has a winning personality. You can't teach that, that is something you are born with. He is very strong mentally, he is the kind of player you build championship sides around.

Of course, the two players who attract the most attention are Cole and Ferdinand. I respect them tremendously as footballers and I love them both as people, which is why, when I speak about them, I do so as an older brother. I want to see them succeed, I want to see them fulfil their tremendous potential. Few people have the talent they have, but that will not be enough to make it without a cartload of hard work.

Cole is one of the greatest talents not just of his generation but of the past twenty years. I played with Alessandro Del Piero when he was Cole's age. In terms of ability, they are similar, though perhaps Cole has an edge. Cole has more pace and greater mental toughness. I also played with Roberto Baggio and, I can tell you, Cole is a stronger version of Baggio.

I see him do certain things with the ball and I have no clue how he does them. The way he spins off tackles, the way he dances through traffic reminds me of a scaled-down Zinedine Zidane. His movements are natural, feline: he's like a young tiger. He shows you the ball and then makes it disappear, like an illusionist. At the same time he has the grace and control of a ballet dancer, no muscle is out of place in his body.

I've had friends and former teammates come up and watch West Ham train. They say: 'Paolo, he's just like you were at his age. And just like you, he never passes the ball!!'

That's a little unfair, but Cole does tend to hang on to the ball a lot. He uses up a lot of energy just dribbling around. You don't want to curb that instinct, because, with his skill, many times it's better for Cole to have the ball surrounded by three opponents than for another, less skilful player, to have it unmarked.

Having said that, I don't think midfield is his best position. It's simply too risky because if he gives the ball away, the opposition picks it up with only our defenders to beat. I'd like to see him further up the pitch, where, even if he does lose the ball, our midfielders can recover it. Also, if he played in the hole, he would only have to beat one or two opponents before having the opportunity to take a crack at goal or set up a teammate. Right now, playing in midfield, everything gets congested. Even if he beats a few men, he still has opponents all around him.

To play there however, he needs to mature physically. At his age, and with his physique, he doesn't need some 6ft 4in central defender kicking lumps out of him. He would still have to learn that withdrawn striker position I play. The key thing would be for him to understand that, even before he gets the ball, he should identify three or four options. Great footballers always see more options than average ones. He has the talent and vision to do that, but it seems that too often his natural instinct is to receive the ball, dribble into space and then decide what to do.

Apart from his ability, what I admire most is that he has absolutely no fear. He is not afraid to make mistakes, he is not afraid to try new and different things. His coaches have been wonderful that way, because they have encouraged him, just like Volfango encouraged me to attempt new things. A more traditional coach (and, indeed, most Italian ones) would have told him not to take the extra dribble, not to try the difficult pass, but to play everything safe.

I am not praising him because I want to hype him up. But, the point is that Cole needs to be challenged, he needs to be stimulated. Coaching somebody like him is difficult, but you cannot apply the same standards to everybody.

You need to make him feel hungry, you need to make him feel like he still has a long way to go, which he does. It is not sufficient for Cole to become a Premiership player or an England player or even an England star. He has the opportunity to become one of the top four or five players in the world.

I spend a lot of time talking to him, teaching him what I have learned. I desperately want him to succeed, for his own sake and for English football. More than Michael Owen, more than David Beckham, he is the future. Beckham and Owen are outstanding footballers, but their style is quintessentially British. There's nothing wrong with that, but the Premiership has changed, English football isn't the way it was ten or twenty years ago. Today it can produce a player like Cole and he has a chance of being the symbol of the new English game.

That's because he is a modern footballer, he is free from the old British stereotypes. He approaches the game in a totally different way. Some may call it a more continental approach; indeed, his skills seem South American at times, but it doesn't really matter how you define it, what matters is that he can combine that with the best traditional characteristics of the English game: spirit, work rate, commitment.

He takes advice very well, which is very gratifying to me. For example, I advised him not to hang on to the ball in midfield in the first ten minutes of matches. That's because, in the Premiership, the early stages are always very frenetic, with tackles flying in and players scurrying about furiously. It's not a good time to dribble. You may beat a few players and get the applause of the crowd, but it's easy to lose the ball or, indeed, get injured. It's better to keep it simple in the opening ten minutes, I told him. Receive the ball, play it on to a teammate and get open again. Be patient, pick your spots. Once the pace of the game has subsided, then you can start thinking about running with the ball. Your opponents will be more tired, they will be less inclined to fly in and hack you down. And your teammates will have settled into the flow of the match as well.

He took my advice to heart. I saw him actively following my instructions in the next few games. I can't describe how much it meant to me. He could have been arrogant about it, he could have said: 'I'm Joe Cole, I will become a star regardless of what Di Canio tells me.'

Instead, he learned from me, tapped into my experience. That's a sign of intelligence, but also a sign that he wants to emerge, he wants to fulfil his potential.

He's a good worker, but he can improve that aspect as well. He needs to eat right, train professionally, concentrate on his fitness. Unfortunately, poor training is often a function of having grown up in English football. You're not going to find too many players in this country who are willing to take care of their bodies, who are willing to bust their butts in training, day in, day out.

Which brings me to Rio Ferdinand. Now, I believe that Lazio's Alessandro Nesta is the best central defender in the world. He has pace, he's good in the air, he has good vision, he wins every tackle, he is comfortable on the ball and he is a natural leader. Right now, he is the benchmark against which all defenders must be judged.

I think Rio can become as good as Nesta, maybe even better. He has all the skills to do it, but he needs to go to the next level. He needs to develop that hunger, that drive, that personality which great players have.

Rio could be the best, but he isn't, at least not yet. He's 22 years old, he has a dozen England caps, he has three full Premiership seasons under his belt. He's not a prospect anymore, it's time for him to be a star. Last year he made mistakes, he suffered lapses in concentration. That's fine, but he has the ability and intelligence to cut those out. Rio is a special person, not just in terms of athletic ability, but in terms of intelligence as well. He can do better.

I try to talk to him, try to impress the importance of improving, but it's difficult. Sometimes, when you feel important, it becomes hard to listen to what others tell you. It's not arrogance, it's a function of knowing you are a star. Maybe he thinks he's good enough already, maybe he thinks he's the best English defender around. He may well be, but is that enough? He can be number one in the world.

Believing you're the best cuts both ways. On the one hand, it gives you the confidence to achieve great things. You're not afraid of anything, you go into every match, every endeavour, believing you will succeed. It's a huge psychological edge.

On the other hand, it can sap your will to improve. If you think you're the greatest, why should you work harder? Why should you try?

It would be a shame if Rio had taken the latter interpretation of being the best. It would be sad if he thought that because he's already great, he doesn't need to push himself further.

Rio shouldn't be saying to himself: 'I'll start for England in a few years and be one of the best in the business in six or seven years' time.' A footballer's career is too short to think that way. He should be saying: 'I want to be recognized as the best defender in the world, right now!'

After signing a huge long-term contract with Lazio, Nesta turned in the finest season of his career. Why? Because he had the drive to want to prove to the world that he was worth it.

I offer these words of advice to Rio because I care about him, because I want him to be the best. I speak the way an older brother would speak. I wish I could take him back in time to Milan's training camp, five years ago. I would make him watch Franco Baresi train. At the time, Baresi was 35, he was in his last season, he was the club captain and a living legend. He had nothing left to prove. And yet, he trained viciously, he worked religiously, he was fanatical about every detail. In short, he was an absolute professional about everything he did.

If Rio could learn from that, there would be no stopping him.

In fact, Rio doesn't even need to go back in time to see a sterling example of how a professional footballer should behave. He's got one right under his nose: Stuart Pearce.

Last year, I was in the West Ham dressing room after training. I was looking at Stuart Pearce. Years of proper training and dedication have given him the body of a man ten years younger. That is how a professional behaves.

'Psycho man, you're a beast,' I said to Pearce. 'Look at you. You're 36 years old and you still have a perfect body.'

He looked at me with a little grin.

'Actually, mate, I'm not 36. I'm thirty-eight years old.'

'Wow!' I said. 'Well, I'm thirty-one. I'm not doing too bad for my age, am I?'

'Perhaps, but you had better keep it up,' he said.

He pointed across the room to where Neil Ruddock, clad only in a towel, was shaving.

'Otherwise, if you're not careful, you'll end up looking like him!' he added, winking mischievously.

'Hell, no!' I said. 'I don't want to look like Ruddock even when I'm fifty!'

The point of this story isn't to make fun of Ruddock. To be fair, we all have different body types, even if he locked himself into a gym for two years he wouldn't emerge looking like Stuart Pearce. The point is that a guy like Pearce is a true warrior. To me he embodies the English ideals of spirit, attitude and commitment. But most of all, he is all about hard work. You cannot play professionally at 38 years of age if you don't treat your body like a temple.

I wish Rio could understand that. I wish he could understand that hard work is all that stands between him and superstardom.

Ultimately, it's up to him. He can choose to not change his ways. He'll remain a hero to West Ham fans and, if he stays at the club his entire career, he'll be remembered as a legend.

But he will never become a truly great player.

Or, he can discover the hunger to emerge. He can begin to train hard, to eat properly, to work on every detail of his game. It's not that big a commitment. If he just develops the resolve to devote himself completely to training, to hard work, he can become a true, world-class defender.

It's up to him.

That summer of 1999 I received a call from Gianluca Vialli. Chelsea had finished third the previous season, their best finish since 1970. With Gigi Casiraghi out for the indefinite future, Vialli needed another striker to complete his attacking corps of Tore Andre Flo and Gianfranco Zola (he would eventually sign Chris Sutton from Blackburn Rovers for £10 million).

'Listen, Paolo,' he said. 'How would you like to come and play for me at Chelsea?'

It would have been a wonderful opportunity on paper. Chelsea were playing in the Champions League, it was a chance to show everybody back in Italy what I could do. Financially, it would have made sense as well, I could probably have got a better deal.

Still, I wasn't totally sure. Vialli was in the market for a big target man as well; if he signed one, there would be four strikers competing for two starting positions. Not to mention the fact that Vialli told me he didn't have much money to spend and I knew that West Ham would only let me go for a sizeable offer.

'I don't know, Luca,' I replied. 'I don't want to be part of a squad rotation system. At my age, I want to play every single game. Besides, I had a good spell at West Ham after coming over from Sheffield Wednesday. I'm enjoying myself and I'm not sure you can afford to buy me.'

Luca was unfazed. As he often does, he went straight ahead with his pitch.

'What if I offer Redknapp Dan Petrescu in part-exchange?'

'Luca, I'm not sure, it's going to work out,' I replied. 'Petrescu is a great player, but I think Redknapp really rates me.'

'Paolo, will you talk to him for me? Will you sell him on the idea? Think about it, you and I together at Chelsea in the Champions League. Wouldn't it be great?'

I never spoke to Redknapp about it. Maybe Chelsea did, I don't know. I never followed it up because deep down I had serious doubts about moving to Stamford Bridge.

Months later, when Chelsea were struggling in the league, I had dinner with Luca.

'Paolo, I'm a moron,' he said. 'We re-signed Petrescu, he's a good guy, but when I think that we could have had you instead . . . It would all have turned out differently with you in our squad. You're consistent, you play hard in every single match. Why, oh why, didn't I do the deal with Redknapp?'

'Listen, Luca, perhaps it all worked out for the best,' I replied. 'I thought about it a lot and I'm glad nothing happened. It would not have been a good idea. You and I are friends, true friends and I'm not sure what our relationship would have been like if I had played for you. I value our friendship too much.'

I meant what I said. First and foremost, I am happy to be at West Ham. While it would have been great to play in the Champions League, playing at Upton Park has been incredibly fulfilling.

But beyond that, I fear my friendship with Luca might have embarrassed him. It might have got in the way of his job as manager. I still believe that good managers often need to behave badly. I didn't want Luca, who was my friend, to have treated me that way, even if he thought it was for the good of the team. I want Luca as a friend, not as a boss, not as somebody with whom to have a confrontational relationship.

Of course, in September of 2000, Chelsea came back in for me. This time, the impetus did not come from Luca (I think he knew how I felt) but from the club itself. They made a £4 million offer, and, from a personal standpoint, I could have probably doubled my wages.

Harry said I wasn't for sale, at any price. I felt honoured that he valued me so much, especially because I know that West Ham are not a wealthy club.

But even if he had agreed, I would have turned Chelsea down. West Ham is my home, this is where I belong. I've only ever felt this way about one other club: Lazio. And that's probably because I grew up there and was a fan before I became a player. At the end of the 2001/02 season, I will have been at West Ham longer than any other club. I think that is part of the reason I feel so attached. It takes time for relationships to grow, maybe if I had been at Celtic or Napoli for more than a season I would have grown to love those clubs the same way. As it stands, I have fond memories and they will always be in my heart. But Lazio and West Ham are something special, something different.

The chairman's office at Upton Park is full of football memorabilia. There are all these trophies from the 1920s and 1930s, photographs of Bobby Moore, Trevor Brooking's England shirt, even the first ball ever kicked at Wembley. It is the very heart of West Ham, our history packed into one room.

One day I noticed that the club had added a photo of my goal against Wimbledon, the strike that was voted Goal of the Season. I am the only player from the modern era, since Brooking, to be up on that wall. When I first noticed it, I went weak with emotion.

I was up on that wall with the legends who had written the history of West Ham. It isn't a question of ability. While you can't compare different eras I know that, in terms of talent, perhaps I am in their league.

But it's a question of longevity. I had been at West Ham less than two full seasons when they put me up on that wall. I think I have given West Ham a lot, but this show of love, of recognition, was unexpected. After all, I am a foreigner, I don't have the years of service which others have put in.

I don't know who was responsible, whether it was the chairman or the directors, but it was an immense show of love. West Ham recognized what I had done for the club and, from my perspective, all I wanted to do was give back even more. They rescued me after my ban, when I desperately wanted to stay in the Premiership but only received offers from abroad.

That's why I will forever carry this club in my heart, regardless of what happens. One day, perhaps in thirty years' time, I'm looking forward to coming here and seeing myself on that wall. I will know I have a second home at Upton Park.

Gratitude is a rare currency in football, and Luca Vialli's sacking, just a few days after Chelsea's failed bid for me, was further proof of this.

I felt sorry for him, though Luca is not the kind of guy

who needs pity. He will bounce back, there is no question. At age 36, he has already won five titles in two and a half seasons.

At that age, Sir Alex Ferguson had not won anything and neither had Jock Stein or Bob Paisley. Giovanni Trapattoni was a year away from his first title. Only one man in history has won more than Vialli so early in his managerial career. That man is Sven Goran Eriksson, who had two Swedish Cups, a Swedish title, a UEFA Cup and two Portuguese titles to his name. But, with all due respect to Sweden and Portugal, Vialli won his trophies in England and Europe, which is a whole other matter.

In the end, Luca had to deal with several unhappy players. To do this, a manager needs the support of the chairman and I think it was lacking. If a guy like, say, Franck Leboeuf, criticizes the manager, the club must be united in dealing with it. Instead, Vialli had to go out and discipline Leboeuf on his own, without knowing if the club was behind him. It's inevitable that the situation deteriorated, because there was a lack of unity.

Luca was undermined, he needed a strong club behind him. Chelsea may be a wealthy club full of wonderfully skilled players, but it is not a strong club. It's a question of mentality. I don't think this would have happened at a club like Manchester United.

The environment at Upton Park is perfect for me. Sure, I still get mad at my teammates. I yell at them, I criticize them, I even curse them when they do something wrong. I am not afraid to do that, though perhaps, now that I'm older, I probably hold back a little.

I think they understand that when my outbursts occur, the intention behind them is noble. I yell because I want my teammates to do better, to push themselves harder. Harry tells me: 'Paolo, you can't get mad at them. They don't have your vision, your ability . . .'

That's fine. I'm used to that. I don't get angry when people try and fail. Everybody misses penalties, even I do. What I'm talking about are mistakes that can be traced directly to poor work habits or lack of commitment in training. That is what makes my blood boil.

Some players think it is enough to give 110 per cent in games. That simply isn't true. If they run their heart out in a match and then come up short, the typical English thing to say is: 'Unlucky, son. Good effort.'

That makes me angry. Because it may have been a good effort on the day, but what went on in training during the previous week? Did the fact that he did not train professionally make him marginally slower so that, no matter how hard he ran on match day, he would not get to the ball first?

People see me yelling at my teammates and think I'm a whinger or an egotist, but they fail to see the bigger picture. I yell when I think the mistake is a direct result of what went on in training, not because I enjoy screaming at my teammates. In short, I get angry at teammates when I think they could do better.

You won't see me yell often at Steve Lomas, for example. That's because the guy is a committed professional who works his butt off every single day. I realize he may not be very skilful, I don't hold him to the same standard I might hold others. Technique may not be his strong point, but his contribution is immense nevertheless.

He can do some things better than I can: tackle, run his heart out, take on bigger opponents and never get knocked off the ball, etc. I can do things he cannot. The issue isn't about skill or lack of it. The issue is about how hard you work, how much you want to translate your talent into production on the pitch.

Another example is when we're two or three goals up in the final minutes of the game and players begin to screw around. Last season, I got furious with a teammate for just that reason. We had a three-goal lead in the dying minutes of the match. He and I were on a breakaway, he beat the defender and had a crack at goal, even though I was wide open, calling for the ball. His effort finished wide and, as we jogged back up the pitch, he got an earful from me.

The press picked up on it and, naturally, had a go at me. They said I was being selfish and an egotist for demanding the ball. We won the game anyway, why not let a teammate have a chance at a goal?

That's a silly argument. The point is that when you're on the pitch you must be a total professional, from kickoff to the final whistle. And that means putting the team first. In that specific instance, my teammate should have passed me the ball because I was better placed to score the goal. Full stop.

It's a question of professionalism. It's a mind frame you get into. In that instance we had the game won, but if you begin messing around, if you begin chasing personal glory, there's a chance you'll do it with the game on the line as well. And that is simply unacceptable.

My second season at West Ham was a resounding success for me personally. I scored fourteen goals and, while the club didn't finish as high as it should have, we still held our own.

The year was marred however by one ugly incident which received a lot of attention and for which I, as usual, was depicted as an evil maniac. It was January and we were playing Aston Villa. Three days earlier, they had knocked us out of the League Cup in an ill-tempered affair in which I won (and later missed) a penalty. Villa goalkeeper David James brought me down that day and after the match he publicly attacked me, saying I was a diver and a cheat.

Now, I couldn't care less what David James says or does. When a player gives away a penalty, he instinctively complains about it. Given my reputation, his instinct was to complain by insulting my integrity as a footballer. I guess that is just the kind of person he is. As far as I was concerned, the incident was over and done with when we met in the league the following Saturday.

The game finished in a 1–1 draw and I scored the equalizer. After the final whistle, I went up to James to shake hands, just as I would do with any opponent. Now, I'm an intense competitor on the pitch, the opponent is my enemy and I will fight him with every shred of energy I can muster. But when it's over, it's over.

I offered my outstretched hand and James just turned away. This cretin would not shake my hand. At that point, I felt like slapping him around, the way you would with a spoilt child. I got very angry.

Perhaps I view it as a foreigner, perhaps I'm just a romantic, but to me sportsmanship is a value I associate with British football. And part of that means shaking hands with your opponents after the match, regardless of what went on in the previous 90 minutes. I love the way people in this country can beat each other black and blue, insult each other viciously, and then, at the final whistle, it all ends in a handshake and a pint in the players' lounge.

By turning his back to me, by stomping off in a huff and refusing to shake my hand, this moron James was presenting two fingers to the whole British culture and tradition of sportsmanship.

It's the very same culture of sportsmanship which I have tried to learn and absorb in my time in this country and the very same culture which I have grown to respect and admire. And now, David James was walking all over it.

I grabbed hold of his arm and said: 'F**k off, you! You are not a man! You are nothing!'

Various other players came in to separate us. I was furious, but nothing actually happened, though naturally that didn't stop the press from having another go at me for supposedly 'assaulting David James'.

Believe it or not, that wasn't the highlight of the match as far as the media were concerned. A national newspaper published a photograph which showed me holding up a middle finger behind my back.

I was immediately accused of making an obscene gesture towards the Aston Villa fans. Again, there was little proof but that did not stop the Football Association from following it up with religious zeal.

I say there was no proof, because, simply put, there wasn't. First and foremost, that gesture could have meant anything. I could have been scratching my back, I could have been signalling to teammates, I could have been doing absolutely anything. But because it's Paolo Di Canio, people assumed the worst. It had to be an obscene gesture.

I was honest about it. At the hearing, I admitted that I had made the gesture towards an Aston Villa player. This was a guy who had insulted me constantly both in our league encounter and in the League Cup. He had called me a 'cheating Italian bastard', we were chattering back and forth and I got my own back. It was something between players, nothing to do with the fans.

Making a gesture to the fans is indeed a serious thing. It can incite a riot, it can lead to violence. Insulting an opponent (whether by giving him the finger or otherwise), while not very elegant, is something which, rightly or wrongly, happens at football matches, at any level. It is a totally different matter.

In this instance, the fans in the background of the picture were blurry. You simply couldn't tell who they were. Which meant I could have been facing any direction. There simply was no photographic evidence proving that the gesture was intended for the fans or indeed that the Aston Villa supporters even noticed it. In fact, to my knowledge, none of them complained.

The Professional Footballers' Association backed me entirely, but even then it was not enough to escape punishment from the FA. They fined me £5000 and told me that at the next incident I would be suspended.

Not only was this another colossal injustice courtesy of the FA, it also reinforced the notion that some players are more equal than others. Arsenal's Emmanuel Petit made an obscene gesture to Aston Villa fans a month later. This time, he admitted making it directly to the supporters, because he felt they had insulted him racially.

Obviously, that was serious, because that could have incited violence. Who is to say that some skinhead lunatic, sitting among the Villa fans, might not have gone berserk seeing Petit giving him the finger and rushed on to the field to attack him?

Yet, what happened?

Petit was slapped with a £5000 fine, exactly like me. And I don't think he was threatened with a suspension at the next incident, like I was.

Where does this injustice come from?

Simple, I am Di Canio and I play for West Ham, whereas he played for Arsenal. Different players and different clubs are treated differently, by now I am used to it.

I think my reputation helped cost me other awards, like the Footballer of the Year award. I don't like to blow my own trumpet, but I believe I had an outstanding season in 1999/2000, yet it seems that few even considered me seriously.

I have no argument with Roy Keane winning the award. I myself voted for him and I think others like Kevin Phillips or David Beckham were very deserving. But when I saw some of the other players who were nominated, I felt a little snubbed.

CHAPTER TWELVE

FROM DEVIL TO SAINT

The first season of the new millennium did not start well. Part of the problem was that we had a number of key players who were carrying injuries over the summer and thus missed much of pre-season training.

It's funny, in Italy pre-season is sacrosanct. You work your butt off, you have fitness trainers who monitor your every movement, everything is done precisely and scientifically.

Here in England, many treat it as an afterthought. Bradford City, for example, played in the InterToto Cup just a few days after they reconvened after the summer break! That would have been unthinkable back home.

Your body has natural rhythms, it's normal to have ups and downs over the course of a 10-month season. But you need to plan it out. Guys like Joe Cole and Rio Ferdinand simply did not have the opportunity to prepare, not because they were lazy, but because they were injured.

When I pointed out that they would have to work that much harder to make up for it, the media had an absolute field day. They wrote that I was 'criticizing Harry

Redknapp's training methods'. At the same time, they took what I said about Rio, that he would have to continue to work hard to be the best in the world, and made it seem like I was slagging him off.

It was a turbulent month and I realized again how the media works. I'll give a legitimate interview with someone and, the next day, the papers will pick up a quote or two, run a huge headline and build a story around it.

But it doesn't end there. The fallacy continues day after day, in every story about West Ham. If it's a story about how we're playing well, then it's 'in spite of Di Canio's vicious attacks on Ferdinand and Redknapp.' If it's a story about how we're playing poorly, then it's 'Di Canio's vicious attacks on Ferdinand and Redknapp have not helped.'

It wouldn't surprise me if they wrote a story about Bobby Moore and threw in a line about how Moore 'had never viciously attacked his teammates the way Di Canio has done in recent weeks.'

The silly thing is that when it comes to my views, I don't think there's any need to sensationalize or take them out of context. If anything, I'm too blunt and there are times when it would be easier to keep my mouth shut.

Harry's reaction to the stories confused me a little. Surely a guy like him would know how the media works. Surely he would have known that those quotes were taken out of context and that I was not attacking anyone.

Instead, he fell into the journalists' trap. He told reporters that I 'hadn't spoken in months and now was opening my mouth every day.'

I assume he knew what was going on, that the media

were simply writing the same things over and over again. Instead, he gave them a reaction, which is precisely what they wanted and the papers were full of stories about tension between myself and Harry.

It would be wrong to blame Harry for responding to the media, however. Unless you're in his shoes, unless you're facing the pressure he faced, unless you understand fully the context in which the question was raised and in which he answered it, it's difficult to pass judgment.

The press and the footballing world enjoy a delicate symbiotic relationship. Without us, they would have nothing to write about. Without them, we would not have the publicity that creates fan interest; there would be fewer supporters attending games, fewer viewers in front of the television sets, fewer hits on club websites and fewer people buying football-related merchandise (including this book). Everyone in the football world owes part of his or her livelihood to the press, and vice versa.

Having said that, the media is not just motivated by a desire to inform, it is motivated by profits, which are driven by circulation, which in turn is often fuelled by controversy. As a manager, you need to know how to handle the media's insatiable appetite for a 'good story', which often means reporting on tension or controversy. You can't always just ignore things, even when they have little basis in fact, because they may well come out anyway, perhaps in a more damaging way.

That's why shrewd managers, like Harry, have a number of trusted journalists they speak to regularly. They need to cultivate and nurture those relationships to ensure that their side of the story gets reported fairly and accurately, at least from their point of view. This is how the system works, these are the rules of the managerial game. Being a good manager is not just about picking a starting XI and buying and selling players; there are dozens of other aspects and this is just one of them.

What I do know is that I probably could not behave like that. I am too blunt, too direct, often for my own good. I suppose these are the kinds of things I would have to learn if I were to go into management one day.

A similar situation occurred in January, when I was taken ill and missed a few games. Stories began to appear suggesting I was pretending to be sick. Harry's words in the newspapers unfortunately did not help matters. He was quoted as saying things like 'Paolo claims he has a cold'.

First of all, I don't understand why he used the word 'claims'. Language like that simply makes it seem like I'm conning the club, pretending to be ill.

Second, I did not have a cold, I had a streptococcus virus which is very serious. It's not something that comes and goes from one day to the next. And the club knew that, since their doctor would come by to see me twice a day.

Perhaps when Harry made that comment he was unaware of the seriousness of my illness. This was unfortunate, because it led to more media speculation about my condition (or suspected lack thereof . . .) and snide implications that I was bottling it.

I won't stand for that. If there is one thing that even my harshest critics (and I have many) will admit about me is that I am a good professional. I take great pride in my training and in my effort on the pitch. The fans know that, that is why they are with me.

The whole business was ridiculous. Some people claimed I had feigned my illness just before New Year's Day, so that I could miss our 1 January clash at Old Trafford against Manchester United.

Pretend to be sick? Yes, of course that's something I would do, considering the fact that I had arranged tickets, hired a mini-van and booked hotel rooms in Manchester for a dozen or so friends and relatives who were in England for the holidays. Now why would I do all that if I was planning to take New Year's Day off?

I missed just seven Premiership matches all season. Given my age and the virus I suffered in January, I don't think that's too shabby. I've played when hurt, I've played with painkillers, I've put my health and my body on the line time and again. One would think I would not have to prove myself year after year.

But then, that's how the media works.

Towards the end of the season, Harry suggested that it was difficult for him to play myself, Frederic Kanouté and Joe Cole at the same time – a fair statement given that we are all players of a similar style. The implication was that one of us would have to be either dropped or sold. A reporter asked me how I would react if I were the odd man out. I told him that, as a professional, I would accept the decision.

So, of course, the next day there were headlines saying I was ready and willing to step aside.

Ready and willing?

Paolo Di Canio steps aside for no man.

All I said was that it was the manager's prerogative to drop me and that it was my duty, as a professional, to accept the manager's decision. After all, if we do poorly as a result, it's the manager's butt which is on the line, not my own.

That's very different from saying I was ready to drift into the background. Besides, it would have been a very risky and brave decision to leave me out.

I don't want to boast, but the fact is that I am an important player for West Ham and, according to the statistics at least, we are a better team when I am in the starting XI. West Ham gained 39 points in the 31 matches I appeared in the 2000/01 Premiership season. That's an average of 1.26 points per game. In the seven matches I missed, we obtained just 3 points, or 0.43 points per game.

When I'm on the pitch, we average 1.3 goals per game (40 in 31). When I don't play, we average 0.71 goals per game (5 in 7).

For some reason, we also seem to defend better when I'm in the line-up. With Di Canio, West Ham conceded 1.13 goals per game (35 in 31), but when I wasn't playing, we let in 2.14 goals per game (15 in 7).

All this means is that when I'm on the pitch we score more, concede less and obtain more points. Perhaps it's just a strange statistical coincidence. But perhaps not. I just wish people would look at the evidence before passing judgement. Some stereotypes are repeated so often that they take on a life of their own, and, in a way, become the truth.

Maybe that was part of the reason why it was such a great feeling to beat Manchester United at Old Trafford in the FA Cup at the end of January.

Nobody believed we had a prayer. Yet, on the pitch, we matched them blow for blow and basically shut them down. This was one situation where, in my opinion, Harry Redknapp deserved a lot of the credit. He gave a perfect clinic in tactics that day.

I know that tactics and strategy are often overlooked in the Premiership, but Harry's game plan against United was spot on. In Italy, he would have been deified for his tactical triumph, in this country he left the limelight to the players.

Everybody knows that United's strength is in midfield, particularly down the flanks with Ryan Giggs and David Beckham. This was especially true against us, because Paul Scholes was absent and his substitute, Nicky Butt, is primarily a defensive midfielder.

So how does the opposition go about stopping Giggs and Beckham? Well, one option would have been to have our wing-backs, Nigel Winterburn and Sebastian Schemmel man-mark them or lie back and give added support to the back line.

This might have appeared logical, but instead Harry brilliantly decided to be counterintuitive. He encouraged Winterburn and Schemmel to push forward as often as possible. At the same time, he told the front players (myself and Frederic Kanouté) to drift wide.

This had two key effects: it put even more pressure on United's flanks (their full-backs, Denis Irwin and Mikael Silvestre, had to worry about me and Kanouté rather than concentrating on supporting Giggs and Beckham) and, at the same time, it left their central defenders, Jaap Stam and

Gary Neville, with no one to mark, which meant they got sucked forward into the midfield.

We kept it tight and defended well, but, more importantly, we were defending 30 yards up the pitch. By attacking their flanks, we forced United's wide players on the defensive and, when they won the ball, they often had to cover the length of the pitch.

Meanwhile, Frank Lampard and Michael Carrick matched Butt and Roy Keane blow-for-blow, while Joe Cole floated intelligently between midfield and attack. Joe's movement that day was exceptional. United did not know whether to track him with a midfielder (which meant his marker often got sucked out of position) or to put a defender on him (which, when Joe retreated up the pitch, inevitably helped create space for his teammates to exploit in the United defence).

Of course, anybody can draw up tactics on a chalkboard, executing them on the pitch is another matter. But we were magnificent on the day, and we had a spot of good fortune as well.

Fifteen minutes from time I managed to spring the offside trap and burst into the area and was left one-on-one with their goalkeeper Fabien Barthez. Now, in my opinion, Barthez is one of the very best keepers in the world, but, on that day, he tried to be a little too clever.

Instead of coming off his line, he simply stood still and raised his arm. You would be forgiven for thinking he was trying to hail a cab, instead he was trying to psyche me out by making me think that the linesman had raised his flag.

It was a trick, a psychological ploy. But it backfired terribly and I slotted the ball past him with ease.

First of all, I knew I was onside. When you are an experienced forward, you know when you're onside and, at that moment, I was 100 per cent sure. Of course, I realize that being certain does not mean much, linesmen are funny animals and often unpredictable. But I also knew that it's better to be safe than sorry and that, I would rather have my goal disallowed than not have a crack at goal.

Some of the press roundly criticized Barthez for trying to outfox me. I disagree. Even if he had come off his line, it would have been nearly impossible for him to stop me from that position. So he took a gamble and ended up looking silly. But, if I had stopped my run, I would have been the one looking really stupid and he probably felt he didn't have much to lose.

It is difficult for me to describe the feelings I experienced when the final whistle blew. Like a dam crumbling under the weight of water pressure, my emotions simply took over.

I ran around the pitch, screaming at our supporters and into the television cameras. 'You see! You see!' I roared. 'Paolo Di Canio bottles it on the road! West Ham cannot win away from home! We don't stand a chance against mighty Manchester United! We're just a small club! You see! You see! Who's laughing now?'

All I could think of were the thousands of Hammers fans. Not just the 5,000 or so who made the trip to Old Trafford that day, but all the other ones who, either because they can't take the time off or because they cannot afford it or because their families will not let them, were unable to be there. This was their victory just as much as it was ours. These are the fans who give up their money, their time, often a little bit of themselves and their families, all for the love of a club and its colours.

They are priceless. And for them, that day was payback day.

I was also happy for Harry. He's such a popular figure that, over time, he has become almost like a character from a cartoon in some people's eyes. Maybe it's the whole East End wheeler-dealer thing, but it seems that often all people talk about are his transfer dealings and the fact that West Ham are like a big family.

All this is true. Harry is an astute man when it comes to buying players and he is not afraid to take a gamble (I am living proof of this). But he is also an excellent tactician and, on that day, he outwitted the most successful manager in history, Sir Alex Ferguson.

That's why I was surprised, even shocked, when Harry was sacked at the end of the 2000/01 season. Only he and the chairman know the real reasons. Granted, we probably expected more from the season in terms of results. And, of course, Harry and I did have our run-ins and we did not always see eye to eye. But he will always have a special place in my heart for it was he who saved my career.

The season also had its high points. One of them was my reconciliation with David James and, I must say, many people were probably disappointed that we made up. They were looking forward to a feud, because feuds sell papers.

After the incident at Upton Park back in January 2000 when he refused to shake my hand at the end of the match,

I called him a cretin and a moron, which was exactly how I felt at the time.

'Does this man not know the meaning of cretin or moron?' he responded via the press. 'A cretin suffers from a thyroid deficiency. In some cases it leads to dwarfism. I'm 6 foot, 5 inches, for goodness' sake. And a moron is an adult with a mental age of eight to twelve. I'm no brain box, but I'm more advanced than that . . .'

James probably thought he was being clever with that response. And I'm sure many observers expected me to go ballistic. Instead, I was rather more measured in my reply.

'David James must have a brain the size of a pea,' I fired back. 'I called him a cretin a year ago so it has taken him a whole year to find out the meaning of the word. My two-year-old daughter could learn quicker than that. In fact, people can go to university and do a whole degree course in the time it has taken him to learn one or two words . . .'

I think James did himself in by taking so long to respond. And I think the fact that we chose to be humorous about it helped defuse the situation.

I'm sure some people wished to see us at each others throats the next time we faced each other at Upton Park in December 2000. Instead, the opposite happened. The game ended with a bear hug and we walked off the pitch together. I think it helped us both put the episode behind us once and for all. And I hope James learned a thing or two from it. I know I did.

Football is a game, it's not a war, though there are times when you need to hate your opponent to succeed. But nevertheless, what happens on the pitch must stay on the pitch and end at the final whistle.

I think this is something of which we often lose sight.

That season, Arsenal faced Lazio in Rome in a Champions League encounter that made headlines for many of the wrong reasons. During one flashpoint, Arsenal defender Gilles Grimandi punched Lazio midfielder Diego Simeone in the face. Then, in one of the most notorious incidents of the season, Lazio's Sinisa Mihajlovic made some racist remarks to Arsenal's Patrick Vieira at the end of the match.

Mihajlovic was crucified for this. In an instant, he became a scapegoat for all that is wrong with football. He received a ban from UEFA and was roundly criticized by just about everyone.

Now, I cannot condone what he did. He was wrong, it was unacceptable and he said so himself a few weeks later. However, I thought that the way the media and other observers manipulated the situation was shameful.

I read interviews in the Italian press where Mihajlovic claimed that he and Vieira had been trading insults throughout the game. I know that Mihajlovic called Vieira a 'black piece of shit'. I also know that Mihajlovic himself, being a Bosnian Serb, has in the past been abused by fans and supporters and that, among other things, he's been called a 'gypsy' and a 'murderer'. I'm sure that having been abused himself he understands the seriousness of racial taunts.

What I don't know is what happened on the pitch and what, if anything, Vieira said to Mihajlovic. But if Vieira insulted Mihajlovic in any way, I have to wonder: is one insult worse than another?

Would Mihajlovic have escaped censure if he had called Vieira a '*French* piece of shit' rather than a '*black* piece of shit'? After all, Vieira is just as French as he is black . . .

Of course, nobody wants to hear players insulting each other on the pitch, especially not if they use ethnic or racist stereotypes. But the truth is that it happens all the time. I've lost count of the number of times people have called me an 'Italian c**t' or a 'cheating son of a bitch' or whatever.

But I've never complained about it.

The reality is that if you put 22 young men on a football pitch and pit them against each other in a high-pressure environment, these things can happen. It may not be nice, but it's human nature, it's the way men are.

The difference is that, at the final whistle, everything ends. You shake hands and go your separate ways.

In England, especially, it has been that way. I've been insulted, kicked and spat upon for 90 minutes, but when the game ended, the very same players who were persecuting me on the pitch wanted to buy me a drink and treated me like a long-lost brother. That's why I love the football in this country. It's still a game.

But the Vieira–Mihajlovic incident was different. By going public with it, one of the basic rules of football was broken: the idea that what happens on the pitch, stays on the pitch.

I'm sure it wasn't the first time that someone hurled racist insults at Vieira. And, sadly, it probably won't be the last. By going public with it however, a dangerous precedent was set and a fellow professional was humiliated (not for the first time).

Go ask Vieira whether he would rather be insulted racially or suffer a knee-high tackle. I think I know what he would answer.

I know that some will argue that footballers are role models and that this kind of behaviour is unacceptable. Well, that might be true if any of the fans had heard Mihajlovic's words. But they didn't. Nobody, apart from the two of them and possibly one or two teammates, had any idea what was said, so it's not fair to say that Mihajlovic was being a poor role model. If anything, by being depicted as a racist, Mihajlovic might have become a hero and a martyr to some people who see him as a scapegoat.

The whole incident was manipulated and, sadly, it deflected attention away from some of the real problems football is facing, in Italy and elsewhere, such as racism and fan violence.

Just as Mihajlovic became a monster, I was virtually canonized at Goodison Park that season, mostly for doing what I would hope any honest footballer would do.

On 18 December 2000 my career in England went full circle.

Eight hundred and eleven days after the Paul Alcock incident, the day which consecrated me as one of the most infamous footballing villains in history, my redemption was complete, as I performed what one newspaper (yes, one of the papers that called for a life ban on me three seasons earlier) described as 'the ultimate act of sportsmanship.'

We were playing Everton away and the score was 1–1 deep into injury time. Their goalkeeper, Paul Gerrard rushed to the edge of the penalty box, to the right of his goal as we were looking, to retrieve a wayward ball. As he ran out, his studs got caught in the turf and he collapsed in a heap.

The ball bounced out to the right wing, where Trevor Sinclair retrieved it and unleashed a picture-perfect cross. I was waiting, unmarked, by the penalty spot and I watched as the ball traced a perfect arc towards me. I'll never know for sure whether I would have scored or not (in football, you can never be certain of these things) but, given the fact that there was nobody near me and that the goalkeeper, instead of being between the sticks, was lying in a crumpled heap outside the box, I certainly fancied my chances.

Everyone was expecting a header, or a quick first-touch and a snap shot rifled into the back of the net. Instead . . . I reached up and snatched the ball out of the air.

Some of my teammates looked at me as if I had just grown a second head. But I knew exactly what I was doing. Fifteen years as a professional have taught me to know right away when a player is seriously hurt.

And when I saw the way Gerrard went down, his foot getting caught, his knee twisting, his entire body weight (he is not exactly a svelte man) collapsing on top of his knee joint, I knew there was a strong chance that he was seriously hurt.

In those situations, immediate first aid can make all the difference. A smart physiotherapist, acting immediately, can prevent permanent injury. Had I taken a shot, it would have wasted a precious sixty or ninety seconds, perhaps even more if one of the defenders had blocked my finish and the ball had stayed in play.

I have said repeatedly that when I'm on the pitch, the

opponent is my mortal enemy. But at that moment, Gerrard ceased being an opponent and became a colleague, a fellow professional, one who, unless immediate action was taken, risked losing his career and possibly his livelihood.

To me, there was no option, there was no choice. Play had to be stopped right away.

Once the crowd realized what had happened, Goodison Park exploded into a standing ovation. It took me a while to realize that they were actually applauding what I had just done.

The response was incredible. The scene was replayed on television stations around the globe. I even received an official letter of commendation from FIFA, signed by none other than Sepp Blatter.

It was unbelievable!

I told people that just as I was not the devil when I pushed Alcock, I was not a saint now, simply because I interrupted play to ensure that a fellow professional could get treatment.

I received around fifty letters from Everton fans, plus dozens more from our own supporters. Some of the Everton letters were really touching. 'Paolo, you are the finest example of sportsmanship we have seen,' wrote one group of supporters. 'Everton will always be in our hearts, but, from now on, so will you. You will always have a second home at Goodison Park.'

Obviously the response from West Ham supporters was a little different, especially because, at that stage of the season, every point was crucial to us. I don't even want to think what might have happened if we had been relegated by a single point and my actions had cost us a place in the Premiership.

'I was angry with you on the ride home from Liverpool,' wrote one Hammers supporter. 'I was really furious, all I could think was that we had just dropped two points. But after a few days I began to see it in a different light. Your actions brought West Ham many more accolades than a simple away victory would have ever brought. People are talking about it all over the world. In a way, it was a victory for the club, perhaps one of the greatest in recent history.'

I stand by what I said. It was a nice gesture, but one that I made without thinking, so I'm not sure how much praise I deserve. I would like to think that other professionals, in that situation, would have acted in exactly the same way.

The way I was deified after the Everton game was just as baffling as the way I was crucified after the Alcock incident. In fact, it was just like the Alcock incident, only in reverse.

The other big talking point that season was the appointment of Sven Goran Eriksson as the England coach. For the first time, the Football Association had gone foreign, a decision which caused great controversy.

Maybe I'm old-fashioned, but I am among those who feel that the national team coach must never be a foreigner. It's a matter of principle, your national team coach is more than just a guy who runs training, fills out team sheets and tells people where to stand. He is a genuine symbol of the country's footballing culture.

It's a tricky role. In Italy, we say that there are 58 million

Italy managers and, it's true, the whole country generally thinks it can do a better job than the national team manager. As you get older, you probably accept that you do not have the skills to be a professional footballer, but few are so humble that they admit that their country's coach is a sharper footballing mind than they are. I know I don't.

That is just one of the many hurdles Eriksson will face. But, having said that, he has all the tools to succeed.

It's amazing when you think about it. Eriksson can't kick, control or head a football, he must be the worst footballer in the game (I know, I've seen him try) and yet he is one of the greatest managers around.

Why? Because he knows how to teach, he knows how to listen and he knows how to handle people. He has the mind of a psychologist. And he's a gentleman. A guy like Fabio Capello might have to rant and rave to motivate players, but Eriksson always keeps his cool.

If the Football Association can surround him with normal, intelligent people then he can achieve great results. Look past the obvious and you'll see that this country is producing an exciting crop of young players and a man like Eriksson can make it all come together.

Being foreign might actually help, because he will not feel indebted to certain players or certain clubs. He can turn the page and start fresh much more quickly than others, and try something daring. I know that he does not need my advice, but, if I may make a humble suggestion, a midfield partnership of Steven Gerrard and Michael Carrick would be difficult to stop.

CHAPTER THIRTEEN

FOREIGN FIELDS

Footballing years are like dog years. Careers are short; when you've been a professional footballer for ten years you feel like a normal guy would when he turns fifty.

You start thinking about the future, about what the next step is. You worry if you've saved enough, if you've invested wisely enough to support your family for the rest of your life.

I still think of it as being a long way off. First and foremost, I want to end my career at West Ham. I don't know if I can play until I'm 38 like Stuart Pearce, but, God willing, I'll try.

This country rejuvenated my career, it introduced me to a new type of football. It was a style of football which I probably carried inside me my entire life, but which Serie A did little to bring out.

In Italy, I was made to feel different because of it. Here, I can be myself.

We are often told that footballers are supposed to be role models. It is like this in Italy too, footballers are everywhere, they talk all the time, but they say nothing. It's all incessant blather.

There's a veto, a national taboo on discussing politics, for example. In 1999, I was interviewed by an Italian magazine. I told the interviewer that politically I was right wing. I'm not ashamed of it, the Right embodies values and ideals I believe in. This does not mean I'm a Nazi or a racist, it just means I identify with the Right. I could say that because I am a West Ham player and in England, there is such a thing as free speech.

Had I said that when I was still at an Italian club, it would have been the end of the world. I would have been in big trouble, I would have been fined, maybe even sacked. I know this because it has happened to me many times before.

Perhaps precisely because I am right wing, I am fascinated by Benito Mussolini. Remember those mobile phone advertisements where they asked people who they most would like to have a one-to-one with? Ian Wright picked Dr Martin Luther King, my choice would have been Mussolini.

I own dozens of Mussolini biographies. I think he was a deeply misunderstood individual. There are two aspects to my fascination with Mussolini.

The first is the way he faced difficulties and overcame them. The first time he went to jail, he was a member of the Socialist Party and was arrested for speaking his mind. Later, the same thing would happen to him on the opposite front, as a member of the Fascist Party. No matter what your politics are, if you speak your mind, the powers-that-be will try to shut you up.

He managed to rally an entire country around him at a time when there was no television, little radio, no mass media to speak of. It's not like today when any politician can give a speech and end up on television. Everything travelled more slowly in those days. He had to rely on word of mouth and his message spread very slowly, up the mountains and down the valleys, rather like the deeds of William Wallace in Scotland. In fact, I think there are many parallels between the two. Like Wallace, Mussolini was a patriot who built something out of nothing, step by step, individual by individual.

While I admire the way he built his power, I am fascinated by the way he wielded it and consolidated it. Mussolini was convinced that he had to save the country from others. To him, the stakes were immense, there was a higher end which justified his means. And yes, to achieve that end, he sometimes compromised his values, his sense of morality.

He deceived people, his actions were often vile or calculated. But all this was motivated by a higher purpose. At stake was the fate of a nation. He sacrificed individuals for what he thought was the greater good. And he did do a lot of good, from introducing national pensions to building hospitals, from modernizing the railways to restoring pride to an entire people.

What fascinates me, and this is probably where Mussolini and I are very different, is the way he was able to go against his morals to achieve his goal. By every account I have read, Mussolini was basically a very principled, ethical individual. Yet he turned against his sense of right and wrong, he compromised his ethics to save the country. It is something I don't think I could do. I couldn't (and haven't) compromised my ethics even to save myself. Too many times I've stood up for what I believe in, only to later pay the price.

Mussolini's other great quality was his patriotism. Like me he was a nationalist. It's sad that this word, Nationalism, has become a by-word for racism and xenophobia. I view it as something positive. To me it's the pride of being Italian, to a Scotsman of being Scottish, to an Englishman of being English and so on. There is nothing xenophobic about that, if anything it shows you are a civilized person, an honest person who understands his history, his culture and his roots.

Unfortunately, few Italians understand this concept. Compare Italy and Britain. We have a history and a tradition which is as rich as any other country's, and yet we don't respect or appreciate it. The British colonized half the world, they built the British Empire which brought civilization and progress to many who today would be much worse off without it. And the British rightly celebrate their Empire and their history, while in Italy we forget about ours or we minimize it in revisionist textbooks.

The effects of these differing attitudes are manifold. Both Italy and Britain are multicultural countries, with immigrants from all over the globe. In many parts of London, for example, there are more blacks and Asians than whites. Yet those blacks and Asians feel British. They have integrated into this country, they are as English or Scottish or Welsh as the next guy, without giving up their own culture. In Italy, too many immigrants come over and act as if they were back in their own countries. They make little effort to fit in and, to be fair, we Italians make little effort to integrate them.

Our government does little for immigrants, so they

simply do things their way. If we're not careful, in ten years' time Italy could be a Muslim country. I have nothing against Muslims, but I don't want my Italian culture to disappear. If immigrants come to Italy and want to be part of the country, want to be part of Italian culture, want to be Italian, that's great. I don't care if they are black, yellow, pink or green. I would love it if an immigrant could come to Italy and, after a few years, say, 'This is my country. I am Italian.'

That rarely happens however. The problems occur when they aren't given a chance to fit in, while, at the same time, not having the will to fit in. They need to be given the opportunities, rights and responsibilities of citizens. Only then could they enrich the country. And, at the same time, those who do not act properly, those who sponge off the government or commit crimes should be mercilessly deported. Not only do they cause problems for the majority of the country, they give other immigrants a bad name and contribute to racism against their own people.

There obviously has been a huge debate in this country and elsewhere about the role and impact of foreigners on football. Some media pundits blame us for teaching English players how to dive. They accuse Michael Owen, David Beckham, Emile Heskey and others of being cheats and they say they learnt it from us.

Maybe so. But if we taught English footballers how to dive, we also taught them how to play football. England may have invented football, but we taught them how to play football. It's the truth.

We introduced Britain to world football. It's a different

game out there and, without us, I'm not sure English clubs would have enjoyed the same success. It's not just those clubs with many foreign stars who benefited. It's clubs like Manchester United as well. They face foreign players week in, week out in the Premiership and this has helped them tremendously.

The flipside, of course, is the glut of foreigners in the game today. The argument is rather more complex than people make it out to be. What is a 'foreigner'?

People complained that Chelsea fielded a side without an Englishman last season, conveniently forgetting that Liverpool did the exact same thing some ten years ago. Sure, they might point out that at least those were British players. But then, where do you set the boundaries?

If you say Chelsea is an English team and therefore should feature more Englishmen, I can say Chelsea is a London team and therefore should be filled with Londoners. Sixty, seventy years ago teams were made up almost exclusively of local players. Celtic won the European Cup in 1966/67 with a team composed exclusively of Glaswegians. Would others have complained if they had been full of Englishmen or Welshmen or, indeed, people from Aberdeen or Edinburgh?

If Chelsea had won the European Cup, with Dennis Wise as the only Englishman in the starting eleven, everybody would have said that they are still an English club. Instead, they lose and Chelsea become a team of foreign mercenaries. Naturally, you can't have it both ways, but people will say and write whatever they want, regardless of the truth. It's the same thing in Italy, we talk incessantly about foreigners, have endless debates, but ultimately it's meaningless hot air.

The bottom line is that everybody would love to have local talent in their side, but they would love watching Rivaldo and Luis Figo even more. Above all, supporters want to see teams that win. I have yet to meet a fan who can honestly say they would rather see eleven local players lose, than win the league with ten foreigners in the lineup.

The real problems occur when you have a lot of foreigners and your team still fails to perform. That's when fans get annoyed and lose interest. Supporters are driven by an unconscious desire or need to identify with their club. People naturally like to identify with winners because it helps them feel like winners, too. That's why they'll happily put up with a team chockfull of foreigners if it is entertaining and successful. Supporters also identify with local players, regardless of whether they win or lose. That's why fans will continue to back a losing team, as long as it is made up of local players. But fill a team with Norwegians, Moroccans and Frenchmen, watch it lose game after game and no Englishman will want to identify with it.

Personally, I'm very concerned about young players. Foreigners are a double-edged sword. On the one hand, they contribute and teach so much; on the other, they can keep promising players out of the side. The trick is buying quality overseas players, guys who entertain and contribute. But since not everybody can do that, you need to set limits. I would favour a cap of five overseas players per club. And I would find a solution to seal the loophole which exists in Britain with players from the Home Nations. It seems silly that players discover Scottish grandparents or Welsh great-uncles just so they can play international football. They're either foreign or they aren't.

Where will I be in five years' time?

I don't know. Until a few years back I would never have considered becoming a manager, for example. I always said that I would never do it. When I hang up my boots for the last time, that's it, I used to say.

Now, I'm not so sure. Working with some of the youngsters at West Ham has been incredibly rewarding. I would have to grow, I would have to mature further, learn to accept the weight of responsibility and learn to deal with a variety of different people and situations. I think that would be the greatest challenge. Beyond that, I think I have the skills. I love teaching kids, I'm a good listener, I've tried to be a leader, I believe I have a good understanding of tactics and, as far as training is concerned, I feel I'm way ahead of the pack.

Another dream of mine would be to open a gourmet food shop in London. It would be a delicatessen, stocked with typical products from Umbria, Tuscany and Lazio. Oil, cheeses, cold cuts, everything would be fresh and imported. I'm not a natural entrepreneur, I'm probably too generous for that, but I do have business experience through my boutique in Terni and I love good food.

Fine cuisine is an art form. What I find interesting is that it can reward you on two levels. On the one hand, you've got elaborate, delicate tastes that are the result of fine, rare ingredients and hours of painstaking labour in the kitchen. On the other, you've got comfort food.

To me, comfort food is the food of my childhood. One of

my clearest memories is returning from training around 6 pm and eating pasta which had been re-heated in a saucepan. It comes out slightly burnt and crispy and it is the most wonderful taste in the world. To this day, when Betta makes pasta, I always ask her to make an extra portion which I can later reheat on the stove.

I highly recommend it. Anybody can make pasta, but few know how good reheated pasta tastes. Forget the microwave. Slap it in a saucepan with a little bit of olive oil and watch it sizzle. You won't regret it.

And I also recommend tiramisu. It's the quintessential Italian dessert. It means 'Pick Me Up' in Italian and, frankly, few names are more appropriate (it's certainly more appropriate than 'spotted dick'). I've developed my own recipe, I make it regularly for Betta and the girls.

PAOLO DI CANIO'S PATENTED TIRAMISU RECIPE:

5 egg yolks, 3 egg whites, 1 lb Mascarpone cheese, ¾ pint of espresso, 1 bar of cooking chocolate, 5 tablespoons of sugar, 20 Savoiardi biscuits.

1. Make a pot of espresso coffee. Or, if you don't have an espresso machine, go to your local espresso bar and ask for about ¾ of a pint of espresso. They may look at you strangely, but just tell them it's for a recipe and, hopefully, they'll understand.

2. Separate the yolk from the egg whites. Take the five yolks, mix in five tablespoons of sugar and beat it with a fork until the mixture is nice and creamy.

3. Take Savoiardi biscuits (available in many supermarkets, you might have to dig around to find them, but it's

worth it) and soak them in the espresso. Don't leave them in there too long, or they'll get soggy and fall apart, but make sure they soak up enough of the flavour.

4. Combine the Mascarpone cheese (again, depending where you live, this may take some effort to find, but it is a crucial ingredient) with the yolk and sugar mixture. Stir gently until most of the lumps are gone.

5. Take three of the egg whites, put them in a bowl and beat them until the mixture starts becoming dense.

6. Gently combine the Mascarpone-yolk mixture with the beaten egg whites.

7. Pour a thin layer of the mixture into the bottom of a rectangular serving dish.

8. Arrange the Savoiardi biscuits side by side in the serving dish, then cover them with another layer of Mascarpone-yolk mixture. Repeat this step until you run out of biscuits or mixture (depending on the size of your serving dish you should have enough for two or three layers). If you have biscuits left over, save them and have them later as a snack. If you have any mixture left over, simply pour it on top.

9. Take the cooking chocolate and grate it over the top layer. Depending on how much you like chocolate you can either make it a light sprinkle or you can cover it entirely.

10. Cover up the serving dish and place it in the refrigerator for about half a day. If you make it in the morning, it's ready by tea-time.

Maybe I can copyright and market my tiramisu recipe.

Seriously, regardless of what I do, I would love to stay in England. Betta and I love it here, Ludovica feels like a child of two cultures. As for Lucrezia, she's still little, but Britain is the only country she has ever lived in.

Whatever happens, I hope to continue living without regrets. I have learned that there is no point in wondering what might have been, especially if you are happy with the way things are.

I hope to continue speaking out freely, no matter what the consequences. When you have faced, and overcome, as many setbacks as I have, you come to realize that no matter how bad the consequences seem, more often than not you can turn them into something positive, either because you learn from them or because you can sleep soundly at night, knowing your conscience is clear.

But most of all, I hope to be able to continue to look back and always remember where I came from and how I got to where I am today.

CAREER STATISTICS

Full Name: Paolo Di Canio
Born: Rome, 9 July 1968
Family: Father Ignazio, mother Pierina, brothers Antonio,
    Giuliano and Dino
Height: 5ft 9in
Weight: 11st 9lb
Junior football: Rinascita 79, Pro Tevere Roma, Lazio
    Youth
Professional football: Lazio, Ternana, Juventus, Napoli,
    AC Milan, Celtic, Sheffield Wednesday, West Ham
    United.

CAREER RECORD

Lazio (1985–90)
Serie A debut: v Cesena (a), October 9, 1988, drew 0–0
1985–86 Serie B, no appearances
1987–88 Serie B, no appearances
1988–89 Serie A, 30 league appearances, 1 goal
1989–90 Serie A, 24 league appearances, 3 goals

Ternana (1986–87 – loan)
1986–87 Serie C2, 27 league appearances, 2 goals

Juventus (1990–93)
1990–91 Serie A, 23 league appearances, 3 goals
1991–92 Serie A, 24 league appearances
1992–93 Serie A, 31 league appearances, 3 goals
1992–93 UEFA Cup 9 apps

Honours: UEFA Cup winner 1993

Napoli (1993–94)
1993–94 Serie A, 26 league appearances, 5 goals

Honours: Voted onto Serie A Team of the Season

Juventus (1994)
1994–95 Serie A, 0 appearances

AC Milan (1994–96)
1994–95 Serie A, 15 appearances, 1 goal
1995–96 Serie A, 22 appearances, 5 goals

Honours: Serie A Champions 1994–95

Celtic (1996–97)

1996–97
Debut (as sub): August 24, 1996 v Kilmarnock (a), won
3–1, scored 1 goal
Full debut: September 7, 1996 v Hibernian (h), won 5–0

Scottish Premier League

Aug 24	a	Kilmarnock	3–1	1 goal
Sep 7	h	Hibernian	5–0	
Sep 14	a	Dundee United	2–1	
Sep 21	h	Dunfermline	5–1	2 goals
Sep 28	a	Rangers	0–2	
Oct 12	h	Motherwell	1–0	
Oct 20	a	Hearts	2–2	
Oct 26	a	Hibernian	4–0	
Nov 2	h	Aberdeen	1–0	1 goal
Nov 14	h	Rangers	0–1	
Nov 30	h	Hearts	2–2	1 goal
Dec 26	a	Aberdeen	2–1	1 goal
Dec 28	h	Dunfermline	4–2	
Jan 2	a	Rangers	1–3	1 goal
Jan 4	h	Motherwell	5–0	1 goal
Jan 8	h	Kilmarnock	6–0	
Jan 11	a	Hearts	2–1	
Jan 29	a	Dunfermline	2–0	
Feb 1	a	Dundee United	0–1	
Feb 6	h	Raith Rovers	2–0	1 goal
Feb 22	a	Motherwell	1–0	
Mar 1	h	Hearts	2–0	1 goal
Mar 16	h	Rangers	0–1	
Apr 5	a	Raith Rovers	1–1	1 goal
Apr 20	h	Aberdeen	3–0	
May 4	a	Hibernian	3–1	1 goal

Scottish League Cup
3rd rd

Sep 4	a	Alloa	5–1	

Quarter-final

Sep 17	a	Hearts	0–1	

Scottish Cup
3rd rd

Jan 26	a	Clydebank	5–0	1 goal

4th rd

Feb 17	a	Hibernian	1–1	

Replay

Feb 26	h	Hibernian	2–0	1 goal

Quarter-final

Mar 6	h	Rangers	2–0	1 goal

Semi-final

Apr 12	n	Falkirk	1–1	

Replay

Apr 23	n	Falkirk	0–1	

League apps: 26, 12 goals
Scottish League Cup apps: 2
Scottish Cup apps: 6, 3 goals

Sheffield Wednesday (1997–98)

Signed: August 1997 (£4.7million)
Debut (as sub): August 9, 1997 v Newcastle (a), lost 1–2
Full debut: August 13, 1997 v Leeds United (h), lost 1–3

1997–98

FA Premiership

Aug 9	a	Newcastle United	1–2	
Aug 13	h	Leeds United	1–3	
Aug 23	a	Wimbledon	1–1	1 goal
Aug 25	a	Blackburn Rovers	2–7	
Aug 30	h	Leicester City	1–0	
Sep 13	a	Liverpool	1–2	
Sep 20	h	Coventry City	0–0	
Sep 24	h	Derby County	2–5	1 goal
Sep 27	a	Aston Villa	2–2	
Oct 4	h	Everton	3–1	1 goal
Oct 19	a	Tottenham Hotspur	2–3	1 goal
Oct 25	h	Crystal Palace	1–3	
Nov 1	a	Manchester United	1–6	
Nov 8	h	Bolton Wanderers	5–0	1 goal
Nov 22	h	Arsenal	2–0	
Nov 29	a	Southampton	3–2	1 goal
Dec 8	h	Barnsley	2–1	1 goal
Dec 13	a	West Ham United	0–1	
Dec 20	h	Chelsea	1–4	
Jan 10	h	Newcastle United	2–1	1 goal
Jan 17	a	Leeds United	2–1	
Feb 7	a	Coventry City	0–1	
Feb 14	h	Liverpool	3–3	1 goal
Feb 21	h	Tottenham Hotspur	1–0	1 goal
Feb 28	a	Derby County	0–3	
Mar 7	h	Manchester United	2–0	1 goal
Mar 14	a	Bolton Wanderers	2–3	

Mar 28	a	Arsenal	0–1	
Apr 4	h	Southampton	1–0	
Apr 11	a	Barnsley	1–2	
Apr 13	h	West Ham United	1–1	
Apr 19	a	Chelsea	0–1	
Apr 25	a	Everton	3–1	1 goal
May 2	h	Aston Villa	1–3	
May 10	a	Crystal Palace	0–1	

Coca Cola Cup
Second round

Sep 17	a	Grimsby Town	0–2	
Sep 30	h	Grimsby Town	3–2	2 goals

FA Cup
Third round

Jan 3	a	Watford	1–1	
Jan 14	h	Watford	0–0	(won on

penalties)

Fourth Round

Jan 26	h	Blackburn Rovers	0–3	

1998–99

FA Carling Premiership

Aug 15	h	West Ham United	0–1	
Aug 22	a	Tottenham Hotspur	3–0	1 goal
Aug 29	h	Aston Villa	0–1	
Sep 12	h	Blackburn Rovers	3–0	1 goal
Sep 19	a	Wimbledon	1–2	1 goal
Sep 26	h	Arsenal	1–0	

Worthington Cup
Second round

Sep 16	h	Cambridge United	0–1	
Sep 22	a	Cambridge United	1–1	

Honours: Player of the season 1997–98

West Ham United (1999–)

Signed: Jan 27, 1999 (£1.7million)
Debut (as sub): January 30, 1999 v Wimbledon (a), drew 0–0
Full debut: February 6, 1999 v Arsenal (h), lost 0–4

1998–99

FA Premiership

Jan 30	a	Wimbledon	0–0	
Feb 6	h	Arsenal		0–4
Feb 13	h	Nottingham Forest	2–1	
Feb 27	h	Blackburn Rovers	2–0	1 goal
Mar 6	a	Southampton	0–1	
Mar 20	h	Newcastle United	2–0	1 goal
Apr 2	a	Aston Villa	0–0	
Apr 5	h	Charlton Athletic	0–1	
Apr 10	a	Leicester City	0–0	
Apr 17	h	Derby County	5–1	1 goal
May 1	h	Leeds United	1–5	1 goal
May 8	a	Everton	0–6	
May 16	h	Middlesbrough	4–0	

1999–2000

FA Premiership

Aug 7	h	Tottenham Hotspur	1–0	
Aug 16	a	Aston Villa	2–2	
Aug 21	h	Leicester City	2–1	1 goal
Aug 28	a	Bradford City	3–0	1 goal
Sep 11	h	Watford	1–0	1 goal
Sep 19	a	Everton	0–1	
Sep 25	a	Coventry City	0–1	
Oct 3	h	Arsenal	2–1	2 goals
Oct 17	a	Middlesbrough	0–2	
Oct 24	h	Sunderland	1–1	
Nov 21	h	Sheffield Wed	4–3	1 goal
Nov 27	h	Liverpool	1–0	
Dec 6	a	Tottenham Hotspur	0–0	
Dec 18	h	Manchester United	2–4	2 goals
Dec 26	a	Wimbledon	2–2	
Dec 28	h	Derby County	1–1	1 goal
Jan 15	h	Aston Villa	1–1	1 goal
Jan 22	a	Leicester City	3–1	1 goal
Feb 12	h	Bradford City	5–4	1 goal
Mar 8	h	Southampton	2–0	
Mar 11	a	Sheffield Wed.	1–3	
Mar 18	h	Chelsea	0–0	
Mar 26	h	Wimbledon	2–1	1 goal
Apr 12	h	Newcastle United	2–1	
Apr 15	a	Derby County	2–1	
Apr 22	h	Coventry City	5–0	2 goals
Apr 29	h	Middlesbrough	0–1	

May 2	a	Arsenal	1–2	1 goal
May 6	a	Sunderland	0–1	
May 14	h	Leeds United	0–0	

FA Cup
Third round

| Dec 11 | a | Tranmere Rovers | 0–1 |

Worthington Cup
Third round

| Oct 13 | h | Bournemouth | 2–0 |

Fourth round

| Nov 30 | a | Birmingham City | 3–2 |

Quarter–final

| Jan 11 | h | Aston Villa | 1–3 |

Intertoto Cup
Third round

| Jul 17 | h | FC Jokerit | 1–0 |
| Jul 24 | a | FC Jokerit | 1–1 |

Semi-final

| Jul 28 | h | Heerenveen | 1–0 |
| Aug 4 | a | Heerenveen | 1–0 |

Final

| Aug 10 | h | FC Metz | 0–1 |
| Aug 24 | a | FC Metz | 3–1 |

UEFA Cup
First round

Sep 16	h	Osijek	3–0	1 goal
Sep 30	a	Osijek	3–1	

Second round

Oct 21	a	Steaua Bucharest	0–2
Nov 4	h	Steaua Bucharest	0–0

Honours: Hammer of the Year 1999–2000, BBC Goal of the Season award 1999–2000

2000–01

FA Carling Premiership

Aug 19	a	Chelsea	2–4	1 goal
Aug 23	h	Leicester City	0–1	
Aug 26	h	Manchester United	2–2	1 goal
Sep 5	a	Sunderland	1–1	
Sep 11	a	Tottenham Hotspur	0–1	
Sep 17	h	Liverpool	1–1	1 goal
Sep 23	a	Coventry	3–0	1 goal
Sep 30	h	Bradford	1–1	
Oct 14	a	Ipswich	1–1	1 goal
Oct 21	h	Arsenal	1–2	
Oct 28	h	Newcastle	1–0	
Nov 6	a	Derby	0–0	
Nov 11	h	Man City	4–1	1 goal
Nov 25	a	Southampton	3–2	
Dec 2	h	Middlesbro'	1–0	1 goal
Dec 9	h	Aston Villa	1–1	
Dec 16	a	Everton	1–1	
Dec 26	h	Charlton	5–0	
Jan 13	h	Sunderland	0–2	
Jan 22	a	Charlton	1–1	1 goal
Jan 31	h	Tottenham	0–0	

Feb 12	h	Coventry	1–1	
Feb 24	a	Bradford	2–1	
Mar 7	h	Chelsea	2–0	
Mar 17	h	Ipswich	0–1	
Mar 31	h	Everton	0–2	
Apr 7	a	Aston Villa	2–2	
Apr 14	h	Derby	3–1	
Apr 21	h	Leeds	0–2	
Apr 28	a	Man City	0–1	
May 5	h	Southampton	3–0	1 goal

FA Cup
Third round

| Jan 28 | a | Man Utd | 1–0 | 1 goal |

Fourth round

| Feb 17 | a | Sunderland | 1–0 | |

Fifth round

| Mar 3 | h | Tottenham | 2–3 | |

Worthington Cup
Third round

| Sep 27 | h | Walsall | 1–1 | |

Fourth round

| Oct 31 | h | Blackburn | 2–0 | 1 goal |

Quarter-final

| Nov 29 | h | Sheff Wed | 1–2 | |

INDEX